ACCLAIM FOR CHRIS BRADY'S
# A MONTH OF ITALY

"Extremely engaging and delightful - a well told story!"
– Chris Gross, CEO Gabriel Media Group, Inc.,
Co-Founder of *Networking Times*

"As a native Italian, I appreciate all the details on my country that bring to life the art, traditions, and values of my land! This is a book every traveler should read and bring along in order to experience the best of Italy."
– Dr. Gaetano (Guy) Sottile, President and Founder,
Italy for Christ, Inc.

"Witty, funny, and at points downright hilarious, but mixed with profound truths shared in a way that makes one pause and ponder."
– Orrin Woodward, Winner of the 2011 IAB Top
Leadership Award

"A spellbinding lesson in learning how to live again, with real purpose. You can't stop turning the pages . . ."
– Art Jonak, Founder of MastermindEvent.com

"I have never read a book that teaches so much while being this fun at the same time."
– Tim Marks, Bestselling Author of *Voyage of a Viking*

"This is the best work Chris Brady has written to date. If this is a vacation handbook, it has redefined the vacation experience."
– Venkat Varada, Silicon Valley Executive

"Vacationing truly is a lost art, and Brady poignantly and beautifully illustrates why it is so vital for driven leaders. A timeless treatise on 'sharpening the saw,' *A Month of Italy* is a book I will sip and savor, ponder and reflect on time and time again. Not only are Chris's insights powerful and refreshing, but his vivid and witty writing is simply a pleasure to read. Reading this book is a charming vacation itself, and it will inspire you to vacation deliberately, effectively, and joyfully."
– Stephen Palmer, *New York Times* Best-Selling Author
of *Uncommon Sense: A Common Citizen's Guide to
Rebuilding America*

"In our hectic lives, we are rarely 100 percent present in any situation. Chris Brady shows that with proper play time, our work time is so much more effective. He has freed my spirit!"
– Jason Ashley, Country Singer/Songwriter *(Texas
Songwriter of the Year 2008)*

"Italy is unique. Moreover, it is a country where the traveler can enjoy the most various experiences. Chris Brady's book has the ability, astonishing even for an Italian, to convey to the reader that variety, that richness of feelings, sights, perfumes, tastes . . . and people."
– Senator Lucio Malan, Senior Secretary of the Presidency of
the Italian Senate

# A Month of

# ITALY

# CHRIS BRADY

# A MONTH OF
# ITALY

## CHRIS BRADY

Second Edition, June 2013
10 9 8 7 6 5 4 3 2

Published by:

Obstaclés Press
200 Commonwealth Court
Cary, NC 27511

Printed in the United States of America

ISBN 978-0-9853387-4-9

*Cover design and layout by Norm Williams - nwa-inc.com*

www.amonthofitaly.com

*You may have the universe if I may have Italy.*
– Giuseppe Verdi (1813-1901) in *Attila*

# CONTENTS

## PART II: ADAGIO

## PART III: DIMINUENDO

# PREFACE

The morning sun is strong now but partially shielded by tall medieval buildings. I rest casually in the shade on old stone steps with no schedule, no plan, and not an ounce of hurry left in my body. It feels strange. I strain to remember if I've ever felt this way before. In childhood, perhaps, but such memories are hidden beneath the dusty veil of time.

A wedding party is kibitzing about the steps on which I sit, breaking up and heading for some tour buses somewhere. I know this because one of the boys yelled it loudly, as if in command of the group, which perhaps he is. One young lady, in the early bloom of her maturity and obviously intending to be sexy, is wearing a dress so tight old women shake their heads while young men find reasons to stop and turn. She pulls self-consciously at the shortness of it in a vain attempt to cover more of herself. I can tell she won't wear it again and smile, thinking that virtue has found her through embarrassment. Or perhaps she simply hasn't struck the right chord, struggling as she is in the space between a girl and a woman.

Pigeons flutter overhead, and doves coo. Old men, as I've seen everywhere throughout this land, have assembled at their posts in little clusters outside bars. They don't begin their card games until afternoon. The mornings are reserved for staring. I find it interesting how they dominate the tables and chairs in front of these little snack shops, but never, not even once, have I seen any of them with a single item purchased from inside. They lay claim to the territory solely on the authority of their age, and I wonder if there is a rite of passage into their silver-haired gang. I daydream about finding out first-hand for myself someday—that is, if foreigners are allowed.

"There are too many Germans in Cortona," I hear a German say in thickly accented English, and I watch as he and others stroll by with shopping bags swinging.

Employees of the museum next to me work lackadaisically to set up street signs in the piazza. A policewoman in navy pants with a scarlet stripe, a powder blue blouse, and a bright white helmet, harasses cars that enter to park. One young man, tall and strapping with long curly hair, jumps out of a Fiat Panda and deploys his flirtatious charisma, promising he'll only be a minute. She succumbs with a smile.

In front of a fruit store, a barrel-shaped old woman angrily sweeps invisible dirt with a whiskbroom, while some middle-aged men in shiny suits sit smoking at tables nearby. Next to me on the steps rests a little jangle of American college students, apparently in town to study something. A tall blonde girl flirts openly with a boy more interested in his schoolwork. He rises to leave and announces he's not quite ready for the test. She mimes disappointment but watches him walk away. One of her friends swats her on the shoulder.

Someone emerges from a ceramic shop and shouts at a man passing by with a dog on a leash. The man turns, smiles, waves, and stops to talk to his greeter. They lean against the building and chat—all the time in the world.

I retrieve my motorcycle from its spot against the stone wall of the old theater and saddle up. I need nothing but its brakes as I descend steep, narrow stone streets and gain passage into the wide-open countryside just beyond the city's ancient walls. I turn onto smooth blacktop and roll on the power, olive trees whizzing past as I head for no destination but just ride.

After an hour, I stop along a quiet road and kill the engine. The sun is hot on my matted hair, and a gentle breeze is too gentle. Digging a camera from my shorts, I attempt to capture the scene in all its glory. A beautiful abandoned limestone farmhouse stands in splendor atop a bright tan wheat field. Dark green cypress trees trace the old lane up to the building and stab the clear azure sky like soldiers in formation. Canopy pines provide shade in a peaceful cluster around the top of the knoll. Rigidly neat rows of grapevines slant across a hill in the background, their obviously manicured condition a stark contrast with the adjacent ruined house. Farther in the distance looms a dull grey mountain range, jagged against the sky. These images comprise a stereotypically stunning Tuscan landscape—the kind that arrests my attention and conjures my wonder again and again.

I zoom in, walk around, and play with the camera but cannot get the lens to capture the full measure of reality. Despite my best efforts, the photographs simply fall short. I so desperately want to share this, to bottle it up and take it back for others. I wish to pour it out for them and show what they too could be seeing, to give them an idea of what is out there and what they could experience. But my efforts are in vain. Sometimes, quite literally, you simply have to be there.

I'll just have to tell the whole story, I think, motoring away. I'll have to tell it in a way that brings it to life for others—enough to inspire them to launch out on their own adventures.

# PART I: CRESCENDO

## CHAPTER I

# PUKING IN A MINIBUS

*In America, there are two classes of travel: First class, and with children.* – Robert Benchley

Flying through the night is no big deal because you can sleep on the airplane. That is almost as big of a whopper as the one about politicians serving the public. For some reason, most flights to Europe from North America are scheduled for departure in the late afternoon, which, with a six hour time change or more, means you land when the Italians are finishing their cappuccino and getting down to some serious consideration of the fact that they might ought to start doing some work at some point that day: in other words—late morning. The pressure to sleep on the flight will be incredible, that dark monster called Jet Lag lurking in the back of your mind with threats of crazed sleepiness at inopportune times of the day.

We popped our melatonin (supplements that supposedly reset one's biological clock) and began the eight-hour wrestling match with our seats. Meanwhile, our four kids (ages 13, 10, 7, 5) did what kids everywhere have done with parental advice since the beginning of mankind: they ignored it. They played the free video games and watched movies and did just about anything they could . . . except sleep.

Finally, though, we landed—groggy but happy. After all, we were in Italy!

We went through the rituals of waiting in lines, telling the Immigration officer we were there for a month, assuring the Customs officer we hadn't recently wrestled with livestock, and trying out new Italian phrases such as, "*Si*." Most of our Italian didn't work too well, so luckily, most everyone we interacted with spoke at least a little English. This would be less and less true as the trip wore on.

Getting the rental car was a fiasco. We shuffled our way into a hot, crowded room that was kind of inside, but not really. The sweltering Italian summer crammed its way into every space of that room, inducing sweat and stink on travelers who were doing their best to look fresh after an all-night flight. A baby was screaming in a stroller while the mother snored in an adjacent seat. Everywhere, without any apparent organization, people waited patiently. I couldn't figure out where the line ended until, after at least fifteen minutes, I realized it was a take-a-number affair. Feeling like a traveler from another country that didn't speak the language, I sheepishly ripped off my little paper ticket and sat on the floor to wait. Man, was it hot. My kids tried to sleep on the floor and said their bellies hurt. I glanced at the number on my ticket: 4175; then I looked up at a digital display: 94.

After forty-five minutes in the free sauna, I ambled to the ticket counter and spoke some Italian I'd learned. My pronunciation must have been pretty good, because the man answered in a flurry of words I couldn't come close to understanding. Noticing my blank stare, he quickly switched to English and handed me some keys. By now I was sweating so profusely and feeling the effects of being up all night that I didn't even think to ask what kind of car I was being assigned. He made some mention of how to find the car, and I listened about as well as I did to the safety demonstration at the beginning of the flight. After all, how tough could it be to find a car? I'd even been here a time or two before. "Come with me, kids; follow Daddy to our car, and we'll get this trip under way!"

"Yay, Daddy!" they said, jumping to their feet.

A half hour later we were still circling a random parking ramp, sweating even more and putting needless miles on the wheels of our luggage. Daddy wasn't so much of a hero anymore, and at least one of the kids needed a bathroom. Another was still complaining of a hurting stomach. Daddy was getting a headache and couldn't bear the thought of waiting through that long line again just to get directions he should have listened to the first time.

When we finally found our vehicle, it wasn't anything like what we thought we'd reserved. Properly called a minibus (pronounced meanie-boos) by the Italians, it was long and white and huge, with some clunkiness thrown in just for style. It was parked on the top level of a two-story ramp because, supposedly, it was too tall to fit inside the main one. Everything the guy had said was slowly coming back to me. *This?* I thought; *I'm going to drive my family around Italy for a month in this?* The only thought that seemed more oppressive was going back through that line to exchange it for something else. I chose the lesser of two evils, rightly concluding that taking this minibus was the fastest route to getting some sleep. Next to that consideration, everything else was starting to take second place. I knew we were in trouble when my wife Terri had to climb out at the exit from the parking ramp to direct me around a tight turn with high concrete walls on each side. Without her help, I would have scraped our new vehicle within the first tenth of a kilometer of possession.

Finally, though, we were under way. "Hey, kids," I yelled loudly so as to be heard way in the back, "We're in Italy!"

"Yeah!"

"I know!"

"Cool!"

"My tummy hurts!"

"Just let us get under way, and we'll stop for food and a bathroom. Okay?"

"Okay, Dad."

Our trusty GPS, brought from home and preloaded with Italian maps, was doing its job wonderfully, and in no time we were trucking down the Autostrada heading south and well on our way.

"That wasn't so bad," Terri said.

"Yep.  Only I'm having a hard time seeing myself driving this box on wheels for our whole time here.  This isn't exactly what I thought we had reserved.  It was supposed to be the smallest vehicle they had with six seats.  This thing seats nine, and there's room for a couple of refrigerators in the back.  For Italy, this thing is enormous!  I'll bet we won't be able to park it anywhere!" I complained.

"We can go back and swap it for something else," Terri offered sincerely, clearly demonstrating that she was indeed in my boat, but also that she had no fear of overexposure in a sauna.

"No way.  It would kill me to sweat my way through that line again.  We'll just have to deal with it."

Just as with many love stories that start on rocky terms, that's how my affair with the minibus began.  I hated her upon first sight, but as we got to know each other and share experiences together, I grew so attached to her that by the end of the month I was trying to figure out how to stuff her into a third suitcase and take her home with me.  If it weren't for my rule of packing light, I just might have done it, too.

But that would all be some time in the coming.  Right now we were somewhere in the crowded area around Naples when, for the sake of proper initiation, Casey our oldest puked on the floor of the minibus.  Dad had ignored one too many cries of "I'm feeling queasy." Not only was this van big and clunky, but it was making my kids motion sick as well.

Then it started to rain.

CHAPTER 2

# SANDALS AND SMART CARS

*To awaken alone in a strange town is one of the pleasantest sensations in the world.* — Freya Stark

Italy has a magnetism that's hard to explain. Tired, lagged, and hot, we were still thrilled with the fact that we were here, and the humongous trip we had planned for so long was truly under way.

Jet lag is not that hard to beat if you adjust your sleep patterns correctly. Here's how it works: when flying east (and, therefore, advancing in time), it is helpful to stay up until the locals go to bed. In Italy this is pretty tough, though, since they don't even start dinner until eight o'clock. *Okay*, we thought, *maybe we can at least hold out until their first course.* We were aided in this by the World Cup soccer games on television, and we caught a match at the hotel's poolside bar. *This is perfect*, we thought. So we ordered pizza and fell asleep on our plates.

Next morning we took a stroll through the busy streets of beautiful Sorrento. Since as a young man back in Flint, Michigan, I had taken all my high school dates to a restaurant of the same name, I was particularly interested in seeing a place famous enough to inspire a backsliding industrial town to name something after it. We mostly just saw the inside of a hot little shoe store, however—one specializing in sweat and customers bumping into each other. For some reason, it was a huge priority to get my six-year-old daughter Christine some sandals. There was a near outbreak of pouting as Nathaniel, the ten-year-old, failed in his bid for a new pair of Nikes, but this was fixed by setting him out on the curb to wait in the baking sun. In five minutes, he looked as lethargic as a desert lizard at the zoo. I took a mental note of this parenting technique, certain it could again prove useful on this trip.

After being in the store long enough to celebrate birthdays, we set out to explore Sorrento's charms. This lasted only so long, as we were proving just how difficult it is for a family with four kids to pass a restroom. We found ourselves utilizing the kind of unspoken economic exchange that involves swapping a purchase of food for directions to the bathroom. *Dove il bagno?* was instantly one of our most important Italian phrases. The only difficulty with this method of restaurant selection is that those with the most conveniently located bathrooms don't automatically have the finest cuisine. This discovery occurred to me as I wrestled with my sandwich, a hard-bread/sausage affair slathered in peppers and olives, which, I learned, is called pepperoni. The owner of the little place was wonderfully helpful, however, speaking a little English and trying his best to accommodate the life-threatening food allergies of my ten-year-old son, the lizard.

Terri had planned ahead by typing up a document explaining our son's food situation and politely asking for help in preparing a suitable meal. She had then proceeded to have it translated by taking it to the best resource for international languages in our town: the soccer fields. Sure enough, one of the coaches was fresh from Italy and cordially provided us a typed translation. Terri subsequently carried this little piece of paper all over Italy, and it never failed to elicit kind assistance and sincere help. Not once did we experience the rolling of the eyes, deep sighing, or throwing back of the head common in the responses of American waitstaffs. This first lunch was only the beginning of the lesson we would get in Italian congeniality.

It was also the first restaurant I'd patronized where both a beggar and a stray dog came in to solicit. These two events happened maybe five minutes apart. The beggar, a fairly young boy, was turned away harshly. The dog, apparently using a better approach, was thrown a scrap of meat.

Next the cops entered and chatted us up so amicably we thought they were part of an official international welcoming committee. It was one of those stimulating conversations in which neither side speaks the other's language. As this realization dawned on the officers, less and less words were spoken and more and more gestures were made, gestures being at least fifty percent of the Italian language anyway. By the end we looked like a bunch of deaf people who hadn't yet learned sign language. Smiles all around and pats on the heads of our children. *Americani? Americani?* Smile, pat, smile, pat. I couldn't help thinking this is probably the exact way police in the United States react to a bunch of non-English-speaking Italians in a restaurant.

As the officers departed, I said to Terri, "We're in Italy, for sure. And now that they've given us our official greeting, let's do this place!" She rolled her eyes like an American waitress who's been told about food allergies, and I herded the kids out onto the sidewalk. As we left, the restaurant owner sent us off like family he wouldn't see for years.

"*Ciao! Arrivederci! Ciao!*"

"We're definitely not in Kansas anymore, Toto," I said to Casey.

"Look at that car!" he answered, totally engrossed in his dad's humor.

It was one of those super-tiny Fiats from the '50s, small even by European standards. Casey couldn't wait for me to take his photo standing in front of it. Terri ducked into a tantalizing little fruit shop while the kids and I began ogling the odd assortment of vehicles parked along the streets and zipping in and out. There were Opels and Fiats and VWs and Toyotas, every one of them small enough to fit in the back of our Ford Expedition back home. Motorcycles and scooters filled all the empty space cars hadn't taken. But the one vehicle that never failed to elicit joy from my children was the Smart Car. These cute little two-seaters were intelligently designed by Mercedes Benz to be short enough to fit into a parallel parking spot by pulling straight in. Back in the States, they look like a toy roller skate. Here in a cramped European town for which they were designed, they looked simply, well, smart.

It was at this moment the four of my children banded together for the monumental task of counting the number of Smart Cars in Italy, or at least the ones within view of the Bradys. This produced a month-long version of Slug Bug without the slug. It didn't matter where we were, what we were doing, or who was talking, if a Smart Car drove by, invariably one of our children would shout it out with authority. It became a comical, cute, annoying ritual that smacked of some kind of unusual Tourette's Syndrome. Once this game was unleashed, it was impossible to prohibit or regulate in any way, like the song "It's a Small World" running through your head after a day at Disney's Magic Kingdom—it just couldn't be stopped. What's more, there were many fights and disputes as to the "official count" and rules of the game growing ever more complicated as the trip wore on. Over time, however, the Brady kids developed into a highly trained, laser-sighted, Smart-Car-counting machine. If nothing else, this trip qualified them for future employment at the Census Bureau.

We climbed back up the hill to our fancy hotel, the one featuring English-speaking employees, marble columns, and drop-kicked baggage. As we loaded our stuff into the minibus and I pulled out the trusty GPS with our next stop already pre-programmed, it became apparent someone at the hotel had dropped my bag, apparently from the roof.  The GPS's touch screen was completely and inoperably shattered.

Also, we didn't have a map.

## CHAPTER 3

# LIVING LIKE (EXILED) KINGS

*I travel for travel's sake. The great affair is to move.*
– Robert Louis Stevenson

We were driving along Italy's Amalfi Coast which is famous for gorgeous mountain peaks rising right out of the Mediterranean, breathtaking sea panoramas, humongous lemons, and a road just wide enough for two mopeds. I am quite certain that at no time during the construction of route SS163 did any engineer or architect envision a clunky minibus full of Bradys passing through. But that's just what we were doing: careening around those tight little corners with mountain cliffs on one side, concrete walls on the other, and always a motorcycle or scooter trying to squeeze past. We whipped the minibus around those turns and up and down those hills like mountain goats.

Every now and then, we would pass through a little town with medieval buildings flanking both sides of the road. Space was so tight that often we had to stop to allow opposing traffic to pass. Incredibly, in many cases the front doors to these buildings opened right onto the street. Say good-bye to the visitor who steps out for a breath of fresh air and forgets that crazed vacationers from

America just might happen by with a clunky white minibus full of kids yelling "Smart Car" at the top of their lungs. Many of these buildings housed quaint little restaurants, though where one was supposed to park to patronize said establishments was a huge mystery to us.

Driving conditions were so tight we went for kilometers and kilometers without the driver (me) being able to peer out at the scenery for even a moment. One look away from the road and there could have been an immediate white smear on the side of some mountain or a very bad day for an opposing motorcyclist. Most challenging, though, were the Audi drivers. For some reason, Italy is densely populated with Audis. There must have been some huge bargain basement bin sale on them just before we arrived. Ownership qualifications must have involved some sort of prior Grand Prix racing experience because it was always the Audi owners with their fluorescent headlamps who zipped around us in a flurry and disappeared as quickly as they'd come. After a while, the sequence became a sort of cadence, the kind of rhythmic pattern produced when driving over periodic cracks in the pavement on a road in need of repair. Only instead of *bump, bump, click, bump, bump, click*, it was something like *motorcycle whizzes by, scooter hums past, Audi whips around*, and then over again. If there came a stretch of road where this wasn't happening, I lost my sense of comfort and started feeling insecure. After an hour or so of this, I became more relaxed, eventually able to sneak a quick glance out the side window and verify that, yes, that flash of blue I saw was, in fact, a sea.

We had been driving for what seemed a really long time, as indicated by the number of times we heard, "I need to go to the bathroom" and "I'm feeling a little queasy," when Terri reasonably asked, "What is the name of the town our lodging is in?"

"I'm not sure," I answered.

"Okay, we've got no map and a broken GPS. How do you expect to find it?" she countered.

"I think it's just after the town of Amalfi," I answered.

"Think?"

"Yeah. Pretty sure."

"How far past?"

"Dunno. But don't worry. I saw it on Google Earth a few months back when we were making the reservations. I'm pretty sure I'll recognize it."

This was not a very foolproof method of finding one particular resort in a coast of thousands of them, but such a fact did not even dent my confidence. Besides, there was really only this one road, the scenery was gorgeous, I had been through here once before, and what were the odds that we'd have a child throw up in our rental car two days in a row?

This plan worked fine until I lost my nerve. Hesitating for a moment, I tried to turn around in a little town whose name was as of yet unknown to us. This maneuver merited some *attaboys*, as I had to somehow spin the minibus like a top without hitting buildings, concrete walls, motorcycles, other cars, and the little old lady stepping out her front door with a basket of vegetables. After a few curves back in the direction from which we had come, I realized I shouldn't have turned around and was forced to execute the maneuver once again. Gradually, I was becoming comfortable with the clunky minibus. I didn't realize it yet, but the deep-level bonding between man and machine had begun.

Terri pulled us through with some guidance from a travel book and a very intelligent phone call to the villa management asking for directions. Not that this was at all necessary, just so you know. I would have found it. After all, we had a whole month. However, I will concede that Terri's contribution to our successful arrival was probably the only reason we didn't repeat the previous day's episode of child carsickness. And sure enough, we came around a super tight corner and, just like that, I recognized the doorway to our villa! And that's all it was—a doorway. With parking across the street in a little niche carved into the rock face, the entire resort was perched on the ocean side of the road, hanging off a cliff with ninety percent of it below street elevation.

Now, how to turn the minibus off this tight road and into the very narrow opening to the parking area? Traffic backed up in both directions as I negotiated a very close fit. It was to be my last driving heroics of the day. And incredibly, all of my adventures behind the wheel of that minibus for our first two days had elicited not a single blown horn, flipped bird, or angry hollering voice. Everyone exhibited the patience of Job with my Italian driving indoctrination, and I was glad for it. Was everyone as nice as these drivers around here? Discovering the answer to that would be one of the missions of this trip.

*Villa Scarpariello* resort is a stair-lover's paradise. No need for step aerobics when staying here. From the moment one enters through the metal doorway (which is perched exactly over the edge of the road, inches from vehicles speeding by), one is confronted with stairs. This is not apparent at first, however, because one is also overcome by an incredibly scenic view. In the foreground are replicas of statues and medallions and architecture that make no sense but somehow thrill the eye with columns and friezes and arches. These range from many different periods and probably shouldn't be mixed together, but somehow they make for a beautiful combined display.

Flowers of many types and colors are thoughtfully arranged around various elevations and terraces. Pergolas are covered with lemon trees, and large, ripe fruit hangs ready for the picking. The original castle keep, one of fifty-two built as lookouts along this coast by the extremely well-traveled Vikings, rises into the piercing blue sky. Its old stone, castellated top, and vine-covered surface is beautiful in the afternoon sun. Rumor has it that the king of Italy exiled himself here when World War II started going badly for fascist Italy and Mussolini was given his rope necklace. Understandably wishing to avoid a similar fate, the old king checked himself into our resort. We couldn't help wondering if he used the name Bob Smith. By far, though, the most breathtaking part of the view is the calm, dark blue Mediterranean Sea stretching to the horizon. Pleasure boats rocked gently on the rollers of the flood tide, and off to the left and right, gorgeously jagged cliffs cut steeply to the sea below. It looked as if we had landed in the middle of a postcard.

*This is going to be awesome*, I thought.

Then we heard the explosion.

## CHAPTER 4

# CELEBRATING HOLIDAYS
# AND GROCERIES

*The world is a book and those who do not travel read only one page.* – St. Augustine

"Daddy," Christine asked cutely, "how are we going to celebrate the Fourth of July if we're in Italy?"

"We'll just have to have a private little celebration, I guess," I answered.

"But how?"

"Maybe we'll bang on pots and pans or something."

This conversation, held days before the trip began, was long forgotten. That is, until we heard the clanging of bells on the distant hilltop followed by a booming, echoing explosion.

"What was that?" my kids asked in unison.

"I don't know."

For several more days, right up until the Fourth of July, it turned out, the bell ringing and booming explosions continued sporadically. Then, as we were reading bedtime stories one evening, a massive fireworks display broke out over the sea right in front of our villa.  It was big, boisterous, beautiful . . . and close. We ran out and stood at the stone's edge, watching flickers and flashes, not sure that we weren't perhaps under attack.

"I guess they are celebrating the Fourth of July!" I said, half joking.  But the celebration went on and on, much to our enjoyment, taking on the aspects of an official observance.

"This place is amazing," Terri said. "First, they send us an official police welcoming committee; then, they arrange for a private fireworks show to celebrate one of our national holidays.  I think I like it here."

We never did find out exactly why the town of Minori hosted a fireworks show, or why the town of Ravella up on the cliff above us had been ringing the bell and firing off explosions of their own. Later in our stay, once we had made friends and connections, we forgot to inquire.  It could have been a festival celebrating the birth of a cow to a local noble three hundred years ago, for all we knew, or the most important event in Italy's independent history.  It was also possible that the two were one and the same.  But during those early nights of adjustment to a foreign land, this little celebration in perfect coordination to our own holiday back home was a welcome touch—as if we needed any more reasons to fall in love with Italy.

"Why do you love Italy so much, Dad?" one of the children had asked before we left the States.  I recognized it as one of those little teachable moments parents crave with their children.  I had concocted this whole trip with at least some intention of it being educational for my kids, and this was as good a time as any to tell them why.  I endeavored to explain how Italy had a deep, rich history, featuring mysterious civilizations like the Etruscans and famous colonization by the ancient Greeks and later the Normans. Then it had become the cradle of modern civilization with the Roman Republic—later, Empire.  The apostle Paul was taken there as a prisoner and then executed.  Then there was the incredible birthing of the Renaissance. Finally, World War II saw major action in Italy. And this was just the *history*. There was also the abundance of art, architecture, music, literature, cuisine, wine, olive oil, fashion, exotic sports cars, fast motorcycles, leather goods, textiles, and a wonderful climate. Top it all off with some of the most awe-inspiring natural topography, and you just about had it all.

"Yeah, Dad, and pizza!"

"Yeah, and pizza!"

"Yes, and pizza, too!"

"Can we have some pizza when we're there? Can we, Dad? Please? Can we?"

"Sure, lots of it, and their special ice cream they call *gelato*, too."

"Yay! Dad is the greatest!"

My vision of this trip had involved doing some cooking on our own, as Terri, already a fantastic cook, learned the local recipes and shopped at fresh markets. Of course, it wouldn't involve me very much; my culinary experience consisted of making toast and burning popcorn in the microwave. But, always the good husband, I was entirely willing to have Terri slave away to make us some Italian delights.

To do this, however, we would need provisions. Food. *Alimentari*. Perched over the sea on the side of a cliff, all the buildings and towns we had been through similarly constructed, we wondered just where and how to find food, much less the sprawling, open-air produce markets of my visions.

So I asked Pietro, one of the hosts at *Scarpariello*. In his friendly manner, he took me into the little reception office atop some steps (like everything at *Scarpariello*). Pulling up Google Earth, he zoomed into street-level views to show me where to park and which shop across the street sold groceries. He was most helpful. One thing he forgot to mention, however, was that in Italy most stores aren't open.

At least that's how it feels. I am sure for Pietro, the obscure and mystifying habit of *siesta* or *pausa* (in which stores of all kinds shut down moments after they open and then do not reopen until you're way too tired to drive back into town) is just so much a part of everyday life that he didn't even think to mention it. Somehow, though, in the same run of luck that had produced a police welcome and a celebration of our national holiday, we managed to get to the store moments before it closed. I wouldn't find this out until sometime later, however, as I could find no place to park the minibus and had surrendered to the idea of dropping Terri and our two older boys at the curb. In some famous last words, I said something silly like, "I'll find some place to park and come join you."

It was words like these that I learned to say less and less. Circling the crowded little town of Maiori on a Sunday at noon during July taught me that the phrase "Lord willing" is much more intelligent. All of Italy and half of the rest of the United Nations had apparently descended upon this seaside town for a day at the beach. People were everywhere. Motorcycles and scooters zipped in and out of standstill traffic. Police officers enthusiastically blew their whistles and waved their hands—gestures largely ignored by the population as a whole. I turned up a side street only to find myself leaving town, apparently headed for some radio antennas placed high atop the mountains.

"Where are we going, Daddy?" asked Christine and J.R., the only remaining passengers on the minibus.

"Oh, just trying to find a place to park."

"Why don't you just go to a parking lot?"

"That's what I'm trying to do."

"I have to go to the bathroom."

This little exchange occurred at least forty times before I got turned around and back into town. Then I managed to turn up another side street and drove down into a cleverly hidden parking ramp. This action was met by a man explaining in fine Italian that it was full, to which I responded in the worst Italian that I was sorry but could never turn my minibus around and would, therefore, be donating it to the owners of the ramp. He kindly assisted as I extracted our clunky vehicle by pulling forward and backward sixty-three times.

"Where are we going, Daddy?"

"Oh, just trying to find a place to park."

"Why don't you just go to a parking lot?"

"That's what I'm trying to do."

"I have to go to the bathroom."

Finally, I found a section of road along the front of some apartment buildings that offered a bit of space. Someone else had staked out this same territory and was sitting in a little Fiat with the driver door open, apparently in a holding pattern for a passenger, much as I. Quickly, I tucked in behind and copied his example.

"Okay, kids. We'll just wait here for Mommy. You can jump out if you'd like."

"Yeah, Daddy!"

"I still have to go to the bathroom."

This last request I solved creatively with the privacy screening of an open van door, and so put to rest half the topics of conversation for the day so far. We then played Simon Says and watched the many pedestrians eagerly heading to the beach. We also had to avoid the water dripping down from clothes being hung out to dry two floors above. Then I got to converse with a police officer directing tow trucks in the extraction of illegally parked cars. Somehow I convinced him that we weren't worth towing because he smiled, waved at me, and then walked on.

"What did he want, Daddy?"

"Yeah, what did he say?"

"I think he asked if this van is our car, and would we be staying with it. But he might also have said that Godzilla is coming through here destroying the entire city and we should run for our lives. I'm not sure, really; my Italian isn't that good."

"He didn't say that really; did he, Daddy?"

Then we got to meet the fine officer again as we caused a traffic jam along the beach while Terri and her two assistants lugged massive bags of groceries into the open side door of the minibus. Our getaway time was horrible, and I made a mental note to scratch bank robbery off the list of desperate possible future activities for the Brady family. I kept looking in my rearview mirror nervously and saying helpful things such as, "Hurry!" The officer simply presided over us by watching and every now and then giving a furtive wave of the hand. Interestingly, he wasn't that upset by our unplanned rudeness, and neither was anyone else, which is pretty amazing, given that we had stopped up the whole town with our caper. He even nodded a friendly good-bye as we finally got underway.

It was right about then that I began to realize and appreciate the general level of goodwill displayed by the balance of the Italian population. I couldn't help being grateful for the many patient and horn-resistant folks we had encountered that day. I was also grateful we had groceries—it had been two and a half hours.

CHAPTER 5

# OBSCENE CUISINE AND THE ITALIAN RESTAURANT THING

*When I started this memoir I swore I would not clutter it with dissertations about food, but I soon realized that writing about Tuscany without talking about food is like writing about the Titanic without mentioning that it sank.*
– Ferenc Máté

I'm known for it, really. Food is not my thing. I've often commented that I eat to live, not the reverse. However, with the rapid onset of "older-ness," I find myself tilting at least a little toward the throngs of folks who sit around at lunch salivating over what they'll have for dinner. In Italy, the tilting turned into a total collapse, a full-scale structural breakdown, making the Leaning Tower of Pisa look as true as a plumb-line.

What could possibly be said about the food in Italy that hasn't been said before? Probably nothing. However, from one such as myself, who until recently (and certainly before Italy) was almost—and I say *almost*—as happy with a ham and cheese sandwich as anything fancy from a five-star restaurant, any comment about food should be earth-shattering. "Who, him? The food Neanderthal? Comment about cuisine? Why, he doesn't know *prosciutto* from bruschetta!" [Not true, by the way.] Perhaps one of the most surprising things about this trip was the total transformation in the likes of yours truly when it came to matters of the palate.

I remembered the food in Italy being extraordinary. But in pass-through visits like those of my previous experiences, one singularizes such observations into compartments: "That was a good meal," or "I really liked that ristorante." However, one can't possibly get the overpowering feeling of fresh, delicious, locally produced, healthy, simple, expertly prepared delicacies when one is speeding through like a teenager in a McDonald's drive-through. One must *experience* the food of Italy, as do the Italians, to truly get the real flavor of the place.

That, at least, was my plan. As authors Louise Fili and Lise Apatoff wrote, "Where else is a meal remembered with the same tenderness and passion usually reserved for a lover?"

*Okay*, I thought, *let's see what all the fuss is about.* And in such a mindset, I put on my best food attitude and got ready to learn— um, eat.

Most of my first samples came from our cramped little kitchen at *Villa Scarpariello*, with Terri preparing the very items with which we'd so painstakingly absconded from the busy beach town of Maiori. She had no spices, only limited utensils, and sparse knowledge of many of the ingredients. Still, the little meals she concocted for us were sublime, delicious, and not overly filling. How had she done it?

"I think it's the ingredients," she responded. "They don't seem to have milk and eggs and butter in everything like we do. And there's way more fresh stuff. Whatever the difference, it's certainly noticeable."

I, the food Neanderthal, agreed.

Also, we began getting the hang of the "Italian Restaurant Thing." This is the term I will use to describe the entire gamut of the Italian dining out experience. You see, back home, it's as easy as pulling into a parking lot, waltzing up to the hostess stand, getting a seat, reading a menu, eating the food, paying the bill, and leaving. In Italy, not one of those steps happens quite that simply.

Lemmesplain.

The Italian Restaurant Thing begins with understanding the hours of operation. In Italy (and this applies to stores, as well), restaurants open when the proprietors decide they're open. Seriously, that's what it boils down to. Sometimes there will be a sign on the door indicating hours of operation, but this has little or no correlation to actual practice. Many times we walked into a restaurant only to be told it was closed. "Come back in half an hour," or "Not open till seven-thirty," or "Why would you want to eat dinner so early?" were the typical responses. Parking, as with almost anywhere quaint and desirable in Italy, was also a problem. We found the best practice to be dumping our minibus at the first available spot and then hoofing it to dinner. This made targeting specific restaurants difficult but, luckily, nearly all of the restaurants in Italy are excellent. Just drive to a certain town, park in some farmer's field if you have to, and start walking. Sooner or later you'll come to a restaurant, and more likely than not, it will be great.

Choosing the exact restaurant may be a bit of a challenge, however, especially if you are in one of the larger cities populated by many excellent choices. Rome, near the Vatican, for instance, presents its own kind of carnival atmosphere outside the storefronts of its restaurants. This is because proprietors stand out among the passersby summoning them into their particular place as if Catherine de Medici herself were in the kitchen cooking. "*Prego, prego,*" they'll say, putting their arm around you and steering you inside. Their tone of voice is a practiced, persuasive, and an "of course this is where you want to be" sort of thing, as if they were offering you their very life savings, so why wouldn't you want to take it? They'll stick menus in your hands and push chairs under your rumpus before you even know what's hit you. It's hard not to succumb to such endearing entreaties, and you start trying to convince yourself that, yes, in fact, you really do want to eat at this particular place and now, come to think of it, you've known it all along.

Ordering is really no big deal. In fact, like many travelers before us, no doubt, we discovered the first Italian we learned to speak fluently was that relating to food and ordering in a restaurant. By the end of the trip, we were spouting off food items and preparation preferences like John Gotti at his corner *trattoria*.

Although France is oddly more famous for its multiple courses and long dining experiences, it was Italy that showed them how to do food. First is the bread and olive oil. This is followed by the *antipasti* (although, bewilderingly, sometimes this goes at the end of the meal). Next comes the *prima piatti* (first plates), followed by the *secondi piatti* (second plates). Finally, there is the *dolce* (dessert), then espresso, and then *grappa* to wash it all down. Wine flows throughout this whole ordeal. There are also variations and extensions of this general structure, but this is normally how it is done. With so many steps (and all of them wonderful), one really begins to feel far away from home. There is never any talk of "low-cal" or "carbs" or "proteins." For Italians, dissecting foods into these vulgar terms is as offensive as breaking sexual intercourse down into steps and sub-components. In Italy—and I can't emphasize this enough—eating is part of living life the way it is supposed to be lived. It is an experience. It is a way of life. It is the culture itself, all embodied in one act. The ingredients are fresh, local and for the most part, healthy and devoid of the preservatives, packaging, transportation, display, handling, chemicals, and the like common with most North American foods. In fact, one begins to wonder if food like that in Italy is even *possible* back home. My hunch is no, it's not. This type of food, closer to real, organic, and authentic than anything we had ever experienced, could be consumed in greater quantities with far less consequences than we expected. This was a relief to discover because, in no time, we were eating like pigs and loving every minute of it.

One word of caution: because of the strength of the euro as compared to the US dollar, a phenomenon rooted in the monetary policy of the United States and the relative profligacy of our government for spending and printing money, eating in Italy will be expensive. It will be worth it, to be sure, but plan on laying out some cash. Or just perhaps, by the time you read this, the European Union will have advanced in its own profligacy for spending and the currencies will be more in line, all being right with the world once again.

Perhaps no part of the dining experience will be as expensive as drinks. And by this, I don't even necessarily mean the wines, as soft drinks and even water at the table are very expensive. There won't be any free glasses of ice water delivered to the table at a constant flow like back home, where to have a glass of water run dry is the greatest offense. Oh, no. Water, either sparkling or natural (*senza gas*), is precious to the last drop. Our kids had to learn not to glug it like they were getting it out of a tap. Large (*grande*) bottles would be brought to the table and rationed throughout the meal. Coffee is a whole different affair, with espressos being tiny, hard-hitting little buggers instead of twenty-ounce monsters like back home, while cappuccinos are so rich they are considered food. But the wines are the most incredible. Local and wonderful, the quality and variety in Italy is staggering. And for the most part, the prices one finds are incredibly reasonable. In most restaurants, the best deal is their house wine, *vino della casa*, usually unlabeled, non-bottled wine that is delicious and cheap.

This brings us to the desserts (*dolci*). For one accustomed to sugared-up, super-sweet American fare, Italian desserts hit the palate in a less impressive way. They seem simpler, more straightforward, and not so heavy. At first, I didn't get it. Eventually, though, I started thinking of the entire meal as a piece of music. In America, the meal builds throughout the experience and crescendos to a climax at the end with a super-sweet, humongous, and filling dessert of sinful proportions. In Italy, the meal climaxes somewhere during the second plate, and the desserts are simply a soft fade to the finish, as a diminuendo.

Another stark difference between the dining experiences in North America and Italy is paying the bill at the end. Back home, waitresses and waiters bring the check in a bit of a hurry, often before they've even asked if dessert is desired. This is because other customers are waiting outside, and the faster they can clear the table and seat the next patron, the better. In Italy, however, crowds or not, it seems as if they never want you to leave. You will likely have to ask for the bill (*il conto*) several times. Eventually, they might even bring it to you. Itemizing the meal is also a curious affair; prices and totals often seem arbitrary. Charmingly, this usually worked in our favor. The times when we inquired if the totals were correct, we were answered with friendly *prego*s and assurances that all was well.

This was not the case in some parts of Rome, however, a place where the dining experience can sometimes be confused with a Mafia shakedown. We learned painfully that the best way to approach a meal in these larger, tourist-trap places was to be certain how much we were to be charged before sitting down. But this is the exception, not the norm. Most restaurants, if properly understood, provide the patron with an experience par excellence.

One tourist family told us they had developed a habit of checking the menu in front of a restaurant for prices before deciding to go inside. "I'm not hungry," one would say if the prices seemed high. This sounded like sage advice. But after a while, it began to seem as if all the prices were pretty much the same, anyway. Sure, the *coperto* (cover charge) varied based upon the setting, but even this added up to less than tips back home. When it came right down to it, the average price for a meal for the six of us didn't fluctuate much, and the food and service were nearly always excellent.

We read somewhere about the different types of restaurants. There are *ristoranti*, *trattorias*, and *osterias*, each with a specific purpose, target customer, and price range. This may be true in some way, but we couldn't tell much of a difference anywhere we went—we loved them all. We were also informed there is often "local" pricing and "tourist" pricing but had no problem with this concept.

Then there is the whole food allergy thing. When I was younger and much less compassionate, I told Terri I thought allergies were a figment of people's imaginations. It seemed to me allergies were for high-maintenance types, attention-getters, and hypochondriacs. "All in your head," I told her. Then one day I went to a doctor to get some antibiotics for a pesky flu I couldn't shake. Instead of prescribing pills, he gave me a shot. Within hours, I was itching like a tree frog. The worst part was the reaction set in while I was in the hot tub with friends. In the heat of that water, my discomfort grew. I fought the urge to itch until it pushed me to the edge of sanity. I sprang out of the water to go inside and see just what was going on. I was covered in a red rash that made me look like the bad guy in a super hero movie.

My next comeuppance occurred after driving a dune buggy through tall spring weeds. I sneezed incessantly, my nose ran, and my eyes swelled nearly shut into little slits. I looked like Rocky Balboa saying, "Cut me, Mick!" Incidentally, that night Terri rented the movie *Hitch*, which features a scene in which Will Smith has an allergic reaction to shellfish and his face puffs up exactly like mine was at that very minute. I must have looked like the Elephant Man as I laughed and laughed through my disfigured face.

The real lesson, however, came in the form of Nathaniel. When he was twelve months old, we discovered he had life-threatening allergic reactions to milk and beef. This immediately made our restaurant experiences a complicated affair. First, the waiter or waitress needs to be informed about the situation. Next, we have to figure out what he can eat. Usually this involves the waiter running back to the chef for a consultation. In the early days, we experienced a lot of people like I had been: totally uncompassionate and unhelpful. As the years have gone by, however, we have run into less trouble. So naturally, one of the concerns we had when planning this trip was how to do all this in a foreign language and keep Nate safe. Terri's prearranged explanation in Italian on a paper we could show upon entry into a restaurant worked beautifully for a couple of reasons. First, the ingredients in Italian cooking are simple and rarely ever include milk or butter—the bread, too, something almost unheard of back home. But the other reason is what I attribute to Italian politeness. Every waiter and waitress, without exception, showed concern and took time to work through the situation.

Language barriers, cover charges, cultural differences, and even allergy considerations do nothing to diminish the charm of the Italian dining experience. Raeleen D'Agostino Mautner wrote, "Mealtime in Italy is a kaleidoscope of sensations, where sights, smells, sounds, and textures come together to sustain the total person." After a while, one realizes that to eat in Italy is to luxuriate. It requires a different biometric rhythm, a slowing down, and an intentional enjoyment of food, companions, and environment.

There is only one problem: Stepping back into the real world after a meal at a restaurant in Italy is a bit of a letdown. There, life, with its responsibilities, heavy issues, and pressures, goes on. Alas, it hadn't disappeared after all; it had merely waited outside the door.   At least there is the next meal to think about.   And it was amid realizations such as these that we began to comprehend at least a little of the secret of Italian life.   It also dawned on me that I was becoming like everyone else when it came to food.   Maybe there was hope for me after all.

CHAPTER 6

# HUNTING A GPS AND RUINING RUINS

*All journeys have secret destinations of which the traveler is unaware.* – Martin Buber

The view from the balcony of our villa at *Scarpariello* was a magnificent Mediterranean delight. The calm sea was in stark contrast to the rugged cliffs rising straight to the sky. Scattered across the steep rockfaces were dwellings of all sorts, shapes, and colors. There were homes, villas, hotels, and restaurants. All of them appeared old. And though each was as unique a creation as had ever been conceived in the halls of any civil engineering institute, somehow they all blended together into a splendid symphony of civilization. As with musical instruments as diverse as a kettle drum and a clarinet, beautiful harmony was made by blending the many. Gentle sea breezes wafted through the stone arches of our balcony and into the open doorways of our living room and dining area, filling our space with the salty smell that can only be found along a coast. Occasional noises from pleasure boats and yachts floated up to us in broken pieces, advertising the fun and frolic taking place just offshore. Far to our left, a glimpse of the busy beaches in Minori and Maiori could also be seen, with their many colored umbrellas neatly arranged in rows and a barely discernible moving mass of humanity beneath.

As beautiful as it was, however, I was used to more space than a cliffside perch could provide. In no time, I was stir-crazy and yearning for an outing. A guidebook from reception provided the answer: Poseidonia. I had read briefly about this ancient ruin city before coming to Italy, and of the early Greek colonization of the Italian peninsula. Now it was time to see it for ourselves. Besides, it would give us a chance to stop in a more substantial city, Salerno, considered *substantial* (and necessary) by the very fact that it was likely to sell GPSs. At least, that's what Pietro promised.

So we were off. Still with no road map, we hugged tightly to the coast, counting on the fact that the sea would be our guide all the way to Salerno. If along the way we decided to take a wrong turn and plow up an endlessly snaking switchback mountain road and somehow failed to notice that fact, then we were deserving of our fate. Otherwise, we reasoned, it would be impossible to get lost.

And that's how it worked. We found Salerno with no trouble, descending steeply to the quay and then making our way along the marina and seafront of the tourist district. We knew we somehow needed to find our way into town where they sold GPSs. Terri was on the phone trying to find such a place and, incredibly, managed to make contact with a few different stores. Yes, they sold GPSs. At least that's what we think they said. But they might have been selling goldfish, for all we knew. There seemed to be no one who spoke English any better than we spoke Italian.

"I don't want much—" I said as I drove in circles through the very busy city streets, "just a place with a big English sign that says, 'We sell GPSs to Americans.'"

"Where are we going, Daddy, and why are we driving in circles?" from the backseat.

"Looking for a store that sells GPSs."

"Why?"

"Because we're lost and need one to find our way."

"We're lost right now?"

"No, not really. But we will be if we don't get a GPS."

"So we're not lost, but we will be?"

"Kind of."

"How long do we have before we *are* lost?"

Dumbfounded silence in the front seats.

"Oh, and Daddy?"

"Yes."

"What's a GPS?"

And so it went as we jockeyed our clunky minibus up and down the narrow and congested Salerno streets. It began to appear that, even if we found a GPS store, whatever that was, we wouldn't be able to park within an hour of it. I began to hatch schemes in my head whereby I would jump out while Terri circled the block in the minibus—*a la* grocery trip. That's when I decided to take one more lap down by the seashore. And wouldn't you know it? In the amount of time since our last time through there, someone had leveled a huge piece of ground and paved a nice parking lot for us. We couldn't believe our eyes. How in the world had we missed it before? The darn thing was the size of a Wal-Mart and had barely any cars in it. Rubbing my eyes and looking again, I began to think I was suffering from some sort of tourist mirage. *Is this what happens to weary minibus drivers on their eighth lap of Salerno? Am I really seeing this?* I thought.

Sure enough, it was a bona fide parking lot. As I positioned our vehicle carefully so it would hang over evenly onto the parking spaces on either side, a man came up and offered a pre-paid ticket. Apparently, he was leaving and had remaining time on the tab. This was incredible. Moments before, it looked like we would never be able to park. Now we were doing it for free. By this point, we were feeling pretty cocky. Things were rolling our way. We skipped along the sidewalk holding hands with the kids and soaking up the sights, in danger of breaking out into "Zippity Doo Dah" at any moment.

Salerno is an interesting town. It was the site of the World War II Allied landing in the invasion of southern Europe. One can easily imagine the hordes of young soldiers pouring ashore, unsure what to expect. They had recently heard of Italy's surrender, but the Germans hadn't surrendered and were still as hostile as ever. In ferocious fighting that would largely be overshadowed back home by news of the Normandy landing in the north, the soldiers in the Italian campaign slugged forward nevertheless. One of them, Terri's "Uncle Buck," fought with the 36th Army Division and at a family gathering earlier in the summer, had quietly asked me to say hello to Salerno for him when we took our trip. He had been a Jeep driver, often on ammunition supply duty. I wondered what he might have felt and seen along these mountainous shores not so many years before. To us, the scene was beautiful and adventurous. To him, one can only wonder. These were the thoughts running through my thankful mind when Terri nudged me with her elbow and pointed upward to a shop's sign.

"We Sell GPSs to Americans," it read.

Not really, but it should have, as accommodating as it turned out to be. Prominently displayed in the front window were several current model GPS units. With the exception of a motorcycle shop, it was the first store of any kind we had come to, and we were barely out of the parking lot. I made my way inside while Terri and the kids walked to the corner store for some gum.

It took ninety minutes and "What are we waiting for, Dad?" several times before we emerged with a brand new GPS, programmed with Italian maps and English settings. The enormous amount of time in the store was necessary because of the way he worked: *slowly and correctly.* Without any hurry whatsoever, the man I assumed to be the storeowner somehow concluded I was a first-time GPS owner. He, therefore, painstakingly went through every menu and feature, explaining it all in broken English and courteously slow Italian. Then, he uploaded all the latest updates from the Internet, and finally he properly precharged the battery.

It was too early in the trip for me to understand his efforts as anything but an individual characteristic. And while generalizations are dangerous and often oversimplified, I would gradually learn that his behavior was quite representative of the Italian way of life. It seems these wonderful people are not as interested in quantity as they are quality—a fact that exists not as a cliché but rather as a stark reality. If it can be done correctly, why not do so? And if it takes all year, who cares? As long as one doesn't have to miss lunch along the way, that is.

I gradually came to understand this attribute was largely responsible for the abundant and widespread attractiveness of nearly everything here. It seems the Italians can beautify almost anything. I found myself pointing my camera at the most unlikely objects and features, simply because they were so *appealing*—that rock wall, those flowers in a box on a balcony, that archway, those shutters, that foot path, that row of vines, that grove of olive trees, those freshly cut wheat fields. Many times, I felt as if we were walking around in someone's screensaver. My goodness, did these people do *anything* sloppily? No wonder their food tastes so good if they could put this kind of time and care into the simplest, smallest, most ordinary aspects of life. Again, these are dangerous generalizations, but there is some amount of fact expressed in the Italian word *sprezzatura*, which means "loosely": the Italians do it better than most without appearing to try very hard. It's nonchalance par excellence.

The Greeks weren't too shabby, either, as it turns out. We reached Poseidonia (the later Roman name for the city was Paestum) after a short drive south along the coast leading away from Salerno. Mercifully, the switchback mountain roads gave way to flat ground, and we found ourselves cruising comfortably through rich farmland. The sky was deep blue and so clear it appeared to have never had a cloud. And suddenly, we were at the ancient walls. I knew it immediately. The stones had a distinct historical appearance: large, rectangular, weathered, crumbling, and labeled with tourist signs—although not well enough, apparently, as we parked the minibus, unloaded the kids, and promptly walked into the train station. *What? This isn't the ticket office? Um, well, we knew that! Just checking departure times, folks; nothing to see here! (Kids, quickly, get back in the van.)*

Often wrong but never in doubt, I tried my best *sprezzatura* by driving away nonchalantly and entering an archway through the ancient city wall (which I later learned was called the Siren Gate, fifth century B.C.), quite sure it would lead me to the main attractions: the three Doric temples for which Poseidonia is famous. Wrong. Instead, I drove right into someone's backyard. I got out hesitantly, wondering why they would get the ancient walls all to themselves and walked a little farther.

That's when I saw it: the first temple, purportedly called the Temple of Ceres (or Athena). It stood magisterially a hundred yards distant behind some trees, its tan sandstone magnificent in the sun. I nearly ran back to the minibus. Back out of the private yard, out again under the arched entry, past the train station, and around the outside of the wall, and we were smack dab in a little tourist area with a proper ticket booth and all. How we missed it ranks right up there with the mystery of Elvis appearances in Kalamazoo.

Twenty-five hundred years ago, the Greek settlers walked these same streets. After that came the Romans, who made it their own city and expanded it greatly. Then came the Middle Ages when it was abandoned and later became the domain of buffalo farmers. Today, it was Americans. The six of us had the place almost entirely to ourselves. The fact that it was 147 degrees Fahrenheit in the shade may have had something to do with it. We took our pictures, read the placards, and did our obligatory search for a bathroom. We also tried to keep the children from ruining the ruins. For over two and a half millennia these stones had stood in place, through famines and fires and plagues and wars and even the sixties, but in seconds, our little ones were picking them up and whipping them violently at random. I could see it now: American kids detained in Italy for desecrating ancient temples. Maybe they would be *caned*, though I was pretty sure that had happened somewhere other than Italy. Maybe here they would just smack 'em with some pasta. At any rate, I realized there is something innate in little boys that makes them throw stones. They can't help it. I am fairly certain it's hard-wired—kind of the same as old men pulling their pants up to their armpits: some things, no matter how undecipherable, are just part of life.

Destruction abated, we took in the three temples and stared in wonder. They truly are remarkable. Large fluted columns continue to stand firm in their task of upholding entablatures with their cornices and friezes, and here and there one finds small sections indicating just how ornate these mighty beasts were in their heyday. Stark khaki against the misty mountains in the background, with tall cypresses and picturesque parasol pines scattered throughout the ruins, the temples are the centerpieces in an absolutely beautiful scene. The ruins of the surrounding town also transport one back in time. Knee-high walls are all that remain of most of the structures save the temples, but the mosaic floors, patterns still recognizable in domestic designs today, abound. Expansive homes are discernible, complete with courtyards, pools, and atriums. Also recognizable are the central baths, a feature of these old Roman towns that speaks to a significant cultural difference from our own times. As if to accentuate the point about cultures, there is also an arena.

I am fascinated by the peek into the lives of those who lived so long ago and also interested in how much their structures integrated the two concepts of living "outside" and "inside." However, walking around the ruins, one's attention is unavoidably drawn to the temples. One, the temple of Poseidon (or Neptune), built in 450 B.C., is supposedly the best-preserved Doric temple in the world. Of an architecture most famously displayed by the Parthenon on the Acropolis in Athens, Greece, the Doric temple is one of the world's most recognizable ancient structures. Constructed with rows of fluted columns upholding triangular entablatures with sculpted friezes, the proportions and overall beauty produce a timeless appeal. Copied extensively right down to today, the style evokes both an ancient nostalgia and also an easy familiarity. As one begins to remember the strange gods and goddesses to which these works of art were dedicated and the sheer remoteness in time from our own day in which they were built, the awesome sense of time and place hits home. It was also humbling to realize the ancient Greeks got all the way here without a GPS.

CHAPTER 7

# SOME BEACH

*People travel to faraway places to watch, in fascination, the kind of people they ignore at home.* – Dagobert D. Runes

I grew up on the shores of the Great Lakes. If you've never been there, particularly Michigan's west coast, picture one of the famous California beaches: pristine sand stretching for miles along endlessly pounding surf, thousands of people, girls in bikinis, mountains in the background, sunshine beaming brightly, sports cars driving along the boardwalk, and surfers out in the waves. The beaches of Lake Michigan are exactly like that, except for the surf (fresh water chop instead), people, bikinis, mountains, sunshine, sports cars, boardwalks, and surfers. If you next dropped the water temperature twenty degrees, you'd have a pretty clear picture. The shores of Michigan are stunningly beautiful, largely abandoned, and frigid as all get out. Every now and then, however, you catch a few pretty good days. At such moments, a Great Lakes beach can seem like heaven on earth.

So I consider myself at least a little bit of a beach veteran. In addition to the extensive Michigan experiences, I have also enjoyed beaches from Japan to the Caribbean, Florida to Hawaii, and in Bora Bora. Nothing, though, could have prepared me for the experience of a beach visit along Italy's Amalfi Coast.

After a day of touring ruins, I thought a little break might be a good reward for the kids. So the next day, we packed up the trusty minibus with towels, sunscreen, balls, and sunglasses and drove into Maiori, scene of the famous grocery heist just days before. It was early morning and a work day for most, so the town was significantly transfigured from the jam-packed beach festival we had earlier encountered. There were still quite a few folks about, but we were actually able to find a parking spot right along the beach. Little did we know it would be the last good real estate we'd acquire that day.

I had a bit of an inkling how this was going to work. I'd seen it all along the French Riviera a few years before. Whereas the beaches of most of the world are wide-open, free-range sort of affairs, for some reason, many beaches along the south of Europe get a little strange. Maiori would be no different. With the exception of a little postage-stamp sized "public beach" section (usually at the end closest to the messiest boats and worst seaweed and largest dead fish), the entire beach is occupied by businesses. I don't mean businesses *along the beach*; I mean businesses *on the beach* itself. Almost all the way to the water's edge, umbrellas are arranged neatly in rows, crammed together so their brims almost touch each other. Along both sides of such a property extends a chain or rope cordoning off that business's section of beach from the neighboring competitor. One can easily keep track of the different sections because the umbrellas are color coordinated: all red in this section. Next door? All green with white stripes, etc. You show up at the curb, pay an unposted amount of money, and then someone escorts you to your umbrella.

For us, it was fifteen euro for the whole day. I asked about being in the row in front near the water and was told, "It is not possible." Then we were led down some steps to beach level, out across a wooden walkway, and down between a row of umbrellas all the way to the end along the plastic chain separating our establishment from the one next door. It was like being given the home in the neighborhood that faces the water tower. I looked out toward the sea and saw six or more rows ahead of us. The one along the water's edge was completely unoccupied, as were 90 percent of the spots in the whole complex. Compared to the acres and acres of experiences we'd had on beaches around the world, this was high up on the strange list.

Next I surveyed our "property." It was at least nine square feet, consisting of the aforementioned umbrella flanked by a lounge on one side and a high-backed chair on the other.

I can't help a small diversion describing these chairs . . . Italy is known around the world for its design. This applies to cars, motorcycles, architecture, clothing, leather goods, what have you. There is a style to the things Italians make that is unique and appealing. In most cases, they just get it right. Not so, however, when it comes to beach chairs. Everywhere we went, from the hotel pool in Sorrento, to *Villa Scarpariello*, to this beach in Maiori, and later at our villa in Tuscany, we encountered these same awful chairs. They were everywhere. Pick up any brochure for a hotel, and you'll see them by the pool. Drive by any beach, and it's all they've got. Yet for us, the darn things were impossible. We couldn't figure out how in the world anyone could get comfortable in them. Take the lounge, for instance; it was adjustable to two settings: 1) backache and 2) neck ache. Whoever had designed this highly popular chair had never taken a look at the human skeleton. In the lower position, the lounge required one to bend at the shoulder blades. In the upright position, one was expected to bend at the kidneys. More time had apparently been invested into the contraption that folds up over the head, ostensibly to shield out the sun. Instead, this device invariably ends up in one's face or hair. Eventually, I concluded this handy feature must be there to hide one's grimacing face.

The upright chair was no better. Sitting in it was an experience reminiscent of those baby bounce seats one hangs in a doorway. The baby fits down into it, fully trapped, and bounces up and down. This is exactly how this chair felt, minus the bouncing part. That would have made it fun. Instead, as soon as you plop down into it, you realize you'll need help extracting yourself. This chair, too, has two helpful settings: 1) pinch fingers and 2) pop pelvis.

Terri and I took turns trading back and forth between these two delightful contraptions of our most recent real estate transaction as our children frolicked in the sand. Actually, they first had to snake through the maze of chairs and umbrellas and all the smoking Italians before doing any frolicking. That's apparently one of the largest attractions of the beach: smoking. Everywhere we looked, that's what people were doing. Even the parents. This was far different from Ireland, where we couldn't help but notice how frowned upon smoking was, at least judging by the warning labels on cigarette cartons, which said things such as, "Warning: Smoking has been shown to kill people outright. It is stupid, stupid, stupid!" and "Only an idiot would buy this pack of cigarettes." And those were some of the tamer ones. So I guess what I'm saying is if you are a smoker, you probably want to choose Italy over Ireland. Besides, the beaches in Ireland are probably pretty rainy, anyway.

After assuming our position in the umbrella city, wrestling with the furniture, and observing the smokers, I next was confronted with physiques. It was hard to avoid. For one thing, one-piece swimsuits must be quite out of style. Instead, what's fashionable seems to be flab hanging down over a bikini bottom. And that was just the men. The women's suits were even less modest. I learned more about Italian anatomy in half an hour than any lawn furniture designer ever knew. Apparently, I wasn't the only one noticing. My five-year-old innocently made the comment, "These mommies and daddies don't need to buy trampolines; their kids can just bounce on their bellies!"

I snaked my way through the umbrella maze and joined my children in the water. Here's where the Mediterranean shines. Warm, calm salt water gently carried me along on my back as I surveyed the beautiful mountain behind the small town. I relaxed in total comfort, swimming with my children and gazing all around. *What a beautiful place*, I thought, spotting a castle I hadn't seen before perched high up on a crag.

Back on shore, we kicked around a small soccer ball and then tossed it high to enable heroic diving catches. I took the two younger children for rides on my back out past the swim area markers. Out there, the water grew a bit cooler, offering refreshment against the ever-rising sun. The day was getting hotter and hotter, and I could see the umbrella city filling up ashore. We headed back to our little slice of beach, and our kids began digging a commercial strip mine. They piled the rough, nearly black sand high on four sides of an enormous pit. This overflowed into several other beach sites in the neighborhood, crowding others out and blatantly trespassing—all without a permit—albeit, no one seemed to mind, as between smoke rings, we were given approving smiles and nods. Once again, we were welcomed by the friendliness of the people.

Our children thought it was funny how the coarse sand stuck to them when they were wet, so they rolled around and got completely covered, sand filling each one's face, nose, mouth, ears, and hair—all the places a parent would later have to scrub clean. But for the moment, they were having too much fun to be stopped. We took pictures and laughed, sharing in one of those good family moments vacations are supposed to bring.

It wasn't long before I started thinking about lunch. I was going native. Not all the way, though. I'd have to be in Italy for a hundred years before I'd buy one of those tight, bikini-style swim trunks . . . come to think of it, maybe two hundred.

CHAPTER 8

# FRIENDS IN LOW COUNTRIES

*A journey is best measured in friends, rather than miles.*
– Tim Cahill

There was a sea diving platform at *Villa Scarpariello* that my children just loved. Depending upon the tide, it rested anywhere from about two to four feet above the water's surface. For my younger ones, jumping off the platform represented quite a feat. Neither would do it at first unless I was floating right in their landing zone, arms extended, waiting to catch them. As time passed, however, they got braver and braver, leaping on their own and even naming their creative jumps. For the older two, it was only a few minutes before they tested higher launching points.

The Belgians were to blame for this.

One of the things that attracted us to *Villa Scarpariello* was its seclusion. With only a handful of rooms spread out at different elevations along the cliff face, most of the time, it felt as if we had the place to ourselves. There was one exception to this: the family in the room directly below us. We saw them everywhere we went around the resort. They certainly seemed to be among the most active vacationers there, and very much the most friendly.

Alain, middle aged, bespectacled, and quietly warm with an easy grin, introduced himself and struck up a conversation on the swim platform. He and his family were here on holiday from Brussels, he indicated, making their estimated twentieth visit to Italy. He then made a statement that very neatly summed up my love affair with this fascinating country: "Italy is the world's largest open-air museum." I concurred wholeheartedly. But for the moment, it also appeared to be one of the world's daredevil hangouts. Alain's two teenage boys were testing the limits of sanity by jumping from perches higher and higher up the cliff. I was amazed, Alain shook his head as if some things are inevitable, and my kids had found new heroes.

If you think about it, there are very few good memories that don't involve people. I understand the power of solitude and could even be considered a bit of a recluse, perhaps. But when it comes right down to it, people are a major part of the sweetness of life (although some folks represent other spices in the rack). The good things in life generally involve special moments, bonds, and relationships with others. I understood this, I thought, and had conjured this Italy trip as much for a family bonding time as anything else. What I didn't anticipate, however, was making new friends.

It's funny how you just click with certain people. In no time, my older two were playing fierce games of outdoor ping-pong with their new teenage companions, Vadim and Sascha. These weren't lighthearted, easygoing affairs, but full-on grudge matches. Hours and hours passed as the boys gave in to their competitive natures, unaware of any age, language, or cultural differences with their newfound mates. It was a fierce international ping-pong championship, right there under the lemon tree pergola.

The next morning, we were making our way across the resort, a little unsure of the day's schedule but ready to continue exploring, when we happened upon their whole family also heading out for the day. They were planning to take a bus or taxi or some such vehicle, but we informed them we just happened to have a bus of our own. So we piled in together and drove to the very touristy town of Amalfi. They were planning on taking the ferryboat to Positano and invited us along.

Why not?

Carolina and Terri hit it off in a big way, and Alain's easygoing style and unassuming conversation was very endearing. Their two boys were also very impressive young men, taking time with our little ones and buddying up with our older two. While my natural instincts are to usually keep to myself, Terri is just the opposite. She loves meeting new people and never was part of a social event she didn't like. If there were visitors in our house 24/7, she would be in her glory. For her, chumming around with new friends is what makes for a perfect day. As this particular day progressed, I couldn't have agreed with her more.

Positano is one of the scenic little towns through which we'd driven on our way to *Scarpariello*. Crammed into an indention in the mountains, it sits in a crescent shaped cove around a small patch of beach. If it was scenic when we drove through, it was downright gorgeous as we approached from the sea. Nearly everyone on the ferryboat had his or her camera out snapping madly as we pulled into port. The day was a little overcast, soft clouds colliding with the mountaintops, while shafts of sunlight broke through and il-luminated the many colored buildings along the steep hills of the town. Like layers on a wedding cake, elevation after elevation of buildings cascaded from the side of the steep hill in pleasing har-mony. Pinks and reds and yellows and peaches and all shades in between colored these buildings, and most had flower-drenched balconies. In fact, flowers were everywhere in Positano. Bright pink bougainvilleas dominated, shining forth from archways and arbors. In the crux of the crescent formed by the mountain, nearly down at beach level, rests the dominating structure of the golden-domed Positano Parish church, while way up high, craggy cliffs jut over the town and reach up to the swiftly moving clouds. We had heard Positano was one of Italy's highest-priced real estate markets, and we had no trouble seeing why. First of all, there is precious little of it. Second, it appears that every single building has a fantastic view of the calm expanse of the Mediterranean. And third, who wouldn't want to live in a wedding cake?

It was warm, to be sure, but the bit of clouds gave us some reprieve from the hot July sun. With no plan, no destination, and no schedule, we wandered up into the narrow streets to begin our adventure. I love discovering new things, seeing new sights, and just plain exploring. I was not to be disappointed because almost immediately, I saw something I had never seen before. There, directly in front of the entrance to one of the fanciest restaurants in town, a group of four adults decided to change a baby's diaper. It was as if a whistle had blown, and they were in a competition for the fastest change. One of them whipped out a blanket and threw it down, and another plopped the kid onto his back, while a third whisked off the soiled diaper and hurled it into the hands of a fourth, who shoved wipes and a clean diaper back in the direction of the child. All the while, the maître d' stood ramrod straight, pretending not to notice the vaudeville act happening a mere three feet from his doorway. The four adults completed their task, dismantled their changing station, and stood up quickly. They had done it: one more baby's bottom was clean, safe from rash, and the world was a better place.

With no agenda or particular place to be, we wandered the narrow, steep streets and peered in at the shops. At one point, all the boys and men in our group stood in wonder at an odd assortment of items hanging on the outer wall of one of the stores. "What do you suppose this is?" asked Alain, to which I could give no intelligent reply. I knew what I *thought* it was, but I was hesitant to express it. Certainly it was too small for, um, well . . . The others seemed to be considering the same line of reasoning but also held back due to the instinct that these items were just too small to be used for *that* purpose. Finally, the store's owner came out and explained in broken English that they were thongs for flip-flops. None of us had been thinking about footwear.

The art galleries enraptured my six-year-old daughter. She walked into her first with a twirl and look of wonder. She seemed awed that such places existed. I stammered out an answer to her question about why there were paintings of naked women and steered her back out into the regular world.

My boys were coaxing for a soccer ball, as they had lost the tiny one that had served as an instrument of trespassing on the beach in Maiori. Europe being Europe, we found one for sale within three steps, and they hungrily made the purchase. Now we walked as a clump of two families while our mix of children juggled a soccer ball amongst the crowds on the narrow streets. This wasn't nearly as annoying to our fellow tourists as the political conversation we got into at a tight twist in the walkways in front of yet another art gallery. A painting of the United States Presidential seal had prompted it. Sascha and Vadim were curious about my particular assessment of American domestic policy, so I gently enlightened them on my very astute and entirely correct viewpoint. This provoked more questions and my inquiry into how things were working out in Belgium. We were enjoying ourselves quite thoroughly, learning about each other's countries and obtaining the inside scoop. However, some American tourists squeezing by the tight corner barked at us in their charming manner, "I don't think this is the place for it!" None of us could be sure if the endearing women were referring to our choice of conversational topics, our viewpoints, or more simply our obstruction of the walkway. So we ducked into another art gallery, this one featuring modern art, and left without understanding anything but still feeling somehow enlightened, and by now, also hungry.

We had lunch on a balcony overlooking the beach a hundred feet below and took photographs of bougainvillea growing extensively on latticework overhead. We told stories and exchanged laughs, posed for group shots, and had no trouble attracting volunteers to snap the photos. During a relaxing and delicious pasta lunch, Alain discussed his favorite Italian wine, and we coaxed Carolina to tell us the story of how the two had met on a train to Florence. We had them describe their house and garden in Brussels, and we likewise depicted our own hometown. We even covered religion at one point. Having broken all the rules of civility by discussing both politics and religion on the first date, without consequence I might add, we happily spilled out of our lunch as one family unit and climbed all the way to the top of the town. This felt necessary after the pasta, but the heat and sweat made it less desirable as we ascended, especially since Christine and J.R. were by now reduced to ballasts and insisted on being carried. So we hiked back down in search of resuscitation-by-gelato. One learns quite quickly here to chase calories with calories, with the ready excuse of "We're on vacation" near at hand.

The kids took up a game of soccer in the main square near the edge of the beach, kicking, scuffling, scrambling, and laughing. Even my little ones joined in the fray. And when the maître d' looked uncomfortable with the commotion in front of his fancy establishment, I gave the kids a wink to keep on playing. It wasn't like they were changing diapers.

CHAPTER 9

# A HERCULEAN EFFORT TO FIND HERCULANEUM

*Tourists don't know where they've been; travelers don't know where they're going.* – Paul Theroux

In 79 A.D. Mount Vesuvius erupted and created havoc among the local Romans. By this, I mean it killed them all—except for Pliny the Younger, that is, who wrote his observations of the great event from a position of safety aboard a boat in the Mediterranean. Like a good reporter, he kept his professional distance, allowing others like his uncle to die by going ashore to help the victims. Pliny's questionable heroism aside, we are still regaled by his rendition of what happened, and seeing firsthand the enormous size of Mount Vesuvius and its obvious missing top, one shudders to imagine what the eruption must have been like.

Two towns in particular were surprisingly well preserved by the geological event. Volcanic ash literally buried the city of Pompeii in short order, thereby preserving its buildings and much of the detail of Roman daily life. A slightly different variation similarly preserved the small coastal village of Herculaneum: it was buried beneath an enormous mudslide. Experts say Herculaneum, due to the nature of the mud, is even better preserved than Pompeii. Having seen Pompeii on a previous visit and, indeed, being duly impressed by the condition of the souvenir shops, parking lots, and bathrooms, I decided I'd like to sample Herculaneum this go around.

To get there, we had to jockey the minibus up and over the mountain range to our rear and descend into the enormous sprawling city of Naples (Napoli). With our trusty GPS, we headed out bravely, certain nothing could go wrong. Lunch at a tiny pizzeria at nearly the highest point of elevation only served to increase our comfort and positive attitudes. This was not damaged in any way by the fact that the pizzeria informed us it had no pizza. Its pasta was excellent besides.

Things went well at first, even getting fuel for the minibus. There are things you take for granted back home that play a major part in properly obtaining and paying for fuel for your vehicle. Like being able to read. Without this subtle skill, one is left to take note of color-coding and similar symbology. In a foreign country, it seems as if every station has a different convention. Green means regular gasoline; blue means diesel; black means some other kind of diesel, and yellow means . . . I don't know what it means, but I never used the yellow. Just when you think you have all this memorized, some station has its own very different color scheme. Blue means regular gas, black means diesel, and they don't even have a yellow! Also, in Italy, full service is still in vogue at most stations, and this became one of the biggest unsolved mysteries of the entire trip. It seemed no matter how well I thought I read the signs, "Self Serve Over Here" and "Full Serve Over There," I always, and by always I mean *always*, ended up receiving full service. I could be dead sure the sign said something along the lines of "Broke, cheap people over here," and yet a man in a little grey uniform would saunter out to me and begin filling my tank. Even Terri and her Spanish couldn't seem to figure it out. So I got quite adept at saying "diesel" and *"completo per favore."* Being an American, and one born much after the popularity of full-serve service stations, I have absolutely no idea why anyone would want someone else to pump his gas for him and, more importantly, what to do while that someone is doing the said pumping. It really accomplishes nothing, as far as I can tell. It's not like I can be doing something productive with that three minutes of time someone else is doing my work for me. Do I stand there and watch? Do I sit in the car and wait like an aristocrat? I was never sure. This was compounded by the fact that the minibus couldn't receive fuel unless the driver's door was open. I pretty much had to be out there with the uniformed agent the whole time. So now two of us were standing there doing nothing while the fuel pumped in. Not being able to conduct any small talk only multiplied the sense of discomfort. Usually, I would end up just standing there watching the digital readout count upward like it was the most fascinating thing since the mobile above my baby crib. Finally and mercifully, the pump would switch off, and the whole ordeal would be over.

*"Grazie, signore."*

*"Prego."*

*"Arrivederci."*

*"Arrivederci."*

Of course, all of this applies to those times when I was actually fortunate enough to find a gas station that was open. Most of the time when I needed fuel, this was not the case, gas stations being like everything else in Italy: closed most of the time, and especially when you need them. In such circumstances, I learned to operate the pre-pay mechanisms, which, of course, differed from station to station. But the general gist of the game was to pay ahead of time, specify which pump and how much fuel was desired, and pump away. Any excess payment was indicated on a receipt so that, theoretically, if you could ever return at a time when the gas station was open, you would be reimbursed. I saw this as quite the nice little scam and made it a sport of actually catching the stations open at a later time and getting my bits of euro back. On this day, however, the entire refueling thing went smoothly.

So we descended into the streets of Napoli in anticipation of seeing Herculaneum. I thrilled the children with a verbal history lesson while we drove. We were in high spirits. We then noticed our exit was completely ripped up for construction and closed. No problem, our GPS was already proposing an alternate route. We would soon learn, however, that this alternate route stuff was not one of its greatest strengths.

Taking the next exit, we followed the new purple line provided by the GPS. Also, I could see the sea in the distance and reasoned that we were headed in the approximately correct direction. I would simply use my own navigational skills in conjunction with the GPS to keep us on track.

Allow me at this point to give a note to future travelers. If you are driving in Napoli and your exit is closed, the best thing to do is to turn around at the next available exit, get back on the highway, and go back home. You don't have a chance.

I didn't know this at the time and, therefore, ended up plunging us into the strangest streets I've seen in twenty years of foreign travel. We soon came to realize that whoever had programmed this particular GPS had never ever been to Naples and probably had never even heard of it.

The streets got narrower and narrower, while the buildings around us got older and older. Eventually we ended up on a one-way street so narrow we had to pull in our mirrors on both sides. Cars were parked everywhere around us in haphazard fashion. People milled about all over the place. Scooters zipped and buzzed like flies. All the while, our GPS confidently led us onward as though this were the most normal route in the world. *This is how people get to Herculaneum?* we wondered.

Finally, we had to stop because a construction site blocked the road. It consisted of one tiny truck and a man with a jackhammer. A chain link fence surrounded the man and his little area. So the GPS proposed another route. This one took us through an archway between two buildings that was so narrow we almost scraped both sides as we went through. That was nothing, however, compared to what would stop us next: clothes racks. It seemed we had landed in the middle of some sort of outdoor shopping bazaar. Clothes on racks and carts were everywhere. Stands with leather purses filled one side of the road while shoes on display filled the other. There was no way we could get through, even though the man tending the clothing rack was kind enough to roll it out of our path.

It had now been hours since our non-pizza lunch at the pizzeria, and some of the passengers in the minibus were getting cranky. Several had been making bathroom requests for at least an hour. One had stopped making bathroom requests entirely, which was particularly worrisome. It was time for a decision. Unanimously we voted for heading home, or to a good restaurant, whichever came first. So once again we turned to our GPS, absolutely refusing to believe the unit was a creature straight from the bowels of Hell as all evidence was beginning to suggest. It promptly led us to the highway, which, of course, was completely barricaded for even more construction. I stopped, got out, and took a picture just to prove it. After driving through so much construction for so long, we began to realize the extent of the damage caused by Vesuvius, especially to the local highway system. Things were still being repaired two thousand years later.

It was at the precise moment when I whirled the minibus around and switched off the GPS that Terri spotted a sign for *Ercolano* (code name for Herculaneum). Following the sign led us to some other little brown signs that guided us straight to the attraction.

There. That wasn't so bad.

Herculaneum is a staggering site; the mudslide caused by the volcanic eruption of Vesuvius had indeed bestowed a remarkable degree of preservation on this two-thousand-year-old Roman city. It is subterranean: That is to say, it sits at least a full story below the ground level of modern day Naples (visible all around with its laundry flapping out its windows) and appears to be carved down into the ground like a town made by tiny hands in a sandbox. Even some of the original wood furniture and building materials are still intact and in place. Extremely impressive was a wooden screw press which had been used for getting the wrinkles out of clothing (laundry being a big thing around here for centuries, apparently). Also, paints, paintings, water pipes (both hot and cold), food in clay jars, and skeletons wearing jewelry (which, to be honest, didn't help their look all that much) were all found in abundance at Herculaneum. Flooring designs, wall decorations, and architectural layout indicate quite clearly that this was a very advanced civilization, in many ways quite similar to our own. Walking the old Roman roads, one is transported back in time and can almost imagine clothing and shoe racks out on the sidewalks and laundry flapping out of windows.

But strangest for me was the fact that Herculaneum had been a coastal village. Entering the dig site through a tunnel in the terrain, which in fact was the mud from the slide, the shoreline of the old town is obvious. The arches of the wharf and the entrances up to the town from the water's edge are clear. What is incredible is the distance Herculaneum now is from the sea. One could not even see today's coast from the upper sidewalk viewing areas overlooking the dig. The radical change to the topography by the eruption of Vesuvius is almost beyond comprehension, even when seen firsthand.

In my opinion, Pompeii gives one a better picture of the layout and size of a typical Roman city, while Herculaneum fills in the details. The two together make an unforgettable experience, mixing touring with a lesson in history, the shock of natural disaster, and the sublime sense of a time long lost. I would strongly recommend both to anyone, with the traveler's tip to allow a full day for touring and at least two for driving through the construction.

As was fast becoming a theme of this trip, our time in Herculaneum involved looking for bathrooms as much as it did learning from the rare and unique surroundings. We had some eruptions of our own to consider.

## CHAPTER 10

# TOSCANA: LIVING IN A MURAL

*Travel does what good novelists also do to the life of everyday,
placing it like a picture in a frame or a gem in its setting, so
that the intrinsic qualities are made more clear. Travel does
this with the very stuff that everyday life is made of, giving to
it the sharp contour and meaning of art.* – Freya Stark

Our first week had been quite wonderful, actually, and my
Monte Carlo-like driving skills had improved tremendously. It was
becoming second nature to squeeze the minibus into the smallest
of areas and whip it around like a stunt driver in a getaway scene.
As my father would say, I was *driving it like I had stolen it.* Before
we knew it, though, it was time to make the drive north into Tuscany for the next installment of our adventure.

Truly, the Tuscan portion of this trip was what had originally
lured us to Italy; the Amalfi week was thrown in at the last minute
just to broaden our exposure. As such, it had been a complete
success. With new friends, new knowledge, and hundreds of new
photos and memories, we checked out of *Villa Scarpariello* and
crossed the mountain, once again descending into Naples. This

time, we stuck to the main highway and scooted through as quickly as possible, leaving clothing racks undisturbed.

North out of Naples and up past Rome, northern Lazio starts to show the topical changes that eventuate into Tuscany. The hills begin to roll in undulations, copses of trees add patches of lush dark green, and wheat fields look like golden patches lain down from the sky by huge children making an art project. Vineyards start to become more prevalent, and their neat and tidy rows in perfect alignment over every type of ridge and rise are enough to impel even the staunchest teetotaler to yearn for a glass of *vino*. Punctuating this patchwork quilt of colors and shapes are the famous cypress trees, green pointed spires planted strategically along driveways and farm paths and almost always decorating the approaches to terracotta and stone villas.

It's the villas that get me. Everywhere I've ever been, from Bora Bora to Nagasaki, from San Paulo to Kilarne, I'm a sucker for architecture. Take me into an art museum or cathedral, show me frescoes and Madonnas that have thrilled art critics for centuries, and I'll soon grow weary and fussy, like a toddler with a chafing diaper. But get me around buildings, and I can walk among them all day, thinking about their architect, envisioning the masons who cut and placed the stones all those centuries ago, and admiring the endless additions and modifications required to preserve and prepare the structure for my later-day viewing. Maybe all that time in engineering school wasn't totally wasted after all. And maybe it's the engineer in me that can't stop ogling the endless villas and ruins of villas scattered throughout the hills of Tuscany. To me, these are the master brushstrokes in the painting of the landscape that round out my infatuation with the place. Each one of those abandoned ruins is a mute story, the scene of lives lost to the cold silence of the stony walls. Indeed, there are lots of beautiful places in the world, both from God's creative handiwork and from man's emulation, but for me, the Tuscan landscape takes the cake.

We have long called our home in Florida the "Tuscan Villa," inspired by a mural painted in the three modest arches of the great room, high up and baked in the tropical sun beaming relentlessly through the upper windows. The real estate agent had told us it was an authentic landscape from Tuscany, and we bought it—both the house and his bit about the mural, which shows green undulating hills with pokey green cypresses on inclined paths to inviting villas. Many a time have I craned my neck upward and wondered if it was based on an actual hillside somewhere with buildings from centuries ago. Could any place really look so inviting? Driving upward into the Valdichiana that morning confirmed that the mural was a fake. It didn't even come close to accurately representing this gorgeous place.

Terri grabbed my camera and attempted to get photos of the passing beauty. I hadn't seen her do that yet on this trip and took this as a good sign. As I said, this whole month in Italy thing was my concoction, a boondoggle dreamt up in the mind of a man with perpetual and unquenchable wanderlust. But my wife is more down to earth, more anchored and—well, okay—more stable. Her dominant weakness is that she's fallen for me. "I'd follow you to India if I had to," she'd said during the dating years to reassure me that my crazy dreams wouldn't scare her off. True to her word, too, that woman. I have dragged her from one end of the globe to the other, and she is still by my side, flashing that permanent smile of hers and digging right into this trip as if she had planned it herself. Still, I knew she would much prefer growing roots deep down in one spot, settling into a hometown in which she knew everyone and could sip iced tea on a porch with neighbors who would never leave. That's why her growing enthusiasm was a welcome sign: maybe she'd be overcome by it, too. Maybe I could still corrupt her. Maybe, just maybe, some day one of these villas would be ours! We'd have sweeping views from the veranda, cypress trees lining our driveway, some canopy pines shading an outdoor lunch table, and a neighbor named Francesco with tree-trunk arms and a farmer's walk who'd bring us over his home-made wild boar sausages . . .

"I have to use the bathroom!"

"Me, too!"

"I feel queasy."

I came out of my reverie and slipped back into daddy mode, pulling into a gas station just off the Autostrada. Conveniently, it had bathrooms, beverages, and dirt bike motorcycles for sale—everything necessary for refreshment.

Then we found our exit and looped around a little town called Terontola, looking for the train station. Here we met Daniela, a septuagenarian with a beaming smile and pretty white summer dress. She spoke exactly no English, but gestured toward a small brown Fiat with a bald man at the wheel and indicated we were to follow him. We did so, just out of town and onto a dirt farm path, upward on dirt switchbacks through a large olive grove, higher and higher we went. In the background, from side to side, grew a widening view of Lake Trasimeno in the distance. With off-road adventure and views like this, what could be better? Three weeks here and they'd never be able to get me to leave.

And it just kept getting better.

After at least two miles of crazy washed-out dirt road, climbing steeper and steeper, we stopped to wait for the opening of an iron gate. The villa was visible below grade on a perch into the side of the hill. Olive trees, 700 of them we would later find out, graced the terraces all around. The stone villa with shaded overhangs was beautiful—even better than it had looked in photos on the Internet. We were at *La Contea.*

The bald man in the car was Giulio, the owner, who had conceived the villa and built it thirty years before. He also spoke no English. So we sat at the long rectangular oak table in the kitchen and communicated like Native Americans meeting the pilgrims: all hand gestures and baby talk. When it finally ended, deposits given and papers signed, he left. Just like that, we were alone, temporary custodians of a corner of paradise.

"Can we swim, Daddy? Please?"

Four excited children broke swimsuit changing records and ran to jump into the pool in unison. The air was stiflingly hot, so I couldn't resist joining them and spending most of the rest of the afternoon splashing around, too. We were here! We had made it. The real part of our adventure, about which I had dreamed so long, had actually begun. We were ensconced as a screaming, giggling, "look at me," "watch this, Daddy," family on an Italian hillside covered in olive trees.

Tuscany was ours for three long weeks.

We were living in a mural.

CHAPTER 11

# RIDING FOR RUINS

*Anyone with a whole soul and even the dimmest passion for adventure will find his own way through Tuscany.*
– Barlozzo in *A Thousand Days in Tuscany*
by Marlena De Blasi

On a subsequent trip to Italy, I waited at the baggage claim at Fiumicino airport long enough to read all the way through *War and Peace*. During this extended campout, I struck up a conversation with an American standing next to me. In his latter middle age, he was taking his first trip to Italy with his grown kids. They had two weeks and were renting a car.

"How's the driving?" he asked.

I thought about the Amalfi Coast, Napoli, and downtown Rome and looked at him inquisitively. "It's not bad," I finally said, comparing it in my mind to England or Japan where the additional challenge of driving on the left side of the road was thrown in for spice. "But I would highly recommend a GPS," I said.

"Oh, thanks, I hadn't thought about that," he replied.

It was then I knew I had to write this book.

Driving in a foreign land is one of those rare things in life where one can receive much more credit than is due. It's a little like your mother-in-law coming to believe you were the inventor of the Post-It note. There are so many less challenging ways to travel through Europe that renting a car with all of its unknowns seems extreme—an accomplishment of bravery and intelligence. What about getting lost, finding fuel, understanding traffic signals, driving so fast? Truth be told, however, it's really not that tough.

Driving yourself through Italy is one of life's most rewarding endeavors—seriously. Remember the exhilaration you felt when you first got your driver's license as a pimply teenager? Oh, the freedom! You could drive to the corner convenience store all by yourself and procure a gallon of milk and bring it home like a hunter from medieval times slaying a wild boar for the family's sustenance. It's a little akin to that.

Having your own car in Italy allows tremendous explorations and the chance to truly get off the beaten path and discover the country as it really is. Just imagine setting off into the hills of Tuscany without a plan, agenda, or schedule. There is no tour guide, train schedule, or route. You just go. Turn by turn you traverse, *oohing* and *aahing* at breathtaking beauty, going through roundabouts without a care in the world, snaking your way up a switchback road to a thousand-year-old town you've never heard of positioned precariously on the side of a cliff. You park illegally a hundred times before you figure out the ticket system, accidentally drive through forbidden areas, and just generally make a mess of it. But remember, it's Italy. Nobody will really get mad at you once they realize you're a crazy foreigner who has somehow lost his way from the beaten path. They may shake their heads and give you directions on how to leave the area, but deep down inside, they will respect you. You care enough to discover their country and culture for real.

Some of our best memories of that month in Italy are of us all packed into the clunky minibus in a happy little family clump, winding our way across the Valdichianna, playing classical guitar music in the CD player as the sun beat down on lavender, sunflower, and wheat fields. We stopped in town after town, got lost, ate gelato from a bunch of different little roadside places, took pictures of everything, and became totally enamored with the views. I would recommend it to anyone.

Motorcycling, though, is reserved for the insane few. At this point, dear reader, you may be tempted to think your harmless little escapism reading has fallen off the cliff into pure fantasy . . . and who could blame you? But renting a motorcycle anywhere in Europe accomplishes something that can be had in very few places: a chance to act like a complete idiot and be totally accepted for it. With the possible exception of Uncle Charlie's wedding reception, where else can you accomplish such a feat? Allow me to elaborate.

When riding a motorcycle in North America, you are expected to behave entirely as though you are still in a car. What's the difference, after all, between two wheels and four? You are to stay in your lane, maintain safe and polite following distances, and only pass on the left in ample space on a dashed yellow line. Should you violate any of these restrictions, there are numerous law enforcement officers all too happy to have a roadside conference with you and explain the requirements. Motorcycles, after all, stand out in America, and highway patrolmen are quick to scrutinize them. In Europe, the game is totally different. It isn't only allowable, but it's downright expected that you'll pull right up on the bumper of the car ahead of you and zip past on either side as soon as you get even a credit-card's width of space. This is usually recommended on tight, blind corners. In fact, if you don't behave in this manner, you will get run over by the scooters and motorcycles coming up behind you. And how about law enforcement officers? For some unexplained reason, they are entirely blind to the behavior of motorcyclists.

Motorcycling in Europe can clearly be demonstrated by a situation that happens in downtown Rome a thousand times an hour. A stoplight halts six lanes of traffic and all cars stop. Instantly, motorcycles and scooters of every variety rush up into the space between the cars, edging to the extreme possible front of the stopped traffic, gunning their engines and waiting for the light to barely turn green. At that moment they all rush forward like a swarm of bees, leaving the cars in their smoky wake. These aren't merely crazy teenagers and daredevils with death wishes, but secretaries in nice dresses and nuns in their habits. In this one little illustration can be seen the entire difference in concept between motorcycling in North America and doing so in most of the rest of the world. Motorcycling back home is for the enthusiast: someone who loves and appreciates motorcycles and pretty much just wants to enjoy their usage—or at least wants an excuse to wear black leather and impersonate a criminal for a few hours at a time. In Europe, motorcycles are a necessity and often a mere commodity and, therefore, are ridden by nearly everyone. Advantages range from better gas mileage to quicker maneuvering through thick city traffic to easier parking. But for the tourist, all these attributes play to advantage. All the freedoms obtained by renting a car are completely amplified by riding a motorcycle. Because of their prevalence of use and all the norms of their operation, a North American loose in Italy on two wheels will just about have the time of his life.

My BMW 600 GS was delivered by carrier van to the train station in Terontola. This is because the driver couldn't find our villa, hidden as it was up the side of a hill at the end of a washed out, washboard dirt road, with no official address and snipers guarding its approach. Fortunately, an American kid from California was working at the motorcycle shop in Florence responsible for renting me my steel steed, and he called my cell phone to tell me Riccardo was lost and could I please meet him in town. No problem. When I got there, the bike was already off the truck and parked under a pine tree. Several helmets were neatly lined up across the back of the truck for my perusal and selection. I just love the flair Italians have for doing even the most rudimentary of tasks with a flourish.

Riccardo was exactly as I would have expected: lean and wiry, like most true dirt bikers, with not an ounce of body fat. He had a wide, bushy moustache, a tuft of hair under his bottom lip, piercing blue eyes, an enthusiastic tattoo collection, a chain from his pocket to his wallet, and black combat boots. He moved with deliberate precision, not wasting a motion, almost as a pastry chef wrapping tiny treats. His English was broken but good, and we hit it off immediately. Motorcyclists know their own kind. I chose my helmet, and Riccardo mounted up and followed me back up the dusty road to our villa. I signed a few documents, gave him a deposit, and then returned him to his van at the train station. Endearingly, he never once said anything even close to "Be careful" or "Take it easy." And just like that, I had my ticket to the loony farm.

I didn't venture too far the first time out, just took it easy and got used to the bike. It had a ton of kilometers on it, and the brakes were squeaky and soft, but I didn't care. I had my magic carpet, and it was time to fly.

I awoke early one morning and set out for my first real adventure on the BMW. Luckily, I had thought to bring along my red leather riding gloves from home, as the handle grips were of a strange ribbed variety that would rub off even the thickest of calluses. Donning the goofy-looking helmet I had chosen as the only one that would fit (I guess I've got a larger sized pumpkin, something I'll take to infer an above-average sized brain rather than a case of just being big-headed), I looked more likely to hand out parking tickets than anything else. Undeterred by my appearance, I set out along the bumpy, steep dirt road winding down from the villa. It was quite challenging. Although this bike is officially advertised as a multi-purpose machine, it is clearly biased toward paved roads. Additionally, the tires were bald from excessive use and its shocks had long since seen better days. On each trip down this hill, I was left to hang on tightly and resurrect every bit of motocross skills I could recover from my teenage days just to keep from sliding out in the corners—the corners being, of course, the only place along this path where any gravel still remained. Ravines and washouts hammered me, and the bike rattled angrily as I navigated through. Finally, I was out onto the paved road and headed north into the small old town of Riccio, whose stone buildings crowd the road on both sides. Roaring past them and into the unknown was a complete thrill.

Still not knowing my way around very well, I tried to take good note of my surroundings, setting my mental compass and looking for landmarks. I would eventually find this to be unnecessary, as each intersection and roundabout in the whole land is adorned with signposts indicating the adjacent towns in all directions. It is darn near impossible to determine a road's name, but the town to which it leads is always well displayed. I grew to love this system so much I found myself on subsequent outings leaving the portable GPS unit behind and bravely punching my way deeper and deeper into the landscape.

I turned at random up a steep roadway between old stone buildings and, within a few hundred yards, was screaming along another bumpy dirt road. This time, it was headed straight up a hill, first past a dirt soccer field enclosed with a twelve-foot rusty metal fence and then through rows of olive trees sloping off to the valley below. I continued higher and higher, pausing only slightly in my mind to contemplate Tuscan trespassing laws, when my fears were put to rest. Ahead came a signpost, one of the brown ones such as I had seen elsewhere, with a symbol representing a church and an arrow pointing farther up the trail. *A church? Up here?* Assured that it was open to the public, I pressed on with more confidence as the terrain got worse and worse. *The only people attending a worship service up this road would be four-wheel drive enthusiasts and Baja racecar drivers*, I thought.

Then at the top of a terrace a mile or so farther, I came upon a partially standing stone structure with one wall jutting proudly and alone into the pure blue sky. In the front was a marquee describing in certain detail the history of the building and all the particulars. At least that's what I think it said, as I, of course, could read only 5 percent of it. I guess it's also possible it was a "No Trespassing" sign warning errant North Americans of the cruel medieval punishments that awaited violators.

Thanks to the Arabic numbering system trouncing the former Roman one, what I *could* read clearly was the date: 1049. Contemplation of this inspired in me a quiet moment of thought as I considered with seriousness just who had built, paid for, cared for, and attended such a humble building in this forlorn location. *Was it a family chapel? A friary? An actual church?* One thousand years had erased almost all the answers. There was now nothing by which to know them but their building and their choice of its location. I felt a connection to these unknown builders and worshipers and enjoyed the serenity of a moment alone on a spot where others had trod long before me. That gravity felt by any fan of history in such places came over me. Place: a concept that still has a power all its own to cause wonder and reflection. Place: the best teacher of history and culture, ever. Place: something so few people take advantage of or understand.

After an indefinite amount of time, I continued higher up the now narrowing trail, hunting a second church promised by signs but never delivered. I searched in vain and ended at a fence across the top of a high ridge. I whirled the bike around and bounced down the rocky incline like a metal goat, feeling as smug as a treasure hunter freshly paid out.

My next excursion was a circumnavigation around Lake Trasimeno. Doing so took me through Tuoro sul Trasimeno, where there are some obscure monuments to Hannibal's defeat of ten thousand Romans in the Punic Wars, and Passignano, where I stopped for a vanilla and pistachio gelato and gazed out across the lake. But Castiglione del Lago, jutting out into the lake and visible from our villa, is my favorite. Its crenellated walls and view of the lake and distant hills are beautiful.

Besides all the other advantages already listed for motorcycling through Italy, there is one other: for some reason, one simply experiences the surroundings better by bike. I can't explain it. Maybe it's the smells, or the hot wind on one's skin, or the maneuverability, but cruising the countryside on a motorcycle gives a sensation that can't be had in a car. It is also the fastest way to learn the territory, and learn the territory I did, in an ever-widening circle from our villa, marking ruins and castles and scenic lookouts in my mind and planning to load up the minibus with the Brady clan and bring them back to share all my discoveries. I was like an advance cavalry scout in an eighteenth-century war, spying out strategic locations and then going back to fetch the army. I felt invincible.

Then I ran low on gas during siesta when none of the gas stations were open.

Lesson learned: Either fill the tanks properly before the country recedes behind closed shutters for its four-hour nap, or memorize where the stations with automatic payment machines are located. Or, I could take a cue from the locals and escape the midday heat by taking a siesta myself.

I chose the latter.

Maybe, just maybe, I have a little Italian blood in me. I had, after all, begun passing on either side of cars in the tightest of turns. When in Rome . . .

CHAPTER 12

# CREATURES AND CREATURE COMFORTS

*Traveling is a brutality. It forces you to trust strangers and to lose sight of all the familiar comfort of home and friends. You are constantly off balance. Nothing is yours except the essential things—air, sleep, dreams, the sea, the sky—all things tending towards the eternal or what we imagine of it.*
– Cesare Pavese

Flexibility is one of the keys to successful travel. With delays, flight cancellations, lines, crowds, unfamiliar places, and, often, bad food, the more one takes it all in stride, the better. It's just not worth getting upset or being in a bad mood. Sometimes, however, this is more easily said than done.

Our first few days at *La Contea* were not exactly love at first sight. Sure, everything appeared exactly as it had in the photos. So far, so good. But I remembered reading in the information I had been sent that even though the villa didn't have air conditioning, this wasn't really a problem because most Tuscan villas didn't really need it. We simply needed to keep the heavy wooden doors and shutters closed against the heat of the day, then open them after dusk for cool evening breezes. Made sense to me.

What makes sense during a quick read in the comforts of home 5,000 miles away doesn't necessarily make sense in practice. For one thing, we hit Tuscany during a massive heat wave. Temperatures were in the nineties by early morning. It was, after all, July—Italy's peak temperature month. Try as we might, though, we simply could not get the place cooled down at night. Now, let me make it perfectly clear that I'm normally not a huge fan of air conditioning. Back home (especially in Florida), there seems to be a competition among restaurants for how cold they can keep it indoors. I have never liked the fact that a coat must be worn in most movie theaters in the middle of summer. So I'm not an air conditioning softie, but even I was wishing we had some during those first couple of nights at *La Contea*.

Walking upstairs to the bedrooms, the increased temperature hit us in the face. We flopped and turned and sweated all over the sheets.

"Are we supposed to open these shutters?" Terri asked, exasperated.

"I think so. Keep them closed during the day. Let the breeze in at night. That's what it said."

"What about all these bugs flying in? There are no screens," she added.

"I think it's a trade-off between heat or bugs. Your choice."

The heat was so smothering that we both chose bugs.

For about an hour.

Several mosquito bites later, we were both awake again. Then Terri froze.

"What the heck is that!?" she pointed. I followed her outstretched arm to a monstrous black shape making its way down the wall directly next to our bed.

"Um, that's a scorpion, I think," I replied, having not seen one in person since my college days in Texas. Its tail curled up menacingly as it inched along the wall. "Don't worry. The manual said if they bite, it is only like a big mosquito bite."

"The same manual that said we don't need air conditioning? That thing is a large animal! Make it go away," she said, scooting backwards across the bed.

I found a shoe and made liquid out of it—a big black and red stain on the white stucco. I was busy wondering how to clean it off while Terri was busy booking out of the room. I closed the shutters. Maybe heat wasn't so bad after all.

"How are we ever going to *sleep* here?" she blurted.

I thought it was a fair question. Another question I considered was why in the world didn't they have screens?

It's not like Italy is backwards or doesn't have technology. They do. It's just that they aren't as in love with it as we are in North America. Usually, that's part of the charm. Where they seem to have a "take it or leave it" attitude toward most modern conveniences, back home we worship, idolize, and incorporate them into our lives like one of the family, never to be without them again. In Italy, air conditioning is hit-or-miss, and even many places that have it don't seem to want to run it. Bathroom fixtures and toilets can be bizarre and often barely work, even in the nicer places. Refrigerators and appliances are small. Washing machines don't seem to work very well. Thousands of places still don't have clothes dryers. And showers are often a trickle. But screens? Why not screens? Even the *Amish* have screens, don't they?

That's when the kids, ever helpful, chimed in.

"Daddy, I'm too hot to sleep," said one.

"Me, too."

"Me, too."

"All right," I said, admitting defeat. "We'll think of something."

I knew I had to act fast. Here we were, barely into the second week of my Italian boondoggle, and the whole family was rebelling. Worst of all, I wanted to join them. I was cracking, and I knew it. I felt a tiny bit of homesickness begin to creep in. There is a law in leadership that states that in order to influence others, the leader himself must first be convicted. I very distinctly felt my conviction waning. What was I doing? Why had I dragged my family a quarter of the way around the world when we had everything so nice and comfortable at home? Why couldn't I have simply been content with a trip to a KOA campground, like most sane people? Why were we spending all this money and subjecting ourselves to—well—who knew what would come next? A viper killing one of us? I read about them being deadly in the same book that said air conditioning wasn't needed, and if they were this far off about air conditioning, how bad was the viper, really? It was probably so bad it could kill you just by slithering past.

I was losing it.

The next law of leadership says that it's sometimes appropriate to make a decision, even if it's wrong. It was a decision that was needed. Period.

So I made one.

"Let's drag these mattresses off these beds and take them down to the first floor," suggested Terri. "At least it's twenty degrees cooler down there."

My decision was to agree with her.

So there we were, living in a mural, lugging five mattresses down tile steps in the middle of the night. And that morning when everyone awoke tired and cranky, we jumped into the clunky minibus and went on a mission to buy some fans.

Back home, this would be a simple matter of finding a hardware store or one of those home-improvement, big-box stores the size of a small city, where you could walk in, locate a huge sign that read "Fans," and pick from seventy-six different kinds. In Italy, it was a slightly different game. First of all, part of the lure of the Tuscan countryside is that it's not littered with big, ugly box stores. So that wasn't an option. Next, the stores they *do* have are tiny, hard to find, and almost never open. They also have signs that aren't in English.

"How are we going to find fans, Daddy?"

"I have no idea. But I saw what looked like a bigger size grocery store the other day while I was on my motorcycle, and I'm going to drop Mommy there. Two of you can go help her, and the other two can come help me find some fans."

"Oh, okay. Well, if you find some fans . . ."

"When," I interrupted.

"Okay, *when*. When you find some fans, how are we going to get them home on the plane?"

"We're not. They'll be a donation."

"Oh."

"We're donating fans to Italy?" one of them said to another.

I didn't care. We were not going to have another night like the last. So there we were, driving around randomly, looking for a fan store.

And wouldn't you know it, I found exactly that within a mile of the grocery store where I had dropped Terri off. I jammed on the brakes, spun the minibus around, and parked in front of a small storefront in the newer section of Castiglione del Lago. There were fans of all shapes and sizes in the front window. With a big smile on my face, I bought three huge ones, already assembled, and crammed them into the back of the minibus. Once again, I was glad we had such a big vehicle. Within literally ten minutes, we were back in front of the grocery store with our treasure, smugly waiting for the admiration from the rest of the family.

The leader of the boondoggle was back in command.

## CHAPTER 13

# PERSPECTIVE IN THE MURAL

*"Ah, signora, you are learning the Italian secret!" he exclaims.*
*"And what is that?"*
*"Our greatest art: the art of living."*
   – Dianne Hales, *La Bella Lingua*

Early each morning at *La Contea,* Giulio and Daniela would show up to clean the pool, straighten the yard, and do all sorts of tidying up. Some days, they were there and gone before we even got up. On other days, we would awaken, open the big dark wooden shutters and doors, and emerge into the bright morning sunlight to find them hard at work, clipping hedges, sweeping stoops, or any number of other things. It eventually became part of our morning routine to get up early enough to interact with them.

Although there was a significant language barrier, Terri with her knowledge of Spanish was usually able to make out what they were saying. Daniela was particularly cute, patiently repeating a key word over and over as if repetition alone would usher in a sudden comprehension. Strangely enough, it often did.

One morning, they told us about an abandoned church ruin marked by a big cross at the top of the mountain behind us. Another time, they gave us information about the fresh market days in the surrounding towns. Giulio was the one to tell me of a motorcycle trail up the mountain behind the villa that followed the entire ridge all the way to Tuoro and the scene of the Roman defeat by Hannibal on the shore of Lake Trasimeno. These conversations were not only great tourist tips, but they built a bond between us.

Giulio and Daniela especially liked our children. Both took special time to point out to them interesting features of the grounds. One of these was the skin or shell of a cicada still completely intact and stuck to the bark of a canopy pine. Another time, Giulio unlocked a door that had been marked "Private" and led all four children down a set of steps into an enormous basement the size of the whole villa, pointing out the fireplaces and stacks of old furniture. At Terri's request, they took the kids into another previously locked section of the house. It was a room with two large stainless steel vats filled with the extra virgin olive oil pressed from the harvest of La Contea's very own trees. With hand gestures and simple words, Giulio explained the process of pressing as he filled a container of EVOO for our use in the kitchen.

The care Giulio and Daniela took with La Contea and with us was what finally eased our anxieties. The hot restless nights, the creatures crawling on the walls, the remoteness of the location, and the thousands of bees circling the swimming pool had been disconcerting. Additionally, traveling with little children is a bit on the nerve-wracking side. There is also the traveler's anxiety that settles in on me at some point during every trip—not exactly homesickness but a discomfort rooted in the abundance of the unfamiliar and the cold hard fact of being so far from hearth and home. But La Contea went from adding to this anxiety to soothing it. We came to realize that being there wasn't so much about accommodations as it was adventure and discovery. We had come to this understanding gradually, through the care of an elderly couple with whom we could barely speak. What we learned was that even without a common language, we could still communicate. Warmth and sincerity come through without words, and Giulio and Daniela had it in spades. We fell in love with them.

We also fell in love with the view. From nearly anywhere on the property, the scenes are amazing. Far to the south sits Lake Trasimeno, a serene blue-gray disc punctuated by the high castle walls of the medieval town of Castiglione del Lago. To the west sweeps the broad Valdichiana, centuries ago a marshland but now one of the most fertile farming areas in Tuscany. Beyond it are the smoky gray ridges of mountains running north and south, framing the backdrop of the valley like a novice's painting. From *La Contea*'s elevated perch, the colors and contours of this sweeping vista change with the position of the sun. Early morning produces a gray-green monochromatic look, sometimes with the low-lying areas blanketed by fog. Later in the morning, the scattered little towns and individual stone farmhouses almost twinkle, the whole area being an explosion of vivid colors: the tans of the wheat fields, the platinum of the olive trees, and the deep sage of the woods all punctuated by the dark green cypress spires. The hours before sunset are the best, though; the farmhouses glow as if they are lights plugged in for some special occasion.

The sounds, too, are inviting. In the morning, it is quiet except for the birds and an occasional church bell clanging up from some unidentifiable place in the valley below. By midday, the cicadas have taken over, grinding angrily with what sounds like broken bows on rusty steel strings. Occasionally, the rumble of the train to Florence rises from Terontola, accompanied by a distinct bell ringing for the street crossing. Many times at night, especially on weekends, music from parties and live performances comes in broken pieces up to *La Contea*'s terraces, never enough to be disturbing, but sufficient to let one know the valley below is alive, full of action and vigor.

Then there are the smells.  One night, I awoke for a brief moment and inhaled deeply the fresh air drifting in through the open oak shutters.  It was so fresh it actually had a taste.  It was both invigorating and a reminder that I was someplace foreign, remote, alive.  I don't know the names for most of the flowers and trees, but their varied and pleasing aromas waft around me everywhere I go in Tuscany.  Never one to have slowed for botany, I promised myself to expand in that direction.  I simply had to learn more about some of these fascinating species, if only to plant them in my own backyard.

Many times throughout our days, I would be interrupted by the view or caught by a sound coming in briefly from the distance far below.  I never grew tired of standing at one of the wooden railings, no doubt constructed long ago by Giulio himself, and peering out across this panorama.  I became familiar with each little town and farmhouse and could easily spot the train station in Terontola or catch the tiny blip of the train racing past buildings and copses of trees.  The view was always on hand to remind me both that we were far from home and also that we were blessed beyond measure.

As the days went by, *La Contea* began to feel more and more like home.  Our early misgivings and complaints faded away.  We teased ourselves for having been stereotypical American travelers, not happy unless every little comfort and luxury was perfectly provided exactly as we demanded at the moment.  We settled in; we adapted; we began to fit ourselves into the mural instead of trying to wrench it to fit us.  And the more we did, the more comfortable we became.  The bees at the pool largely left us alone.  The scorpions were rare and never did bother us.  The villa was still hot at night, but we didn't care anymore, sleeping on our mattresses downstairs like it was the most normal thing in the world.  Eventually, gradually, and thankfully, we began to feel more of our blessings and less of our needs, gaining one of the biggest features of a vacation of this nature: perspective.

What is travel if not a chance to change? What good are experiences if they don't make us better? What good is solitude if we don't use it to think and reflect? These and other realizations crept in unseen but still absorbed.

We grew to realize something about Italy as well. The rhythm of the place was entirely different from that to which we were accustomed. The allure of this place wasn't only its landscape, history, beauty, food, and art, although there are enough of each of these to keep any traveler busy for a lifetime. What was so special was how different everything was at the core. It wasn't just a change of scenery featuring good museums and monuments, but a different way of life. People in Italy lived *differently*, and in many ways, we came to believe that they lived better. I have traveled all over the world and had never been as struck by this as I was with the Italians. Their siestas, their harmless displays of anger at each other (usually ending in laughter and hugs), their relaxed schedules, the complete absence of hurry (except on curving mountain roads), their focus on togetherness, their patience with foreigners mumbling through an order at a restaurant or a purchase at a grocery store, their courtesy, their slowness to embrace or idolize technology, their love of talk, their seeming abundance of time available for another person, and their utter habit of beautifying everything they touch, from a plate of food to a stone farmhouse, all began blending into a mosaic of their way of life in our minds. Looking back, I know now that this is what we were really there to discover. In my previous rushed trips through this land, perhaps I had sensed it. Maybe it was what had made me want to come back, and to do so at a deeper level. I was on a treasure hunt, grasping for some fuzzy image of value I knew was there beneath the surface, unreachable when following along behind a tour guide, sticking to highly traveled tourist paths, or adhering to a rigid itinerary. I had left the well-worn path of shallow sightseeing and discovered the proper tools for digging—and I had struck gold.

My real attraction to Italy was its people and their ways. It was, I became convinced, the secret to the country's lasting allure. The merry Etruscan blood, the colonizing Greek blood, and the organizing Roman blood, the conquering Norman blood, the creative and expressive Renaissance blood all still flowed through Italy's veins. So much had happened here, and so much had been left as proof, from ruins to buildings to sculptures and tombs. But the biggest legacy was the people themselves, the best monument of all to the many lives that have been lived here before. This was Italy's real secret.

I thought about these things and how the next generation is the best message we can ever send forward through the mystery of time. This is what Italy had taught me. This is what the Italians had taught me. Then I took a look at my own four precious little children frolicking among the bees in the pool and put down my pen to join them in their play.

## CHAPTER 14

# PRODIGIOUS NOTICING

*Look back at an object until it begins to look back at you. It can be dangerous to travel. A strong reflecting light is cast back on "real life," sometimes a disquieting experience.*
— Frances Mayes

Mark Twain called it "prodigious noticing" and said it was a key ingredient in his work. Truth is recognizable as authentic the moment we take note of it; when we hear or read or learn something that is accurate and true, we know it immediately. If it's important enough, we also never forget it. That's how it has been with me regarding Twain's bit of insight. With this one term, one of America's most gifted creative minds had opened a window into his genius.

Upon reading about Twain's prodigious noticing, I immediately started trying to look at things differently—more deeply—and with different eyes. I attempted to fight the natural mechanism called selective sight that quickly dismisses from our conscious mind anything overly familiar and deemed unimportant. This mechanism blinds us as we age, giving us a sense of "nothing new under the sun." But if we can rewire the mechanism and make it malfunction, we can suddenly see people, events, and all sorts of things around us we've been systematically ignoring. Indeed, *noticing* is one of the keys to thinking, experiencing, and creating. Twain, it would seem, knew his business.

International travel is also a great wrench thrown into the selective sight machine. We are hit with new smells, surroundings, sites, faces, languages, sounds, and cultures. It is the submerging of oneself into an atmosphere so different that our reticular activating system doesn't know what to leave in and what to leave out. It therefore falls to our conscious mind to make all the decisions about the myriad of information coming in. This is what leads to the mixed feelings of exhilaration and anxiety. But it is also responsible for clearer memories and retained experiences. In short, we are usually shocked into a greater state of mental awareness when on an adventure, particularly of the foreign variety.

So much for the psychology.

In practice, during our month in Italy, I began forcing myself to try to take active notice of things, large and small. I spent more time than a busy American male in the prime of his life would ever even be caught dead doing just staring at the landscape. I'd stop my motorcycle at the base of some incredible curve between wheat fields, shut off the engine, and just stare at a ruined farmhouse on a ridge. The longer I would look, the more I would see. At first my eyes would start picking up the flights of birds. Then I'd begin hearing sounds: quails, doves, a distant rooster, wind rushing through nearby fields. I would begin to feel more, too, like the distant warmth of the yellow Tuscan sun on my skin. My eyes would dial into the scene more acutely, and I noticed flowers I would never have noticed before growing around the entrance to the ruin. Were these planted by someone, or had they grown wild due to the lack of traffic on the approach? Then I'd see a jackrabbit the size of a dog scamper from one bush to another. Looking long enough, I could almost see back to the days when the building wasn't merely a pleasant portion of the panorama but, instead, the nucleus of a busy and difficult farming family's life.

Photography also helped. I began using my camera lens to gain different perspectives. I would look through it without snapping a photo, moving it slightly here or there, zooming in or out, waiting for that bird to pass in front of the lens. I became fascinated by doorways, so prevalent, diverse, and infinitely interesting in the many medieval towns throughout Tuscany. I took note of flowers planted around villas, their arrangement and their variety. And, as always, I ogled architecture everywhere, realizing more clearly than ever my complete fascination with masonry and ancient stone construction. Give me that over wood any day.

"People watching" also hit a new level. Always a risky sport, as if one is prying into the private life of another, I treaded respectfully the line between watching and staring. I noticed more closely how people dressed, greeted one another, walked, and chose which store to enter. Sitting off to the side of any number of famous old piazzas, I would relax and just look. It was then that I decided that the best place in the world to be an old man would be in Italy. In the States, they generally gather at McDonald's in the early morning and enjoy the senior coffees and the free refills. Flying my airplane, I would often find two or three of them assembled at little private aviation airports to swap tales and maybe lies about their earlier flying days. But, to my mind, this is all a far cry from the hanging out older Italian men do with each other seemingly all day long at outdoor tables playing cards or at Bocce pits swearing at one another between rolls (or is it pitches, or bowls, or throws?). Everywhere I went, there was always a similar looking cluster of old men sitting together, commenting and talking (probably about the weather and, I like to believe, about old women). Once, I stopped my motorcycle along the road and entered a café for a gelato right in the middle of the afternoon. Politely enough, but with a perplexed look on his face, one of twelve old men at a table got up to help me. It wasn't until he heard my broken Italian that I saw his face let go of the question: *What in the world are you doing buying an ice cream during siesta?*

As for the old women, I never saw them gathered in groups. At most, there would be two. I wondered if this might be a sociological thing, like blue crabs killing each other in a bucket. They were always out and about, though, these elderly ladies (not blue crabs), usually with a shopping bag or a cane or both. Perhaps they were simply looking for their man, trying to find which café was serving as the latest hideout.

Part of noticing is also amplified by recording. I began putting thoughts down in my journal much more regularly and carefully than I ever did in the firefight of the busyness of my life back home. I even drew some sketches, something I hadn't done with that amount of care since adolescence. The more I thought to record, the more I remembered and, likewise, the more I remembered, the more I noticed. I felt as if I had turned on an entirely new sixth sense—something that had lain dormant for most of my life. This Twain guy really was a genius (and yes, he spent a considerable amount of time observing Italy himself).

I also aimed my rediscovered skills at my own family. Familiarity can easily make the subtleties of beauty obscure to us, and nowhere is this more likely to be true than with those we love. Domestic fights and violence are a tragedy that ruins lives and scars souls horribly. Perhaps we could eliminate much of it if we could simply observe more clearly those dear people in our lives who have become too familiar by proximity. In my case, I began to notice little things Terri would do that I had stopped appreciating long ago. There were small moments of incredible patience she would exhibit with each of the children and special kindnesses she would confer on me. As for my children, their freckles, loose teeth smiles, and dark shiny eyes seemed all so much more *there* for my notice than they had been. It saddened me to think how much I had missed of those infinitesimal little moments in between. I began tuning in better to the many cute little things they would say, such as, "Pogo sticks have oily springs so the screw can slide up and down," and questions such as, "Do ants sleep?" and "What do crickets eat?" and "How do ants fight in a war? Maybe they chuck food at each other. I just saw a dead one. Its wife was carrying it home." I also learned that "God sees your underwear all the time." I watched my children thrill over a colony of ants marching with their bread crumbs in a massive procession across fifty feet of portico; watched lovingly as they captured a tortoise and tried to force-feed him half the insects and leaves on the property; and heard them giggle with joy as they tied plastic shopping bags to long sticks, calling them kites, and then ran with them as hard as they could through the hot wind whirling up the driveway.

Leonardo Di Vinci had a mantra: *Saper vedere*, which means, "to know how to see." Yes, this was also why we'd come to Italy: to not only see *it*, but to see more of *each other*, as well, and to do so with new eyes.

CHAPTER 15

# SIENA BY CAR

*Not all those who wander are lost.* – J. R. R. Tolkien

In my planning of this trip, I had purposely located our Tuscan lodging in what looked to be a central location convenient for striking out in all directions to places of interest. *La Contea*, just south of Cortona, fit the bill perfectly. Within an hour or two by car, we could reach Florence to the north, Perugia in Umbria to the east, nearly Rome to the south, and Siena to the west.

Of these, and the many other smaller towns and sites scattered around us, it was Siena I was most eager to see. I had read about it, seen pictures, and heard people talk about it with that far away look in their eyes. The *Palio*, the famous three-lap horse race held twice each summer in the Piazza del Campo (the main square), officially began in 1283, though some think it dates back even farther to Roman military training. This race is more spectacle than sport. The competitors are representatives of Siena's individual neighborhoods called *contrada*, each with their own mascot (such as a Caterpillar, Ram, Wolf, and Panther), colors and symbology, and histories and rivalries. It's a pageant of color and ritual, a citywide party held twice a year, so intense, so inspiring of passion, that it

seems no foreigner can ever entirely understand its parochial appeal
still so reminiscent of its medieval origins.  From the pictures I had
seen of the Piazza del Campo, with its odd trapezoidal shape and
slippery herringbone brick surface, I could not imagine running
horses there.  All these facts combined to make Siena a mystery I
just had to see for myself.  Even though we weren't going to visit
during the *Palio*, what I couldn't have envisioned was that the Piazza del Campo would still be the scene of a spectacle that day, and
*we* would be it.

It started off innocently enough, as these things generally do.
We had gotten a little lazy because of the GPS and would usually
just type in a city name and hit "City Center" on the menu of
choices.  Dutifully, the little electronic wonder would then steer us
with a purple line right smack into the center of said city.  This was
usually all well and good except, however, when the city, such as
Siena, was closed to cars.

Many of these attractive medieval cities throughout Italy work
similarly.  Signs are posted at the ancient city walls indicating that
the only traffic allowed inside is for deliveries (usually in the mornings) and residents themselves.  Everyone else is to park in one of
the 3.5 public parking spaces provided outside the city gates.  On
that hot, clear morning, we approached the entrance to Siena filled
with awe and wonder, peering up at the walls and snapping photos
out the windows of the minibus.  I scanned each of the miniscule
parking areas as we approached and found nothing.  The GPS continued to lead us onward, so I followed.  I felt comfortable driving
under the entrance arch because a sign for public parking (a white
capital P on a blue background) had pointed in this direction.  But
once we drove through the city wall and into the city proper, I
somehow missed any further signage.  There were cars parked everywhere, but no spaces.

One of the advantages of the minibus was its size.  It could haul
our entire family and another, too.  But, as we've already learned,

its size was also its main disadvantage, especially when traversing a thousand-year-old city. As we drove, the walls got closer and closer together, and the crowds of people walking were denser and denser. Slowing down, driving at the pace of a crawl, I allowed the pedestrians to hear my engine purring and get out of the way. I didn't want to be rude.

The farther we went, the more I realized we would be unlikely to find a place to turn the big van around. It slowly dawned on me that we were driving directly into the center of one of Tuscany's most revered treasures—illegally. Eventually, we had to stop because of the press of people all around us.

"Just act like we belong here," I said to Terri and the kids.

"People are looking at us funny, Dad," one of them said.

"That old man is pointing."

"Just play it straight. We'll be out of here in a moment," I reassured them, hoping I was telling the truth.

I looked over my left shoulder at a small road we had passed, a tight opening between buildings that looked as if it might lead down a hill and out of town. I was just considering whether I should back up and somehow negotiate the turn around the hard edges when Casey from the back seat said, "Uh, Dad? There are some ladies trying to talk to you."

I turned and looked. Two elderly ladies, obviously locals, were frantically motioning for me to roll down my window.

There are certain moments where training and experience kick in. When I was taking flying lessons, pounded into us over and over again were the proper steps to take in an emergency. We practiced them repeatedly so in the event of an actual emergency we would be able to keep our heads, refrain from panicking, and follow procedures by habit. It was the same kind of response that kicked in now.

I slowly brought the window down, but as I did so I swiveled in my seat to face Terri and the kids, who were now all out of their seatbelts and crowding forward around the front seats, as children all over the world will do, to get a better look at a calamity in the making. I said under my breath with all the authority a dad could muster, "You guys all hop out, now! Find the Piazza del Campo, get some gelato, and wait for me. I'll find a way out of here, park this van someplace, and come find you."

They dutifully poured out of the van, either demonstrating great instincts for situational awareness or simply escaping the embarrassing situation as quickly as possible. Only Christine paused to look back longingly at her father, as though she might not see me for a while.

Next, I turned to face the music.

In all fairness, the ladies were firm but nice. After all, some tourist idiot had driven his huge minibus smack dab into the center of their beautiful city. At least I looked like a delivery van. And, in fact, I *had* made a delivery—an entire family, to be exact. But I didn't tell the two elderly ladies this. Instead I just smiled, nodded my head, and listened. Despite the enormous language barrier, generational barrier, and cultural barrier, their overall message was loud and clear: "You idiot."

Eventually they softened a bit when they realized I wasn't a terrorist tourist bent on destroying their city by exploding my minibus in the center of their town. My family, thankfully, looked pretty harmless. I asked how to get out of the rat maze I had threaded my way into, and they answered in unison by pointing in different directions. I nodded, gave some *grazies*, rolled up the window, and took the next available right turn. It was a good choice. The crowds thinned, the opening widened, and soon I was dumped out a different city gate onto a downward spiraling switchback road with cars parked in every available spot along both sides all the way down. After at least two miles of this I came to a small town of sorts, consisting of a gas station and two small buildings. Undeterred from my trespassing experience mere moments before, I turned the minibus around and headed directly back up the hill, intent on finding a parking place closer than Minnesota.

Incredibly, I found myself pulling back through the city wall once again, but this time I kept my eyes peeled for those pesky blue and white parking lot signs. I waited for several minutes behind another minibus that was waiting to get into some sort of sub-merged parking structure and then lost patience and pulled back out. Now I was driving along *next* to the inside of the city wall, passing steep streets leading back up into the city, all of which were packed full of cars parked along both sides. All of a sudden, I came to a street with at least ten good parking spaces, all open and ap-parently available. Not able to believe my luck and being quite certain that this was closer than the bottom of the hill would have been, I quickly darkened one of those spaces with the presence of the minibus.

There. That wasn't so bad.

Just another day touring Italy.

Just then, the other minibus I had seen waiting to get into the parking structure came pulling up next to me. The passenger rolled down his window and began speaking to me in broken Ital-ian, and then some really slow English. As he got to the English, his voice got distinctly louder.

"*Scusi, signore*, uh, do you know if we can park here?"

"*Io non capisco L'Englese*," I replied, pouring on my best Italian-sounding tone while indicating that I didn't understand English.

The guy's frustration was percolating over, and he smacked his thigh, about to utter a swear word or two when I cracked up laugh-ing.

"Just kidding!" I said. "I couldn't help it. Yes, I think we can park here. If you want, you can pull right in behind my van there," I motioned.

The man laughed, and then I noticed he was part of a van full of adults.

"Where are you from?" I asked.

"Florida," he replied.

"Me, too!"

And in a moment, we were all walking up the hill together, making our way to the parking payment machine.

I think there were eight of them—four couples. The man I had joked with was nice, and so was the driver. We swapped small talk about our locations in Florida and what a small world it was . . . things like that. But what I remember the most is one of the women from their group. She interrupted us, politely enough, but started tapping her watch and reminding the assembled group that they didn't have time to waste. They only had an hour and a half to see Siena, and then they had to get on the road. They had a wine tasting in Montalcino and something else after that.

As we parted ways, I wished them good luck and counted my blessings. I couldn't help thinking to myself, *An hour and a half to see Siena?* We had been in Italy only about a week and a half at this point; but already, I noted, my time clock had wound down a little. I had already lost some of the hustle and bustle being exhibited by these folks who were fresh in the country. Or, I wondered, maybe their hurry was because they didn't have a very long vacation and, therefore, had to squeeze a lot in. I know I've had those kinds of experiences before, and I wasn't relishing the memory of a hit-and-run approach to sightseeing. Or, maybe, just maybe, they lived their whole lives that way, scrambling to keep up with the clock, cramming in as much as possible, obtaining those huge check marks at the big landmarks and quickly moving on. Or, I guess it's possible that they were having the time of their lives and wouldn't change a thing about their approach to their vacation. After all, they were here, weren't they?

I wasn't being judgmental, just thankful. And I also did a lot of pondering about the *purpose* behind vacations. I realize everyone has his own life to live, and everyone has a different way of going about his business. Still, I was glad I wasn't restricted to just an hour and a half to see Siena. I didn't just want to see it; I wanted to *be there*. I wanted to take prodigious notice of it.

As I climbed that steep street up to the Piazza del Campo and my gelato-gulping family-in-waiting, I thought more and more about the art of vacationing. *People need this*, I thought; *they need a break. They need to sharpen their saws, let off some steam, slow down, and look at the world, look at themselves.* It was the second time on the trip the thought hit me: *Someone has got to tell this story. Someone has got to remind people to go slow in order to go fast.*

I pulled out my phone, opened up the memo section, and began to type myself a note: "I'd rather see Siena by car than try to see it in an hour and a half." And in that moment, this book was born.

"Hey, Daddy! Look at what I've got!" yelled Nathaniel, holding up a Fernando Torres soccer shirt and beaming at his good fortune.

"And I got some gelato!" said J.R.

"Daddy, come look at this!" shrieked Christine in delight, taking my hand and leading me to a souvenir stand with pretty scarves and silks hanging all about.

We had pizza in the piazza (say *that* ten times fast) and then climbed the main bell tower called the Torre del Mangia, supposedly named after the lazy Renaissance-era bell ringer who was "eating" up the profits by shirking his responsibilities. Reported to be the second highest tower built in Italy during the Middle Ages, there are 505 steps to the top, but the view from up there makes the sweat and chafing worth it. It also makes one realize why the bell ringer might have been so lazy. The surrounding countryside, the piazza below, and an ocean of tile roofs fan out like a view from an airplane, producing a mesmerizing spectacle from which you cannot look away. The breeze cooled us slightly, and none of us were in a hurry to go back down.

Perhaps the biggest marvel to me is the splendid Duomo. It is enormous. Even so, the structure that stands today is a mere shadow of what was intended. The original size is evident by the huge fascia built hundreds of years ago and standing as a lone wall off to one end. Also visible in the pavement outside are column bases for the unfinished nave, of which the far wall would have been a part. The side aisle of this unfinished section was given a roof, some sidewalls between what would have been internal columns, and turned into the Museo dell' Opera del Duomo. Had the church been completed as planned, it would have been the largest cathedral in Italy, even bigger than St. Peter's in Rome. This was the direct intent of the ambitious Sienese. But alas, the plague of 1348 wiped out over half the population of Siena, and a less grandiose structure was built instead. That they would leave the original end wall of the nave in place through three quarters of a millennium is proof enough that things are different in Italy. Unless it were a government job, of course, such a thing in North America would be nearly inconceivable.

We walked all around the city and just generally soaked it up. We took pictures of a man dressed in gold paint standing as still as a statue. We chased the pigeons off the Fonte Gaia. We walked under the arched aerial bridges on the Via della Galluzza. We shopped and browsed till our hearts were content and then sat and rested, watching the people in the piazza. We saw Siena, but left realizing we could never see enough of it. We left promising to come back some day.

And yes, it took us much longer than an hour and a half. We needed that much time just to find where I had parked the mini-bus.

# ART, HISTORY, AND
# MICHAEL JACKSON

*Perhaps travel cannot prevent bigotry, but by demonstrating that all peoples cry, laugh, eat, worry, and die, it can intro-duce the idea that if we try and understand each other, we may even become friends.* – Maya Angelou

One of the ways I had sold this whole month of Italy con-cept to Terri was by emphasizing its educational aspects. Partly due to our regular travel schedule, and also the fact that we insisted on living in two states at once, we had thus far entirely homeschooled our children. This had many benefits and effects on our family life, one of which was to turn us into opportunists always on the lookout for ways to teach. So my sales pitch was an easy lob across the plate: What could be more educational than to go and see in person many of the things one normally only gets to read about in books? It was a strong argument, of course.

While in Siena, as we were touring the magnificent town hall called the Palazzo Pubblico, a project to restore some of the build-ing's many fabulous frescoes was underway. Christine stopped cold in her tracks when she noticed a college-aged woman lying on her side on the floor, carefully applying freshening color to a border originally painted over six hundred years previously. This gave us the spontaneous opportunity to explain to our children the process of painting *en fresco,* wherein the artist applies the paint to the wall as its freshly laid plaster is still drying. In this way, the art is applied *into* the wall and not merely *onto* it. For this reason, the art is much more durable throughout the centuries. Fortunately for us—and the world—the Renaissance painters from Michelangelo to Raphael painted almost entirely *en fresco.* This was a moment of art history at its best.

This one little lesson inspired a search for art supplies and resulted in several afternoons of drawings and sketches. Nathaniel and Christine each drew and colored fabulous renderings of the temples from Poseidonia, complete with fluted columns and admiring tourists. J.R. drew a colorful rendition of his own, and Casey took a little table and chair out into the yard and made a nearly perfect sketch of *La Contea.*

On another occasion, right around bedtime, Casey sat on the small love seat adjoining the desk I had set up as my temporary office. "Dad," he inquired, "how come my allowance is worth so much less in euro than it is in dollars?" I was glad he was seated because my answer would take a bit of explaining. As I launched into one of my favorite topics, Nathaniel heard what was going on and joined us. Soon Christine and J.R. were there, too, and now I had eight brown eyes looking at me intently as I explained international monetary policy and the effects of inflation, balance of trade, and currency exchange rates. I couldn't believe their concentration level, their uninterrupted attention spans, the incredible teachable moment. Their questions were pointed, informed, and insightful.

We chatted back and forth for almost two hours when finally Christine said, "Thanks for teaching us about inflation, Daddy."

"How was that for some homeschooling?" I proudly asked Terri after the kids were in bed.

"It was fantastic," she agreed.

"I couldn't believe how attuned they were to everything I was saying. Even little J.R. I think this trip has awakened in our children the hunger to learn," I said, never one to miss a chance to reinforce a sale I had made.

"Yes, I'd agree. But there was also another factor at work," she said.

"And what was that?"

"It was bedtime, and they were stretching it out."

Fast-forward six months after our month in Italy. We were settling into our new surroundings in North Carolina. Terri had taken the kids to an event at a local museum in downtown Raleigh. As a guide led the group around a corner and into a section of Italian art and history, my kids apparently came alive. There was a painting of Mt. Vesuvius they recognized immediately. They were even able to name some of the artists and their works. As Terri recounted this story to me afterward, I couldn't help thinking how satisfying it is for a salesman to hear of his customer's satisfaction.

I have long believed that history is critical to a proper understanding of our human existence. Billions of people have inhabited this place before us, and they have left fascinating clues and hints about the lives they lived. They aren't just names and places and dates; they were real people just like us. They felt deeply, suffered terribly, laughed merrily, loved, ate, traveled, thought, raised children, worshipped, wrote, expressed themselves through art, built wonderful buildings, and wrote penetrating thoughts. I get lost in wonder just pondering the depth and width of human history. It is mysterious because so much of it is irrecoverable. Tiny proofs of it are scattered across the globe, leaving often agonizingly incomplete records of what transpired before us.

History is also one of the most difficult subjects to impart to children. It takes patience and a deep appreciation of it on the part of the teacher to have any hope of transferring its wonder to the next generation. Many times as I relate stories from history in my speeches or writings, I run across adults who say they have never really understood history before. "It was always so boring," they say. But it is not boring. History is magnificent and as full of mystery as life itself. It's a story without full answers, an unfinished work of art still being crafted each minute of every day. It was this depth of appreciation I hoped a slow and easy trip through Italy would impart to my children. But I wasn't leaving it to chance.

In my opinion, perspective is the key to appreciating history appropriately. This must occur through the agency of two other things: geography and a timeline. I love maps. In another life, I probably could have been a cartographer, holding up in a dusty office in Florence or Genoa, working with parchments and ink, and reproducing the territories being discovered by the brave mariners of the late fifteenth century. Timelines too have been a fascination, the way they provide insights into concurrent events or the proximity of one event to another. When looking at timelines, I have often been hit with "aha" moments, realizing for the first time, for instance, that the conquests of Alexander the Great were a great connector between the civilization of the ancient Greeks and the Roman Republic and the Roman Empire to follow. So in the interest of maximizing the impact of our historical touring through Italy, I had decided to use both maps and timelines with the children.

One day, we assembled at the wooden picnic table on the veranda. With a long blank piece of paper, together we wrote out a crude timeline, showing first the ancient mysterious peoples populating the Italian peninsula, then the Etruscans, next the Romans, followed by the Dark Ages and the rise of the official church, then the Renaissance, and onward up to the present day. In one sweep, portrayed with colored pencils in the Tuscan sunshine, my kids were treated to a perspective only obtainable through simplification.

"Now," I asked, "where do the frescoes we saw being redone in Siena fit on this timeline?"

A little finger came forward and rested on a spot.

"Almost," I answered and then was able to give some explanation.

"How about the ruins we saw in Poseidonia? Where do they fit on here?"

This time the point was accurate. I continued with these kinds of questions until I noticed boredom creeping in.

Next, I flipped over the crude timeline and drew an even cruder map of Italy. It was at this point that I was thankful we weren't taking a month in Hungary, or Poland, boots being so much easier to draw than livers or spleens.

"Who can point to where we are in Tuscany right now?" I asked.

Again, out shot a little finger.

"Good. And how about where we were on the Amalfi Coast. Where is that?"

Another nearly perfect point.

I was feeling so good. This teaching stuff was a piece of cake. Then I caught myself and realized it wasn't my teaching ability, and it certainly wasn't my map or timeline making ability; rather, it was the power of being here and seeing it all firsthand. It was the power of *place* all over again.

Next I asked, "And who painted the Sistine Chapel ceiling?" I was certain they would get this one easily. We had been talking a lot about art history, and one of my favorites of all time is Michelangelo. Besides, we were planning to go to Rome soon and had been discussing seeing the Sistine Chapel.

"I know!" yelled Christine full of excitement.

"Okay, sweetheart, who?" I asked, waiting like every proud teacher to hear a demonstration of the growing knowledge of his pupil.

"Michael Jackson!" she answered with all the sincerity in the world.

CHAPTER 17

# STOPPING POWER AND THE ART OF VACATION

*The Italian knows that speed—say, the fitting in of another appointment or hurrying to finish something he can finish to-morrow—will give him not more satisfaction but less, if such preposterous acts interfere with his rituals.*
– Marlena de Blasi

A strange thing happened about halfway through the perfect vacation: we almost ended it early. We were getting more comfortable at *La Contea* and settling in fine but, still, something was gnawing at me. At the two-week mark, I was entering by far the longest break from the rat race of my adult life. In fact, up until this vacation, I was one of the biggest violators of the principles I have been espousing throughout this memoir. I hadn't taken a complete break from all work-related responsibility in a long, long time. And I certainly hadn't done so for four weeks in one whack. Looking back, believe it or not, I think my restlessness had something to do with being an amateur at taking vacations. I had been in the forest cutting trees so hard and so long I couldn't remember how to sharpen the saw anymore . . . and I barely noticed that my blade was dull. I had fallen into the all-too-common trap of working harder and harder, all the while losing ground.

At one point, I went as far as to email my assistant to have him inquire about the cost of changing our flights to come home early. The answer (seven thousand dollars) was enough to drown any genuine thoughts of an early return. I guess when you multiply any amount by six people, it adds up fast.

I pondered the reasons for my temporary and strange malaise. *Is it homesickness?* I was quite sure the answer to this was no. I travel a lot for a living, and I always hate leaving my family. The biggest bouts of homesickness always hit when I'm away from them. But on this trip, I had them with me. I wasn't missing our particular house or streets or neighborhood in the least. Those were only things. The people I loved most were with me in a cozy little traveling cocoon, and that aspect had been wonderful.

*Perhaps*, I thought, *if it isn't homesickness, then maybe it is simply idleness.* Was I bored? It's strange; even as I write that word *bored*, I recoil inside. When I was growing up, it was the worst of taboos to ever announce to my parents that I was bored. Immediately, I would be given a lecture about blessings and how good I had it and why didn't I just go out and do some chores, and my boredom would surely go away. My brother and I quickly developed defense mechanisms to keep from ever using the word for fear of an afternoon spent in penitence pulling garden weeds or cleaning the basement. Besides, how could I be bored when I was truly enjoying the exploration and adventures we were experiencing daily here in Italy? No, I wasn't bored. My parents had trained me well away from that one.

I finally realized there was a necessary and probably predictable adjustment to make when going from a full-speed, high-paced life to a complete respite. There are dynamics to changes in motion, as in the case of a high-performance sports car accelerating quickly or aggressively taking a sharp corner. Every action has its equal and opposite reaction.

I once owned a superfast car engineered to make any passenger throw up within four miles. Despite the hand-built engine and incredible zero-to-sixty acceleration time, what I liked to demonstrate the most was its stopping power. If I remember the promotional brochure correctly, it was capable of slowing from 100 miles per hour to zero in less than a hundred feet, all without skidding or becoming uncontrollable. That's some serious stopping power, enough to throw any unsuspecting passenger violently forward against his seatbelt. Incidentally, this same stopping power would later serve me extremely well. On a beautiful summer day, I had the convertible top down and was going about fifty miles an hour when a silver Buick materialized broadside in front of me as if teleporting from the *Starship Enterprise*. With probably less than a second on the brakes, the stopping power may have made all the difference.

"That guy was lucky he decided to pull out in front of a car like *this*," the sheriff's deputy said to me as I sat fuzzy-headed on the curb. I nodded. The other driver got three points on his record, and I never saw my mangled car again.

So stopping effectively is a useful skill. I gradually came to realize similar dynamics were at work with my vacation. It was a violent clamping down on the brakes in my life, and I was pushing hard against the seatbelt, as should have been expected. But it was *useful*. It was purposeful. When life is a lot like a race, vacation shouldn't be.

The danger in speaking of vacations is that it feeds the tendency in all of us to want too much of a good thing. What I am advocating is not idleness, but rather a respite from busyness. In fact, to me, idleness and busyness are opposite sides of the same coin: disorder.

Some people tend toward one extreme, languishing placidly and wasting the days of their lives. They buy into the lie that pleasure is the ultimate aim, pursuing personal peace, affluence, and gratification as their top priorities. They seek travel and experiences as an end, in and of themselves. There is a dangerous bait-and-switch dynamic at work behind the pursuit of pleasure as an end, however, and it comes from the fact that pleasure doesn't satisfy. Instead, it leads to the pursuit of more and more pleasure, greater and greater stimulation, all the while satisfying less and less. I have read travel books that are plenty dreamy, well written, excellent descriptors of places and attractions, but they are shallow and Bohemian, leaving the reader feeling empty at the end.

Other people—in fact, most from the crowds I run in—suffer from the opposite malady: filling their calendars so full they blast right through years of life without tasting a morsel of food or noticing a sunset. They are busy, busy, busy; scurrying here and there, convinced that if there is a job worth doing, it's worth *over*doing. The crowded schedule and unending demands upon one's time are often displayed as status symbols. Busyness becomes an outward show of importance. The philosophy goes like this: "I am busy; therefore, I am successful."

Both extremes are signs of disorder; it's a fact we know deep down inside. *Get back toward the center,* some inner voice seems to say; *you're wobbling like an unbalanced wheel.* By providing a chance to think, feel, ponder, pray, worship, learn, and realign with priorities, a proper vacation should ideally restore balance by transporting one back toward that center.

It gradually dawned on me that this month of Italy thing was so appealing to me because of the tremendous expectations I had set for it. I wanted to clear my head, spend some quality *and* quantity family time, analyze my priorities, search my heart, read several very specific books, plan some writing projects, and the like. A sabbatical like this was an enormous blessing, rare in a world where so many are less fortunate, and I wasn't taking it lightly. I wanted to wring every last drop of usefulness out of it and emerge changed, stronger, better.

There was another aspect to our respite that was incredibly satisfying. Somewhere, I had read about the idea of "going dark," which meant turning off all electronic communication devices. This turned out to be easy, since smartphone data roaming charges were prohibitive and the Internet service for which we had prearranged was hit and miss. As a result, we grew less and less attached to our email (I deplore email anyway), were able to go somewhere without that desperate reach for our cell phones, and with the exception of watching the final three World Cup games, never turned on the TV. It is amazing how much the cadence of life improved, how much more time opened up for us during the day, how much clearer our thoughts and our genuine interactions were when there were fewer interruptions and less "electronic tyranny." I would highly recommend this technique to anyone truly interested in restoration through vacation. Fire the media—all of it.

Now, it's time to literally shift some gears.

CHAPTER 18

# HORSEPOWER HISTORY

*Only in Italy could the lust for beauty and perfection produce these fantastic handmade cars. Only fifteen cars a day are finished....* – Eric Dregni

It is probably obvious that I'm a gearhead. I went into the field of mechanical engineering, not because I had the foggiest notion of what the field was, but because I enjoyed working on my motorcycles. *Mechanical?* I thought. *That sounds good. I'll take that one.* I have always been interested in horsepower, speed, and competitive motorsports. So in addition to being in love with Italy for its history, architecture, art, and food, there was yet another aspect that had always held my attention: sports cars.

Simply the term *Italian sports car* has a certain ring to it. It conjures images of exotic design and high performance and, of course, brings to mind that distinctive, one-of-a-kind sound. Most of my childhood was spent waking up beneath a poster of a Lamborghini of some kind. My favorite television show as a little tyke (unusual, really, because I've hated TV my whole life) was *Speed Racer.* And the fascination with Italian high performance wasn't limited to cars. During my motocross years, the low-production Cagiva dirt bikes were pleasingly unusual and special, and who could avoid craning his neck to admire a Ducati motorcycle racing by on the freeway?

So for me, long before I understood the deep layers of Italian history, culture, or cuisine, I always thought of it as the birthplace of dream vehicles. It was the quest to see the heart of exotic horsepower in Italy that launched us on our next day trip. We were off to see some sports cars, sure, but not just *any* sports cars. We were headed for the company Enzo Ferrari had built.

Ferrari. Even the word itself sounds fast. Or expensive. Or both. I've never owned one, and right away, that was going to put a damper on our tour, as I learned from the polite lady on the phone.

"Sir? Do you happen to own a Ferrari currently?" she asked in wonderfully accented English, as if owning one was the most natural thing in the world.

"Uh, no, not at the moment," I said almost apologetically.

"Ok, then, sir, no problem. However, the actual factory tour is reserved only for actual Ferrari owners, actually. Still, we have a lot to offer you upon your visit with us. This includes a racing and history museum, a hands-on section for the bambini, and a huge pro shop. Will this be acceptable to you, sir? Actually, I can reserve your tickets for you if you'd like."

*I'd like*, I thought, actually. And so we were up early and ambling down the dusty road from *La Contea* as the sun was just starting its daily climb. None of the kids objected to being roused from bed early. It seems Ferrari has a universal appeal to all ages.

The drive was a simple one, pretty much involving driving as if we were already in a Ferrari on the A1 Autostrada to Bologna. I loved the wide-open speeds prevalent among motorists on this road. Accustomed to its stretch between Rome and Florence, I had never been this far north on the Autostrada and was amazed at the curves and tunnels necessary as we crossed the last of the Apennine mountain range and descended onto the flat, industrial heartland of *Italia*. It was a short drive west from Bologna toward Modena, followed by a little jog south into a town called Maranello. Ferrari fans will be familiar with these town names, as the company has had car models named after each in the past.

Red. The color red. That's my dominant impression of Maranello. Red flags line the road. Red signs with the black Ferrari stallion on a bright yellow background are everywhere. Even the gates and walls of the factory are red. There are gift shops wholly dedicated to Ferrari paraphernalia, most of it—you guessed it—in bright red. Several places throughout the Ferrari-crazed city have cars clustered together under umbrellas and sexy girls standing out on the sidewalk to attract attention (as if the cars needed any help). For enough euro, one can be rented by the half-hour (the cars, that is).

We looped around the town before finally locating parking an easy few-minute walk from the main souvenir shop. Once inside, I tried to take a picture of an open-wheeler racecar on display in the front window. "It is forbidden, sir," said a young woman dressed in red, "unless, of course, you are one of our Ferrari owners."

One more closed door like this, and I was going to buy one, doggone it!

"Dad, you *do* have a Ferrari," Nathaniel said with a fiendish grin.

"Yes, son, but a 1:24 scale replica doesn't count, I don't think," I answered, picking up his humor immediately.

"Come on, guys, let's look around."

The store is a red and yellow blast of eye candy. Everywhere are displayed gorgeous clothes, toys, and just about anything onto which they can squeeze that overwhelming Ferrari logo. The only drawback (besides the discrimination against us non-Ferrari-owners) is that the merchandise is almost as expensive as the cars themselves.

"How could anyone ever accumulate enough money to buy one of their cars if they shopped in this store?" Casey asked.

"Guys," I said to Casey and Nathaniel in particular, "when you are famous international soccer stars, and you walk in to buy your Ferrari, be sure and remind them of this day!"

They both grinned dreamily.

We managed to escape without buying anything, therefore, leaving our family's net worth intact, and next proceeded to the Ferrari museum. Huge logo-drenched poles decorated the parking lot, and a ginormous (as my kids say) black stallion dominated one of the walls to the entrance. I had to admit, Enzo's descendants had retained his touch for the dramatic. Anyone with any amount of car-bug in them couldn't help but be excited entering such a place. Then we got to the ticket counter.

"I'm sorry, sir. Much of the museum is closed today due to a big tour of Ferrari owners coming through."

I couldn't believe my ears. Talk about high-pressure sales tactics. "That's it," I said, taking out my wallet. "I'm buying one right now! Give me a yellow Spider to go!"

"*Scusi*, sir? I don't understand," the beautiful young woman clad in red said in a bewildered tone.

"Aw, nothing. I'm just kidding," I said, wondering why the nice lady on the phone (no doubt, dressed in red) hadn't told me of this several days before when we had spoken.

"What I can offer you, sir," she said, handing me some red tickets, "is a discounted rate for the portion that is available."

I paid her quickly and moved on. Despite shameless "race-ial" profiling (excuse the pun, I just couldn't help it), I was still excited to enter the vaunted chambers of horsepower history.

I am not sure exactly what portion of the museum was closed because it seemed like we saw everything possible. There were race cars dating all the way back to the early days, featuring crazy tailpipes and spoke wheels, long nose cones, and open cockpits. The kids enjoyed getting pictures taken near these. There were strange, exotic, one-of-a-kind racecars, pace cars, and experimental cars. But my favorite exhibit was the twenty or so cars from recent model years, all scattered around on one elevated portion of the museum. Here were the cars in the posters on the walls of countless young boys all over the world. I enjoyed getting my picture taken around these.

At one point, Christine seemed totally occupied at a series of tables near some Shell Oil logos. We sauntered over to find her interacting with a video explaining the workings of an internal combustion engine (an Indy racecar engine, nonetheless).

"See, Terri," I pointed out, "homeschooling strikes again."

As we exited what had been a fascinating walk through automotive history, we spilled into another gift shop. This one was smaller and had no ban on photography. Christine decided to spend all of her souvenir money on a cute little artist's case, complete with little pens, colored pencils, and pads of paper. The whole thing was bright red with a prancing horse on it.

Next we walked the town in front of the main entrance of the factory itself, snapping photos all the while. It being lunchtime, waves of employees were spilling out the front gates, making their way across the street into restaurants and parking lots. Every last one of them was dressed in matching red Ferrari coveralls. It looked as if we were watching an army decamping. Having worked in the U.S. auto industry for many years, I laughed when I tried to envision the United Auto Workers wearing matching uniforms.

We walked a little farther, and then we heard it: That Ferrari sound! Through privacy slats in a chain link fence, we could see a brand new red Ferrari *Italia* 458 emerge from the factory door and literally race along the fence line. We soon learned that it was headed for the test track out back, a facility we could partially see from the road while leaving town. There were five or six brand-new red Ferraris being hot-tested on their very own track before shipping off to actual customers who would be allowed factory tours and photos in the gift shop. Wow. What a sound.

It was enough to inspire an optional appendage to our trip we had conceived only the night before: Lamborghini.

"It's only a half-hour up the road," I said.

The kids looked at each other and then at their mother.

"It's okay with me," she said, "as long as we get lunch first!"

"Yeah, pizza!" said Nathaniel.

"Yeah, pizza! Pizza, pizza, pizza!"

Some things just have universal appeal, like Ferraris and pizza.

Driving north, skirting the eastern edge of Modena, we wound along narrow farm roads slicing through photogenic scenes of fields of wheat. The farther we went, the less confidence I had in the directions I had obtained over the phone. That language barrier thing was always on hand to erode one's confidence and, besides, this just didn't look right. We were out in the *boonies*. An automotive factory out *here*?

We quickly passed through the little tiny town of Nonantola, squirting out the other side onto a little two-lane road. Suddenly, there, right by that little lane, gleamed a long shiny building that looked so out of place in the middle of this farmland I almost thought we were seeing a mirage. We weren't in an industrial park, a factory city, or even a suburb of one. We were in farmer Giovanni's back forty!

A well-dressed young man greeted us at the road's edge and kindly opened a gate to allow us into the small visitors' parking lot. We popped out into the bright sunshine and stared at the long, black, shiny, glass fascia of another of automotive history's revered brands. This scene, even more than at Ferrari, reminded me of visiting Willy Wonka's Chocolate Factory.

Lamborghini has always seemed a bit eclectic to me and slightly more exotic than even Ferrari. The comparison between their two physical plants could not have been more supportive of that impression. I couldn't help but wonder how and why they had placed their factory *here*. The idyllic country setting simply added to the allure.

The Lamborghini museum occupies two floors right along the fancy glass front of the building. Like Ferrari, it houses a stunning history of the progression of their automotive designs over the years. And, matching my impression, it is even more varied than the Ferrari one, and sometimes downright odd. There are cars from the sixties with cross-mounted twelve cylinder engines. I imagined the weight distribution in these babies and how difficult they would be to drive. Then there are humongous twelve-cylinder racing boat engines, farm tractor engines, and my favorite—the predecessor to the Hummer by at least ten years—the Lamborghini LM002. This enormous off-road truck is impossible not to like, looking as it does like something out of a *Mad Max* movie. I took more photos of it than anything else in the museum.

Upstairs features many of the later model cars, including a fascinating handful of one-of-a-kind concept cars that never saw production. Two Diablos literally hang on the wall! The favorite of my kids was the Diablo police car. Toys of this model are in gift shops throughout Italy; now we were seeing the real thing. Each car has a placard telling a little about its history and indicating how many were produced. Most of these quantities are surprisingly small. The police car, for instance was one of only two such cars in existence. Talk about exotic.

The biggest treat was reserved for the end, however. Just as we walked outside to leave, a brand new pumpkin-orange Gallardo was being delivered to its buyer. They started the car, drove it around the parking lot a little and, generally, just put on a show for all of us gawking tourists.

"Cool, Dad," said Nathaniel.

"Yeah. This is the best trip ever," added J.R.

I had to agree.

# PART II: ADAGIO

CHAPTER 19

# AT THE BEHEST OF SIESTA

*The ways of eating and speaking are always what unify a country.* – Guido Tomassi

International travel offers all sorts of intrinsic rewards. Being totally immersed in a foreign culture is one of the most educational experiences one could ever have. It is also one of the most inescapable.

I remember when I first arrived in Japan as a grad student. In preparation, I had taken a crash course in the language but was still hopelessly ill-equipped. I had read books on Japanese history, but I was still in literal culture shock as I tried to figure out what I was eating, how the train schedule worked (very efficiently, by the way), why the pay phones were all Kawasaki green, and why almost all the cars were white. And what was up with the yellow headlights? Even after I became close friends with several Japanese students (and one Japanese-American who had moved to Japan to study), I could still never totally figure out many aspects of their culture. Why, for instance, did the Japanese love Americans and look down on almost every other nation? Why did the women handle all the money and pay at every restaurant stop? And what the heck was Pachinko, anyway? Even after I'd been taken to a Pachinko parlor to play, I still had no idea why it was so appealing as to necessitate gaudy parlors spread across the whole country like eyesore cancer spots. And perhaps my biggest question of all: Why did the background videos that showed the words to Karaoke songs feature full-body camera pans of naked women?

I remember at one point during my stay in Japan thinking through the various stages of travel it would take me to get home to my apartment in Pittsburgh, Pennsylvania. If I recall correctly, there were eleven separate travel steps, including buses, trains, airlines, taxis, and a ride home from the airport, among others. It was then that I felt just how far from home I truly was.

That's how it began to feel during our month in Italy. Most of the time it was a total blast. The complete immersion in a different culture was stimulating and exhilarating. But other times, their idiosyncrasies, at least from the point of view of a spoiled American, could become annoying. There were times we just couldn't escape the fact that we were a long way from home, in many more ways than mere distance.

Primary among these reminders was their custom of siesta (or *pisolino*: nap). I have to admit, it flat drove me crazy. When I was in a better mood, it was cute and cultural—something different to be appreciated. But when it didn't line up well with my personal needs, it made me grumpy and gruff.

There were other smaller features, what I'll call sub-features, of the siesta culture in *Italia*, as well. It eventually occurred to me that we never saw a restaurant that offered breakfast . . . anywhere. This isn't that big of a deal to me, for whom breakfast is a take it or leave it affair. My breakfast is usually no more than a gulp of healthy fruit juice and possibly a protein bar halfway through the morning. For many of my breakfast-fixated friends, however, the complete dearth of public breakfast options in Italy will be a sad surprise. There was, however, one exception to this situation. No matter where we went, how small the town, how backwater on one hand or tourist-infested on the other, there was always—and I mean *always*—a bar open. These bars, though, are quite different from what most Americans would think of when hearing the word *bar*. These are generally dinky little places with a glass-fronted cooler full of soft drinks and soda water (trying to find natural water is as hard as finding an honest politician in an election year) and also a miniscule glass counter containing four or five sad danishes or croissants for sale. Sure enough, behind all this are always bottles of various hard liquors on display on a shelf. I have no idea why these places are the earliest establishments open for business, or why they are the only ones that remain open during the sacred afternoon siesta. But truly, if you find yourself with an empty stomach in Italy any time before 12:30, look for a bar. It will be your only hope. Likewise, if you have the audacity to get your lunch schedule off from that of the rest of the nation by even as much as forty-five minutes, once again, a bar will be your only salvation. Simply saunter in, grab some Cokes out of the glass cooler (where there will only be about three on a good day), buy up all four of the danishes, and you and your family just might make it through until the dinner hour, which starts at 7:00, at the earliest. Of course, should you actually show up for dinner at 7:00, you will be looked at as though you dropped in from another planet and politely asked if you could wait around for "five minutes" (code in Italy for a minimum of a half hour) for them to finish getting ready.

This tight window for meal times, with lunch starting at about 12:30 and being closed by 1:30 and dinner starting at 7:00, but really more like 8:00, is cute for a little while. But before too long, if your family is at all like mine, you will soon be dreaming of the land of 24/7 restaurant hours and greasy spoon breakfasts. In fact, as soon as you hit the tarmac back home, you will likely drive directly for the nearest Denny's, even if you've never been to one in your life, and gorge yourself silly, all the while proclaiming it the best food you've ever eaten. These are the kinds of things that happen after full immersion in the Italian culture. Consider yourself forewarned.

The situation with bars is still a mystery to me. It is these same bars, by the way, where the old men congregate all afternoon to play their still-unknown-to-me card games. The other game they play all afternoon is called "Watch the foreigner by unabashedly staring at him" game. All of them play it well. Of course, I may be a little overly sensitive on this point and, come to think of it, deserving of their stares, because I find these little clusters of ten or twenty old men irresistible for photography. On a couple of different occasions, I actually stopped my motorcycle, removed my helmet, retrieved my camera from some impossibly deep pocket in my pants, and aimed it in their direction for two or three representative photos. They weren't a spectacle to me but a dream of an ideal retirement. Of course, they had no way of knowing what this crazy motorcycle tourist was up to and, therefore, I can easily understand their stares. But at any rate, I stand by my statement that Italy must be the best country in the world in which to be an old man. Whether I end up old and sitting out in front of an Italian bar during siesta or somewhere else on the planet, I hope to learn from their example and surround myself with crotchety friends playing games and making wisecracks at any darn fool rude enough to stop his motorcycle and take photos of us.

For the successful tourist in Italy, the whole "siesta thing" can never be forgotten. As mentioned, your stomach must conform to the national schedule or suffer the fate you deserve by not heeding the advice of this book. But it can also be a significant hindrance to the effectiveness of your sightseeing. For instance, we eventually settled into the routine of getting up a little on the early side and heading out to see some wonderful attraction within an hour's drive or so. This usually worked quite well. If the mood struck us and the time lined up exactly right, we would grab lunch in that particular town. Next, having what, half a day or more ahead of us? We would drive to another attraction a half hour or less away and attempt to see it, too. Only this plan normally didn't work out so well. The reason was the siesta thing all over again. It doesn't apply only to restaurants but to museums, stores, and just about anything else a human might find necessary for basic survival. I hate to think of what happens to the poor sap who injures himself during this precious time of day.

"*Si, signore*, we'll be right there immediately, as soon as siesta is over. We'll see you around 4:30. *Molto benne?*"

One could bleed to death.

Another observation so obvious and well known it borders on a cliché is how most Italians talk with their gestures as much as they do with their words. I at first thought it ironic that cell phones are so prevalent here, until I began noticing how a cell phone conversation proceeds. First, both parties begin by saying, "*Pronto*," as in, "Yeah, yeah, get to it." Then the speaker talks in a very loud and inflective manner, all the while flailing his arms and hands around as if the person on the other end of the connection could see every move being made. Then, while (I can only assume) the other person is speaking, the supposed listener interjects all sorts of sounds and words of acknowledgement. In fact, this particular habit is, of course, not limited to cell phone conversations. Often, whole groups of people can be seen happily talking all at once, waving arms, speaking loudly, in a cacophony of noise and motion capable of baffling any foreigner.

When it comes to gestures, there are a number of pleasing differences here, too. With another reflection on Japan, I learned that gestures are not universal. I was leaving my boarding house on the college campus when the women who cleaned the place showed up. One of them moved her hand as though to shoo me out the door quickly. I tied my shoes even faster and made an attempt to comply. But the more I did so, the more she shooed.

Finally I realized the American gesture for "Get outta here" is the Japanese gesture for "Come here." Complete opposites. I haven't observed any opposite Italian gestures, but there are many that are unfamiliar. When buying some fried potatoes as a snack for the kids at a market stand one day, the lady assisting me dropped one of the euro coins I gave her. Instead of instantly bending to retrieve it, she first stopped and chomped on her index finger. Two index fingers pointing down to the ground means, "May it never happen here." This is used when bad news is received. Putting both hands together almost as if in prayer and while pressing them together pumping them outward from the chest a few times is a sign for hoping something takes place. My favorite Italian gesture, however, is what I call the cab-driver bird: sticking out one's chin and flinging four fingers of one hand from the nape of the neck out past the chin in the direction of the other person. I am not even sure what the literal translation of this one is (something like "I don't care," so I am told), but upon seeing it, the intent is clear.

Gestures aren't the only thing lost in translation. I had a grand old time just taking in signs and advertisements. I have no idea why, but many things which seem aimed predominantly at locals, are often posted only in English. I am certainly not complaining, nor could I do better than the following examples were I charged with translating my everyday English into Italian. However, I chuckled right out loud when spotting flyers posted all over town around Cortona advertising a "Pig Party" presented by the "Pig Family," complete with "A Sexy Show" and "Sexy Wash." Depicted were two women in bikinis crawling suggestively across the top of fancy chopper motorcycles. The musical groups (I think) advertised to appear were Burned Brains, Lost & Found, and Sexy Show. I told Terri I thought I would like to go check out this particular event just to find out what was being advertised. She laughed and said the curiosity was killing her, too, but she was scared I might catch a disease or something if I got too close. However, one evening we were driving home from somewhere and saw cars all over the place. Music was blaring throughout Terontola, and we realized the big event was happening right then! Strangely, hordes of people, many of them families with children, were all headed to the source of the sounds. We were too tired from the day's touring to even pull in and have a look. It is one of my chief regrets of the trip. After all, what kind of a prodigious noticer bypasses the chance to find out what a Sexy Wash Sexy Show is all about?

There were other funny signs, too. Some were downright profound. My favorite of this ilk was in the little burg of Foiano della 'Chiana, over the door of a daycare center. It read: "Baby Parking." True enough, I guess. In Rome I saw one that read: "Baby Leader." On the box of a toy bow-and-arrow set in big script lettering was written: "Archery: The life consist of sport." Even better, underneath that it said, "Do not shoot the person or the animal." At the poolside cabana of one of our villas was a sign boldly proclaiming, "Children Must Be Hold By Parents." A brand of potato chips is called "TeenAgers." One translated menu had for a special "The Pork Chop." Another said, "Pigeon in Pieces Cooked in Red Wine." This was all very entertaining until it dawned on me that I was basically speaking babytalk Italian in restaurants and shops. Maybe I'd keep my chuckles to myself.

## CHAPTER 20

# FROM VIOLENCE, BEAUTY

*Adventure is a path. Real adventure—self-determined, self-motivated, often risky—forces you to have firsthand encounters with the world. The world the way it is, not the way you imagine it. Your body will collide with the earth and you will bear witness. In this way you will be compelled to grapple with the limitless kindness and bottomless cruelty of human-kind—and perhaps realize that you yourself are capable of both. This will change you. Nothing will ever again be black-and-white.* – Mark Jenkins

O ne marvelous feature of the Tuscan landscape is the smattering of medieval (and older) hilltop villages. Many of these are perched like citadels atop atolls and rising hills, and all of them appear the same medium brown color from a distance, contrasting beautifully with the surrounding green and tan farmlands. Against the ever-changing backdrop of the sky, with the sun providing its nonstop changing brushstrokes, these towns never lose their power to make drivers stop and yank out their cameras.

Among these scenic towns, the most photographed has to be San Gimignano. It appears on book covers, travel guides, posters, bookmarks, and tee shirts. Even those who have never been to Italy will likely recognize its profile of varied height towers popping up apparently at random from the surrounding base of terracotta roofs. According to historians, the small town once featured seventy-two such towers. Today only thirteen remain. The towers were originally constructed for defense, providing a high place of refuge to which a family or group of families could retreat when under threat from either a rival faction from within the city or attackers from a neighboring town. Expensive to build, often several families would connect their buildings and share a tower in times of peril. Eventually, however, the towers became status symbols indicating a family's wealth. This caused a race to see who could build the highest tower, a medieval version of keeping up with the Joneses.

Touring the serene Tuscan countryside and visiting towns like San Gimignano, it is hard to visualize a time when tall towers were needed for survival. But these hills have seen waves and waves of violence throughout the centuries. This was Roman-controlled territory once, after all, and the Romans were harsh conquerors of their Etruscan neighbors. The oppressiveness of their rule practically obliterated the Etruscan civilization, which has left us little more than tombs, the term *Tuscany*, and a deep-seated mistrust of anything Roman that persists to this day among Tuscans. I am told local political elections are often determined by who is seen to most staunchly oppose centralized Roman politics. While the Tuscans pride themselves on their honesty, I was told there is a common saying, "Never trust a Roman."

After Rome fell in the fifth century A.D., power migrated to the official church and to local landlords. This resulted in a staggering number of little governments and fiefdoms, each in perpetual struggle with neighbors. As the centuries rolled by, six major city-states emerged in Italy: Venice, Naples, Rome, and the Papal states Milan, Florence, and Siena.  Often these, too, were at war with each other.  As the so-called Dark Ages morphed into the Renaissance, France and Spain began a confusing  series of alliances, invasions, and soirées into the peninsula.  War and threats of war were a way of life.  Dante, Machiavelli, Leonardo da Vinci, and Michelangelo were all either combatants in battles, or called upon to design and help construct defense mechanisms against invasions.

In addition to fighting between cities, often-violent factions and feuds existed within a city's own walls.  Some of these, such as the Ghelfs and the Ghilbellines, or the Blacks and the Whites, among others, were bloody affairs that toppled city governments and swayed back and forth for years like water in a cake pan.  The long rule of the Medici family in Florence, followed by their ouster and then later return, is just one example of the enormous power struggles that took place within what today appear to be serene walls.

All the strife wasn't centuries ago, however, as World War II raged here, too.  The Allies pushed hard against a stiff German organized retreat through these exact hills.  Following Italy's official surrender to the Allies, a sturdy guerilla resistance erupted throughout the region in which local boys risked their lives to help the Allies rid the peninsula of the German army.  This was often followed by violent reprisals from the Germans, a sad situation commemorated with markers and statues that stand in silent salute today.

What was once a necessity for survival becomes a photo op for a tourist.  The terror of one's family in danger from bloodthirsty violence is contrasted against the joy of a man on vacation with his family.  The irony of all of this was not lost on me as I gazed out across the beautiful panoramic view provided from the top of the tallest tower in San Gimignano, the only one currently open to the public.  It is called the Torre Grossa and is accessible through the Museo Civico. We climbed the two hundred fifty steps with ease, even J.R., whose five-year-old legs were the first to complete the ascent. At the top, on a sweltering morning headed for a super-hot day, the gentle breezes wafting in from the west were refreshing. We had arrived early, beating the waves of tourist busses that would soon descend like a SWAT team, and we, therefore, had the tower largely to ourselves. I stood leaning against a centuries-old stone parapet and pondered the ravages of war this countryside has seen—what violence in a setting of such beauty.

I took a few minutes to describe this series of wars to my children. Waving an arm across the landscape and attempting to conjure for them an image of a Sienese army moving northeast to invade Florence. Or the French and Spanish in a huge line heading south to eventually sack Rome. Or the Roman legions kicking up a cloud of dust as they marched for Gaul.

San Gimignano is positioned on what was once the main north-south route for travelers on pilgrimage to Rome from all over Europe. This accounted for its prosperity, but like other places, it was devastated by the plague in 1348 and never fully recovered. After explaining the wars and battles that had raged throughout the region, I attempted to convey a picture in the minds of my children of the pilgrims passing through—how they looked, thought, smelled, and the things they may have discussed. Fortunately, my kids have not yet read Chaucer and were easily enraptured by my plagiarism (edited to Rated G).

Something else dawned on me as I took in the sweeping vista from Torre Grossa: I was getting a little too accustomed to so much beauty. Everywhere we drove, everywhere we looked, we were greeted by sweeping views and gorgeous landscapes. Jagged mountain ranges in the distance, smoky gray to almost a blue smear into the color of the sky, fronted by darker ridges closer in. Set ahead of these were the undulating hills punctuated with farms and towns and ruins. Up close was usually an olive grove or vineyard, or both, juxtaposed as if coordinated by an artist for maximum visual impact. But perhaps no view was as gorgeous as the one we beheld that morning from San Gimignano. It was sufficient to shake us out of the lull so much beauty had induced in us, and I could not take enough photographs. Gazing out across the miles and miles of expanse, I would spot a quaint farmhouse in its own setting of cypresses and think, *I'll take that one. No wonder the Buy-a-Tuscan-villa-and-fix-it-up-to-live-happily-ever-after genre of travel writing has become so popular. Who wouldn't become intoxicated with the thought of calling a little slice of this dreamland home?*

"Oh, honey, we could put in so many flowering plants and annuals and have our own vines. We could decorate the kitchen with that handpainted ceramic stuff called, what was it? Yes, majolica. We could cook with olive oil from our own trees and . . ."

As usual, when such fantasies were running rampant in my mind, fatherhood interrupted.

"When are we going to eat?"

"Yeah, Dad, I'm getting pretty hungry."

"Can we have pizza?"

"In just a few minutes, guys; I want to take in this view a little longer."

I could have stayed for hours.

Eventually, we descended the tower and walked the side streets, always the best way to find the cheapest food, and poured ourselves into a tiny place offering *pizza al taglio* (pizza by the slice). The kind lady running the place spoke no English, but took great care with Nathaniel's allergies, showing Terri containers of ingredients to help make sure we'd be eating safely.

Driving back toward *La Contea,* we decided to make a quick stop at Monteriggioni, a small fortress town built in 1203. It was strategically located as a garrison by Siena at its northern territorial edge to protect against incursions from pesky old Florence—another treasure of beauty left to us from violent origins. Built in the shape of a rough circle and ringed by fourteen guard towers, Monteriggioni is distinctive. Legend suggests its shape was the inspiration for Dante's deepest section of punishment depicted in his *Inferno*, one of three parts comprising his classic *The Divine Comedy*. Inside the fortress walls is anything but a hell, however. Instead, one finds a quaint little town, complete with rounded stone streets, stone buildings, the now-familiar tile roofs, and flowers spilling out of balconies. A couple of restaurants front the small piazza, and one hotel nicely modernized but still retaining the charm of its thirteenth-century architecture is a place I'd love to stay during some future visit.

It was knock-you-down hot outside, and everyone was thirsty. There was nothing open at this hour except, of course, the bar. I scooted in and bought each of the kids the only thing available, a peach drink called *ESTA THE pesca*—a phrase Christine immediately put to song. Soon the other kids joined in, and the drink has since become famous in our family, its consumption always accompanied by the singing of Christine's song.

The highlight of Monteriggioni was walking its walls. Tickets can be purchased at either end, a lift or stairs can be taken to the top, and an expanded metal walkway has been constructed around approximately one-third of the fortress's perimeter. Signs are everywhere warning against climbing up onto the actual stone ledges, so, of course, that's the first thing my children did. But the signs were in Italian, so at least we had plausible deniability. Once again, the view provided is intense. It's easy to see how effective this location was as a lookout. We did quite a bit of looking out ourselves, snapping more photos and taking it all in. But the heat was more oppressive than an attack of Florentines, so we descended and re-

treated to the pool at the villa and a home-cooked meal by Terri.
We came.  We saw.  We *ESTA THE pesca'd*.

CHAPTER 21

# THE JOURNEY OF A WINE SNOB

*"Look at those vines," he said. "Nature is wearing her prettiest clothes."* – Massot in *A Year In Provence* by Peter Mayle

I love bookstores, and I love used-book bookstores the best. Perusing the titles and walking the rows is like a treasure hunt in which any moment could offer up a new favorite volume. Villas that have long been used for vacationers are invariably stocked with interesting little piles of books left by unknown travelers past. There will usually be travel guides, paperback novels, and some classics, and these in a pleasing array of different languages.

I remember a dusty little cottage high atop a dune overlooking Lake Michigan near Grand Haven. In it was the usual eclectic assortment of books in which I discovered an original edition hardcover of *Kon Tiki*, Thor Heyerdahl's true adventure tale of sailing a hand-built raft from South America to Polynesia. I had never heard of this classic before, and now it is a treasured memory as my best beach read ever, as well as a valuable volume in my library. (I sent a check in payment to the cottage's owner, who laughed off my concern over book theft.)

*La Contea* was similarly stocked. Though most volumes were

in Italian, there were some German, French, and a few English titles. One of the latter was an old travel guide. In it was a detailed description of a recommended day drive through the Chianti wine region, with six or eight stops of interest encouraged along the way. I had heard of this area, had read one or two books in which the action was set in its vineyards, and was immediately convinced this would be a perfect idea for our next outing. Terri's buy in was easily obtained; her favorite thing to do in Italy was taking leisurely drives of exploration anyway. The kids I convinced with promises of pizza and gelato. Negotiations always come down to knowing your adversaries.

Things started off smoothly enough. The guidebook recommended launching out from Siena, so we drove the now familiar road and once again mounted the steep hills leading upward to the city of minibus fame. I had thought the route for skirting the city would be obvious once we were on location. I would simply take a road going off to the left or right, wind around the city walls, and be on my way toward Chianti to the north. The only problem was there didn't seem to be any roads going off to the left or right. Either that or I just flat missed them. At any rate, there we were, driving straight into Siena in our minibus once again, the GPS encouraging me every step of the way, just like before. The darn thing has no shame. I began to have visions of hundreds of elderly ladies descending on my driver's window to remind me once again that I was an idiot.

You don't have to tell me three times. I spun the minibus around like I was in an episode of *Rockford Files* and made a quick exit of Siena before the ladies even found out I was there. But I still couldn't make sense of the roads. The points of interest along the way weren't available on the GPS, and besides, by this time my "maleness" had kicked in. What resulted was the infamous "I can find it without directions" machismo.

So we got lost.

Wherever we were, though, it was beautiful, we kept saying to one another. The terrain had changed dramatically. Soft rolling hills had given way to ripples through wheat fields that looked like water frozen in motion. Gray cliffs looked as if they were caused by the ground sinking away just moments before, leaving turf growing on top but the sides exposed as fresh gray clay. As far as the eye could see were bright yellow wheat fields freshly cut. I was back to using the GPS, which seemed to have lost its mind in the heat, and we drove from one gravel road to another, all the while going deeper and deeper into this strange new territory. We would later find out this area is officially known as Crete Senesi, unofficially as the "Tuscan Desert." The more we drove, the more lost we got and the less we minded.

There were small towns consisting of four or five buildings tightly crowded along both sides of gravel roads, beautiful villas in ruin atop golden hilltops, and as always, the ever-present cypress trees standing at attention as garnishment. Occasionally, from who knows where, bicyclists would come racing down a hill or slugging it out slowly up one, dressed in their bright colorful riding gear and nodding with grimaces. One gang of at least twenty motorcycles tooled past in the opposite direction, every one of them waving at us as they went by.

"Where do they make the wine, Dad?" asked Nathaniel.

"Yeah, is this that famous region?" joined Christine.

"Not exactly. This is another famous place, though," I answered.

"What is it?" asked J.R.

"We don't know, but isn't it pretty?" Terri answered.

And on we drove.

Once, we actually drove in a huge circle, jumbling down from a gravel hillock to cross the same dirt road we had seen an hour before.

"This is a heck of a day to have forgotten our map," I said.

GPSs are wonderful, but in times like this, they just don't have what is needed. We had tried following the signs to the nearest town, only to discover the place to be a ghost town or too tiny to have a gas station or anything open. Not even a bar!

"We could just follow these roads back to Siena," Terri suggested. "Once we get there, we'll actually know where we are, and then we can get started again."

I try to be a patient husband.

"If I go back to Siena today," I carefully explained, "the society of elderly ladies will string me up by my fingernails. No way am I spending half my day getting back to the place we started. Nope. What's this town up ahead? Asciano? I've heard that's one of the best places for pizza in the world."

"Yay, pizza!" Christine and J.R. yelled in unison.

Terri giggled.

And we had some of the best pizza in the world right out by the street at a bar-that-was-kind-of-a-pizzeria in Asciano. A man sometimes just has to stick to his guns.

"*Scusi, signore*," I said to the, um, bartender who brought the pizzas to the table, "*dove Chianti vino region?*"

For the uninitiated, that's how Italianglish sounds.

He was initiated.

"Stay on this road and then turn north for about twelve kilometers," he said in perfect English.

Terri's ability to keep quiet in these situations is a marvel.

The Chianti region *is* gorgeous. The guidebook didn't lie (at least, about that . . . not so sure about the driving route thing). Entirely different from the desert we had just crossed, it was, as to be expected, thick with grape vines. Winding, twisting roads had all the kids mumbling, "I'm queasy," from the back seat, and I was simply getting tired of being in the car.

So the driving tour of the Chianti wine region turned into a one-stop deal featuring Castello di Brolio. This, however, was worth the entire escapade. Originally built as a monastery, it was later put to use by the Florentines as another outpost to keep an eye on those wily Sienese. Next, a family named Ricasoli purchased the castle. This particular family is much better at passing along heirlooms than is my own. Whereas we have already lost my great-grandfather's hammer—our sole family heirloom—despite the fact that his name was written in bold ink on the handle, these clever Ricasolis have managed to hand Brolio castle down to each succeeding generation since 1167. Pretty impressive staying power, if you ask me.

Over the years, the original castle was expanded to incorporate a palace, which blends into the castle so well it's difficult to tell where the castle stops and the palace begins. A private chapel was also constructed on the property in the late Middle Ages, and it features some interesting mosaics, an art technique rare in these parts. There is a family crypt below the chapel that is open to the public, should you wish to pay your respect to some of those heirloom-passing Ricasolis.

Manicured gardens surround the castle on a balcony and on terraces below. Their rigid, classic style provides a visual transition from the staunch castle to the rolling lines of vines that begin at the edge of the gardens and drape over hills all the way to the distant ridges. Once again, we found ourselves on an elevated perch, marveling at the view. *How many times*, I asked myself, *have I been arrested by the views here*? Certainly the vistas throughout Tuscany are the largest reason for its fame. Well deserved, too, I might add.

There is a tiny souvenir shop up at the level of the castle's perch, a restaurant halfway down the switchback road through towering pines, and at the base of the hill, an *enoteca* (wine shop). Being in the afternoon, and during siesta, the place looked deserted. But I knew beyond a shadow of a doubt the wine shop would be open because, well, those little bars were open all over the country, weren't they? And my logic followed that the wine shop would be, too. I was right, but this logic only applied to Castle di Brolio, not to any of the other shops we passed on the way home—let the wine-loving traveler be warned.

The shop was a beautiful masterpiece of wine racks, with a counter for tasting and some English-speaking workers. This was extremely fortunate for us because in addition to speaking very little Italian, we also speak very little of the language of wine. At this point in my life, I knew just enough about wine to be dangerous. There was red, and white, for instance. Of that much, I was certain. And I knew there was an interesting job called something French, like *sommelier,* because I had met one once. Beyond this, the whole world of wine, wine tasting, wine making, and especially knowing how to be a wine snob was a complete mystery to me. However, I was interested in learning more because I had noticed that in Italy wine wasn't alcohol but food.

I came to wine through the vines. Those interesting rows of meticulously maintained specimens seemed an age apart from the rest of the world of agriculture. The obvious care, the mysterious science, the lack of agreement on technique, planting, pruning, harvesting, processing, fermenting, bottling, and aging seemed like an entire universe I had somehow missed. The more I learned about wine, and especially the more I saw of vineyards, the more I became attracted. Perhaps, in my years of classifying wine as just another elixir of wantonness and drunkenness, I had missed something. Perhaps there was something much more, well, respectable about it, something mysterious and special, worth discovering and experiencing.

So Terri and I entered with an adventurous spirit and open minds, interested in discovering what so many people we knew and respected had found in this sophisticated world of the grape. We tasted some reds, tasted some whites, tasted from big glasses, and then tasted from even bigger glasses. The glasses kept getting bigger and bigger until I darn near had to stick my whole head inside one just to get a taste. I began to wonder just who in the world washed all these glasses, and did we really need another glass each time we tasted a new wine? I guess so, because each one they offered came with yet another new glass.

When it came to the wines, Terri pretty much didn't like any of them. She's a coffee drinker, after all, and there's nothing so hard to penetrate as the mind that is convinced coffee is the best drink in the world. I, on the other hand, am only a soda drinker, known the world over for being more open-minded than those tight-lipped coffee sippers. Therefore, I actually liked some of the wines. I thought I liked best the Chianti Classico, to which the worker (was he a *sommelier*?) said, "Excellent choice." Incidentally, in all subsequent tastings on this trip, I was always told, "Excellent choice," which led me to believe I had "the wine gift."

"I like the bouquet and think there is a faint patina of satin with a hint of oak," I would have loved to have said, but I didn't have the guts. Instead I said, "Can you ship to the United States? Six bottles, I think. For my wine cellar."

Ha! Wine cellar. Now I was cracking myself up. I did have a basement, however, and why couldn't I put some wine down there? It would certainly impress someone.

And that's how my wine snobbery began. I started the day as a lost tourist and ended it a wine connoisseur. Some of us just have that kind of capacity for personal growth.

## CHAPTER 22

# FREE TIME AND A PLAN TO TAKE ROME

*Man disgraces himself by believing technology brings happiness. Technology has no conscience. It distorts what we need.*
– Signor Api in *Head over Heel* by Chris Harrison

Gobs of free time have a unique effect on a person. I was well into the third week when I noticed a completely different biometric rhythm to my days. I had lost almost every trace of hurry. Interestingly, I was sleeping better and sleeping less. Getting up earlier and earlier in the mornings, I had ample time to think, read, write, and pray before the kids came bounding out to start their days. It was wonderful. It was also nearly unexplainable, even now as I attempt to pen these words.

I remember getting home after this trip and everyone asking me, "So, tell me, how *was* it?"

"It was indescribable," I would say, and then I'd go on about an attraction or a special moment. But what I really wanted to tell them was something untellable. How can one explain what it is like to have day after day without a schedule? Or looking up at the stars at night without a cell phone buzzing with a text message coming in, or worse, a late night phone call? I wondered how to relate what it felt like to go four weeks without wearing a watch, or to wake up when I felt rested and not by the squawking of an alarm clock. The nearest thing I can find to describe it is childhood, when one lived through the days not knowing about deadlines, commitments, or Facebook.

Another product of such time is a large number of smaller moments. I found myself making card houses with the kids or entering into their soccer ball juggling contests. One day, we had the most fun with wooden swords, re-enacting a battle between Florence and Siena, and then the Romans and Hannibal. There were family art projects and tons of card games together. There were games of all sorts in the pool, books read aloud to each other, and reptile hunting that never ceased.

As for myself, there were also random excursions on the motorcycle. Always unplanned and unmapped, these eventually became a near-daily ritual. In the heat of the afternoon when the kids had grown exhausted swimming and headed inside for some relief from the sun, I'd don my helmet and gloves and head out. I'd take winding roads until a certain mood struck; then on impulse I'd act on it and play out the adventure. Sometimes, this resulted in short rides, and other times, I'd head to some distant town and explore its streets.

One major advantage to a motorcycle is its ability to work into nearly any crevice of tight old towns. Parking is a snap, and so the motorcycle became a kind of magic carpet on which I would ride into the main piazza of any town and begin my sightseeing. By doing so, I became quite the shopper, picking up a leather case for Terri's laptop to match her purse bought in Florence years before. After all, there is nothing like Italian leather goods when it comes to gift-giving. Unless, that is, one remembers the silk industry. On another motorcycle jaunt, I ran an errand to pick up a selection of silk scarves from which Terri could choose as gifts for girlfriends back home. She selected the best, and I returned the rest. I would even pack the side bags of the motorcycle full of staple groceries from time to time. Believe me, these types of things would never happen back home. But give me a motorcycle in Italy and, yeah, I'll be your errand boy.

Another advantage we took with our free time was sunsets. Ask yourself, when was the last time you simply looked at the sky? Or counted how long it took the globe of the sun to sink completely behind the horizon? Or forced yourself to stay silent throughout the entirety of the drama so as not to ruin it?

The hill behind *La Contea* leads steeply upward on a surface of worsening gravel and exposed hard stone. It took about ten minutes to walk to the top while coaxing little legs to make the trip. Cutely, Casey and Nathaniel took to carrying the younger two on their backs, Sherpa-style. Once reaching the summit where an old rusted cross stands alone in some brambles, the air moved in from the valley below and provided much-needed cooling. The sweat from the climb evaporated, and the heat from the day seemed to radiate out of us as we caught our breath. If we timed it well enough, we would have time for the kids to explore before darkness fell. On several occasions, we startled huge hares from the weeds nearby, and they ran along the trail ahead of us in a panic. Once, we found a pile of shockingly sharp porcupine quills.

There are, of course, active olive groves all down the northern slope falling away from the place we would usually stand. Atop the hill were some old wooden fences and fields gone to weeds. Sometimes we would find a tractor parked nearby or a horse in a fenced field. Usually, though, the place was completely vacant, offering nothing but an uninterrupted view of the valley far below and Cortona silhouetted on the distant slope.

It was atop that hill, though, where the sky came alive: ruby and rust, streaks of steel, a changing artist's canvas painted by the Master Himself. How sad for it to be so often wasted on a world too busy to notice or too sophisticated to believe. I would stare

into that ever-changing masterpiece wondering why I had ever ignored the beauty on display around me every day.  I vowed that
as I returned to my "normal" life, I would take fewer things for
granted.

The nightly family sunset ritual was one of the things we were
going to miss as we prepared to spend a few days in Rome. "Wait
for us," we said on the night before leaving. *It is amazing,* I thought,
descending in the gray dusk, *that something so beautiful happens every night whether or not anyone happens to be watching.*

\* \* \*

If you talk to people who don't travel much and you happen to
mention the city of Rome, you'll likely hear something like, "Oh,
watch out for pickpockets."

Strange. I've never had that problem myself. When I get ripped
off in Rome, it's always a lot more open and obvious than that.

One time was by the vagabonds dressed up like Roman soldiers
outside the Colosseum.  They get their silly replica hats on you so
fast and pose for so many photos in such a friendly way you begin
to think the Tuscans have it wrong about the Romans.  But when
they demand with the force of a Mafia shakedown ten euro for
every photo taken, you walk away thinking the Tuscans might be
onto something.

Another incident occurred in a little restaurant just across from
the entrance to the Castel Sant' Angelo. (If I could remember the
name of the place, I would gladly publish it in these pages.) While
ordering, two friends and I were offered an additional appetizer
plate of some cheeses and *prosciutto.* We accepted without asking
the price.  Our bad.  When we received the bill, we found that
the two sad little chunks of buffalo cheese and two equally meager
strips of meat were worth fifty euro (about seventy-five dollars).
Mind you, this wasn't a five-star restaurant, where at least a linen
tablecloth and a waiter with a towel over his arm would make you

think it was worth it.  Nope.  Our meals had cost around eight euro each.  What followed was a heated bout of verbal accusations back and forth in which the restaurant's owner informed us that he had "fought four years for his country's flag!"  Not sure what this had to do with anything, my friend (a former Air Force Captain) retorted that he'd fought for *his* country's flag for *seven* years.  This rendition of "my dad's bigger than your dad" finally ended with the exasperated owner handing *me* the bill and saying, "Just write down how much you want to pay.  We Romans are a fair and understanding people."  He was surely related to the fake soldiers at the Colosseum.

So I wasn't really too worried about pickpockets.  In Rome, they rip you off right out in the open.  What I *was* worried about, however, was parking.

I knew we had to have a plan.  About two hours away from *La Contea*, there was just too much to show the family to attempt to travel there and back in the same day.  In fact, the way I saw it, two hotel stays would be the minimum.  Although this is ridiculously short for seeing a city that could take years to explore, we had small children in tow and had to be strategic.  We just weren't going to be able to see everything.

Terri, interestingly enough, had never been to Rome.  On the Mediterranean cruise we had taken, two of the kids were sick on the day the ship docked near Rome, and she "took one for the team" and stayed back on the ship so I could go ashore.  I had thanked her profusely and then scurried out the door before she could change her mind.  On another trip, I had come with my friends who had "fought for their flag."  So this would be her maiden voyage through Roma.  That being the case, I wanted to hit the highlights.  This meant going where every tourist in the world has gone before and, in fact, where they would all be going on those particular days, too.  Crowds are a way of life at Rome's biggest attractions, so one might as well get mentally prepared for it. Parking is primary among these considerations.

Hotels would be my solution. While not all hotels in Rome offer parking (traveler be warned), I managed to find one quite near the Vatican that did. I even called ahead to make sure they had a parking space big enough for a minibus. "*Va benne, va benne, signore*, no problem," I had been told. He could have given me ten *va benne*s, and I still wasn't going to relax about it until I saw it with my own eyes.

Our plan was to wake up early, drive to our hotel in Rome, beg them to let us park early, hours before check-in time, and walk over to tour the Vatican. The second day, we would take taxis to the Roman Forum, where I felt certain I could lead a decent walking tour while at the same time giving the evil eye to anyone dressed as a Roman soldier.

## CHAPTER 23

# REELING TOWARD THE CEILING

*Michelangelo had brought the power, vitality, and sheer magnitude of works of sculpture such as the 'David' into the realm of painting. The art of fresco would never be the same again.*
— Ross King

The Smart Car counting contest had never abated. All four kids were enthusiastic contributors, yelling out things like, "Smart Car number four hundred fifty-one!" without warning. This was normally followed by, "No, I already counted that one!" or "That's number four hundred fifty-three!" These sightings took place entirely at random, all the time, in every town and dale through which we drove. We were never lacking in entertainment or misunderstandings requiring parental refereeing. So, with a sharp eye out for Smart Cars, we drove into Rome.

I absolutely love Rome. It is high on my list of favorite places in the world. If nothing else about Italy has appealed to you thus far, Rome should do the trick. That is, of course, if you don't get overwhelmed.

We entered the city proper at mid-morning, just about the best time to avoid traffic. Finding our hotel rather easily, we inquired inside if we could park early this many hours before check-in and received several more *va benne*s. The hotel security guard motioned for me to follow him outside where he opened a narrow steel roll-up garage door. It revealed what looked to be a dark cave with a floor sloping down into the abyss.

"Is that where they kept the Apostle Paul?" I asked

"*Scusi, signore?*"

"Never mind. *Va benne.*"

He gestured, and I maneuvered. Minibusses have a strong tendency to resist small cave-like spaces; it took merely twenty or thirty wheel cranks and lunges to get it spun around between the rows of cars parked along both sides of the street. Pulling down into the tiny subterranean parking garage was another test. There was a low ceiling and a steel railing along one side, while the other side featured a stone wall showcasing scrape marks left by my predecessors. I was undeterred, however, because I'd been on the Amalfi Coast for a week.

"This is all working out fine," Terri commented cheerily as I re-emerged from the Parking Dungeon.

"Nothing to it."

And we were off to see the Vatican museums on the hottest recorded day since Romulus and Remus had first founded the place in 756 B.C. *Maybe the heat will keep the crowds away*, I thought.

We rounded a corner and were greeted by a mob scene. People were lined up at the museum entrance, out onto the small courtyard in front, down onto the sidewalk, all along the steep stone wall running parallel down the street, and then disappearing around the corner. So much for help from the heat.

The Vatican is a sovereign state all its own, ruled by the Pope and, therefore, Europe's only true monarchy. This city-state has its own money, banks, post office, court system, newspaper, and radio station. To the approximately five hundred people living there as residents, it must feel like an invasion when people from countries all over the world descend daily to smudge up the glass on the museum cases and crane their necks upward at Michelangelo's ceiling. On this smoking-hot day in July, it certainly looked like an invasion. I wanted to quit as soon as I saw the line. There was no way we could stand in this heat for the two or three hours it looked like it would take just to get inside.

I immediately felt like an idiot. In planning this trip, I had, of course, booked the hotel accommodations in Rome in advance. Why hadn't I also thought to pre-book tickets to enter the Vatican? The best way to do this is through one of the many tour groups. They charge a little more but then whisk you in a side entrance and bypass the tourist invasion.

Just then I spotted a tall young man walking the length of the line holding up a brochure. It sounded like he was speaking English.

"What are you offering?" I asked hopefully.

"A guided tour, sir; it'll get you past this line, and you can go through a four-hour tour of the museums with one of our highly skilled and entertaining guides."

I didn't care if their guides were unskilled and boring as heck. If one of them could get me past this line, I was all for it.

"How much?"

I can't remember the price. It didn't matter. It could have been 200 euro per person, and I still would have done it.

"Deal," I said. "Only with the little ones," I said gesturing to Christine and J.R., "I don't think we really want a guide. Can she get us in and then turn us loose?"

"Certainly, sir, anything you want. But you will like our guides. They are highly skilled and entertaining."

No doubt.

"Follow me, sir."

And we were off. First, we cut back through the line, crossed the street, and then went along the line away from the entrance. We rounded the corner and noticed the line not only did, too, but it actually bent out of sight around the *next* corner.

"You are doing well to get the guide," the young man said. By now, we had found out his name was Raj, and he was from New Delhi.

"How much farther?"

"Oh, not much more, sir," Raj assured us. Raj was a nice guy, and we chatted about all sorts of topics. I was sure it was his highly skilled and entertaining technique to keep us from bailing on him once we saw how far away he was taking us. Perhaps he was a con artist leading us to those famous pickpockets.

"Here we are," Raj said, guiding us into a small, crowded, sweltering storefront. "You pay right here. Enjoy your tour," he said and was off. Probably to go get some more suckers for the pickpockets.

We paid an exorbitant amount of money and were assigned our tour guide, a woman named Jennifer from—where else—California! She had long curly hair and mischievous eyes and was quick to smile as we approached and made our introductions. She immediately took command and led a group of about twelve of us back into the blistering sun. We traversed the ground we'd just trod with Raj, who I thought we would likely overtake at any moment. Jennifer told us that as many as 25,000 people a day visit the Vatican museums, and I had no trouble believing her. They were all there already on this day, and it appeared as if each had brought a friend.

Inside was a crowd so thick you could barely move, much less breathe. Jennifer did her best to knife us through, and the air conditioning was a welcome reprieve from the heat outside. *This is going to be just fine*, I thought. Then I realized only the ticket lobby had air conditioning.

The Vatican museums house one of the world's largest and most valuable art collections. This includes, of course, the famous frescoes in the Sistine Chapel, but also the Raphael Rooms, the Etruscan Museum, the Gallery of Maps, the Borgia Apartments, a gallery of modern religious art, the Pio-Christian Museum, the Egyptian Museum, the Pio-Clementine Museum, the Pinacoteca (an art gallery), the Chiaramonti Museum, and something called the Gregorian Profane Museum (but I don't remember what the &*%$#$*&* that was). There are additional museums and wings closed to the public. To try to make sense of this maze of amazement, the Vatican has proposed several color-coded tour routes. This is necessary because, much like the way swine are moved through slaughtering pens, a strict, one-way system is in place throughout the complex. One can choose from several tour options or just hire a Jennifer to hit the high points. This is one reason we decided not to abandon Jennifer after all. The other reason was she threatened us with bodily harm if we left her tour group. Apparently, the Vatican tour guides must account for the radio receiver units they loan out to us. These are equipped with horribly fitting earpieces, theoretically, to allow us to hear the guide's skillful and entertaining information. Throughout our tour, one couple from England kept falling behind and getting separated from the group. So we would have the honor and privilege of waiting for them while Jennifer stewed and stammered nervously, counting the cost of having to replace those radios, no doubt.

If the relentless beauty of the Italian countryside has the ability to numb one's senses, the Vatican museums have double that ability. I love history and art. I truly enjoy it. Seeing artifacts and artwork that not only is staggeringly beautiful, but required mind-blowing skill on the part of its creators, is really a joy. Appreciating the antiquity of some of the pieces gave me another deep sense of the passing of time. It also made me marvel that these items had survived millennia of wars and earthquakes and fires and erosion and politicians so that we could enjoy them in a museum one day.

Museums, however, are a lot like a good meal. At first, one is hungry and can't take enough in. Every display is like a succulent morsel over which to linger. Slowly, though, satiation sets in. The appetite wanes. Then one becomes totally full, subsequently stuffed to the point of throwing up.

Inundated with so much beauty for so long, this process was happening to us. We were getting completely full. Add to this the heat and the crowds. Tens of thousands of sweaty people from all over the world were crammed together in tight places filled with motionless air. By the time we hit the map room, I was feeling as full of art and history as a glutton after his last meal. Jennifer, too, was cracking. She was sweating as much as we were, and the English couple was pushing her buttons. But she soldiered on and had a good knack for when to pour on the information and when to give it a rest.

By now, J.R. was asleep and riding on Terri's back. Christine was sitting down on the cold marble floors every chance she got. Nathaniel wanted a drink, and Casey asked, "How much longer?"

It's strange what happens in situations like this. We had traveled a third of the way around the world to be here in this special place. We had looked forward as a family to seeing these museums, and especially the Sistine Chapel, together. I was the only one among us who had seen it before, and I was very interested in sharing it with my family. In particular, I wanted to show it to Terri, who had missed it due to sick children on the cruise trip, and also Christine, my little art lover. But the "tyranny of the physical" was taking over. The temperature, our feet, our thirst, and our moods were overpowering the sophisticate in all of us. The body was taking precedence over the mind.

It was something you could sense throughout the entire crowd. The whole mass of us began to move more and more quickly, with a goal-oriented determination that would have made Tony Robbins proud. It was as if a hundred nationalities had all united in one great purpose: "Get us to the Sistine Chapel *now*."

This must have been nothing new because the closer we got to the famous chapel, the less and less artwork adorned the walls and rooms through which we passed. By the end, we were traipsing through nothing but plain ole whitewashed dry-walled rooms that looked no better than a hallway in a HUD house.

Suddenly, and almost without any warning, we were there. The air conditioning greeted us like an old friend, and I thought how pathetic I was to notice that first. Then we heard the museum workers shushing the crowd. Signs everywhere warned against photography. But these efforts had no more effect than a row of rent-a-cops trying to hold back a mob of European soccer fans rushing a field. I noticed Japanese tourists secretly aiming their cameras upward and taking flashless pictures, and the whole room was abuzz with excited chatter. Everyone's head was turned upward to get a view of Michelangelo's masterpiece on the ceiling.

The first thing that struck me about the ceiling was its explosive color. The photos in books just don't convey how bright it is, and this is even more amazing given the fact that the lights in the room are intentionally kept dim for preservation purposes. I can only imagine how bright and lively they must be when the room is well lit. The other thing that occurred to me the first time I viewed the room was how little mention Raphael's work on the walls below the ceiling receives and also how much better (I think) Michelangelo's painting *The Last Judgment* is on the far end than his work on the ceiling. But the scope of the work is staggering.

The four years it took to complete the ceiling sounds lengthy until one is standing beneath it. Then it seems miraculously short. *The Last Judgment* took seven years, and this seems a bit more in line with what feels possible to us mere mortals. In a whisper, I pointed out to my children everything I could remember. I told them the story of how Pope Julius II, nicknamed *"Il Pontefice Terrible"* for his domineering manner, all but forced Michelangelo Bounerotti to paint it, despite the fact that, incredibly, Michelangelo protested that he was not a painter. This dim view Michelangelo held of his own artistic abilities with the brush (he staunchly maintained that he was merely a sculptor) was not false modesty. In a poem to a friend he wrote:

"Giovanni, come to the rescue
Of my dead painting now, and of my honor;
I'm not in a good place, and I'm not a painter."

"Can you imagine having to work four years on something like that ceiling against your will? Then, can you imagine being forced back as an old man by another pope and made to paint that huge painting on the far wall? Can you tell by looking at it that the far wall is sloped inward toward the ceiling so dust won't settle on it? Did you know that after more than four years of working overhead on the ceiling that Michelangelo suffered from something called eyestrain, which forced him to read correspondence and drawings by holding them at arm's length above his head?" And on and on I went, suddenly refreshed and back in historian mode. Jennifer, eat your heart out.

Rather than eating her heart out, however, she was forcing us to leave. *This*, I thought, *is the disadvantage of a guided tour.* I wanted to stay for at least an hour. *How does one appreciate art of this magnitude with just a glance?*

Our group slowly departed, and for once, the English couple wasn't last.  I remained behind until the radio-hoarding Jennifer came back and forced me to leave.

"What did you think?" she whispered with respect, noticing my reluctance to leave.

"Arresting," was all I could think to say.

Jennifer nodded with understanding and led me back toward the group where I saw the English couple giving me the evil eye.

## CHAPTER 24

# THE FANCIEST GRAVE IN THE WORLD

*Both a brilliant failure and an extraordinary feat of architecture and engineering, the Basilica of St. Peter was the most monumental undertaking of the High Renaissance, and the story of its construction is as convoluted and controversial as the Church it serves.* – R. A. Scotti

Jennifer wasn't done with us yet, however. She led us through some corridors and into the sanctuary of St. Peter's Basilica. Only by sticking with her could we bypass another set of huge lines awaiting entry to this, the crown jewel of the Vatican's treasures. And with all of us thus tightly gathered, she could retrieve her radios.

We said our good-byes to Jennifer, who really was an excellent tour guide, and to the English couple, who really weren't good tourists, and began strolling through the cool marble expanse of one of the most revered churches in the world. We were finally on our own. Raj had told the truth. Sort of.

The ground upon which St. Peter's stands has a fascinating history, hotly debated and charged with controversy. Originally, it was called the *Ager Vaticanus*, named for the *vati*, or "soothsayers," who practiced augury there centuries before. This was a ritual in which animals were slain and their scattered entrails were examined for portents from the gods. Next, the land was used as a dump for refuse and carcasses, safely located, as it was, across the Tiber River from the city proper. Later, it was converted into a chariot racing ground called the Circus of Caligula. It was here that many Christians were martyred, including (and this is one part that's often debated) the crucifixion and burial of the Apostle Peter. Official Roman persecution of Christians persisted in an on and off fashion for centuries until the Emperor Constantine made a big show of converting to the Christian faith. In one swoop, the power of the empire went from persecution to sponsorship. One of the outward signs of Constantine's newfound faith was to convert the former grounds of slaughter into a place of worship. In 324 A.D., he decreed the construction of a basilica directly on the grounds of the Circus, over the supposed final resting place of St. Peter himself. The basilica, an enormous wooden structure, was the scene of important moments in church history, including the crowning of Emperor Charlemagne in 800 A.D. Incredibly, it was still standing and in use in the fifteenth century when Pope Julius II (known as "*Il Pontefice Terribile*," to whom I introduced the children in the last chapter) began dismantling it to make way for the new one. What resulted was (more controversy) one of the largest scale sanctioned destructions of a historical monument in world history. According to R. A. Scotti, "To destroy Constantine's basilica—a hallowed site almost as old as the Church of Rome—was a desecration. The scandal that his plan provoked only steeled the pope's resolve. Julius imagined the new basilica as the centerpiece of Christian Rome more magnificent and mighty than the city of the Caesars. And the fact that the original St. Peter's was the most revered shrine in Europe, the repository of a millennium of sacred history and art, be damned. He would rip it down and replace it with something more immense, immutable. A new edifice for a new age."

The new basilica was infinitely expensive and its construction dragged on for centuries, involving a procession of thirty popes and some of the best architects and artists of several generations, including Bramante, Michelangelo, Raphael, della Robbia, Bernini, and others. Some say pressure to raise money for the construction of St. Peter's led to an intentional escalation in the sale of indulgences by Pope Leo X, the first Medici pope. This is the same pope who famously said, "God has given us the papacy; now let us enjoy it," and who also had a little disagreement with a German monk named Martin Luther, which ultimately birthed the Protestant Reformation.

So when admiring this particular building, there is much more represented than mere architecture. The ground is literally fertilized by the blood of martyrs, and the building itself is layers and layers deep in history. But oh, what architecture! Marble of various types is used in floors, stairs, and immense columns. Materials were taken from pagan Roman temples and buildings throughout Italy, including the Colosseum, and blended into the whole, providing much-needed material for a building project with an endless appetite for more. Even some mosaic grottoes from the original basilica were salvaged, restored, and incorporated into the new building. The scale of everything is gigantic, and the intricacies of decoration are overpowering. Everywhere the eye lands are carvings, gilded and glittering. Light streams in from windows way up high, adding to the ambience of an already impactful place. The overall plan is of a Latin cross, with a baldacchino created by Bernini standing tall directly below the dome of Michelangelo's design. Its massive bronze columns twist upward and are incredibly ornate. So much bronze was required for this one item that most of the roof tiles from the nearby Pantheon, itself an architectural marvel from Roman times, were pilfered for the purpose. The dome is positioned at the intersection of the cross and is flanked by two minor cupolas. A work of art in its own right, the dome is magnificent.

Although not completed during his lifetime, Michelangelo's design was powerful enough to inspire Thomas Jefferson to copy it for the dome on the United States Capitol building. Bernini designed the enormous semicircular colonnade that encompasses the Piazza San Pietro. Like two outstretched arms reaching to embrace pilgrims, the area between is capable of accommodating tens of thousands of people for religious observances. At its center resides a granite obelisk standing eighty-three feet high. This was originally taken from Egypt as part of the spoils of conquest and had stood in what had once been the Circus of Caligula, erected there to commemorate his achievement in the early part of the first century. For proper placement in the center of the piazza, however, it had to be moved. Michelangelo had flatly stated such a task could not be done. But in a tribute to the ingenuity of Renaissance times and an insufferable pope called Sixtus V, the enormous 320-ton structure was successfully relocated to the center of the piazza, thereby preserving symmetry for future generations.

Another fascinating aspect of St. Peter's is the blending of so many styles by so many minds over so many years. What began early and continued through the High Renaissance was finally completed during the Baroque period. The front façade and atriums by Carlo Maderno and the statuary and other carvings along the front are classically baroque, while the domes have the restrained elegance of the Renaissance.

Also included within is an art museum in its own right. Michelangelo's *Pieta*, carved when he was yet a young man, stands behind protective glass just inside and to the right of the bronze doors salvaged from the original basilica. *St. Peter*, carved by Cambio in the thirteenth century, sits on the right of the entrance to the apse. Bernini's *Cathedra in the Apse*, a monument to Pope Alexander VII, is an enormous, beautifully sculpted one of a kind, depicting Truth, Justice, Charity, and Prudence—with a globe-supported foot resting directly upon England, that recalcitrant Protestant nation.

All of this after the day we had already experienced! Our senses were overloaded.  Christine kept plopping herself down on the marble floor, first in this corner, and then in another.  Her actions were a representation of how we were all feeling: reduced and compressed by the heat.  The beauty, proportion, and over-the-top gaudiness had no ability to penetrate our tourist fatigue. We finally left without climbing to the top of the dome or touring the crypts of former popes below.  I had done these things before so wasn't that keen on a repeat, and the rest of the Bradys needed their batteries recharged.  Seeing the body of deceased Pope John XXIII in a glass coffin didn't even interest the kids. That's when I knew they had had it.

So we exited the basilica, crossed St. Peter's enormous piazza, and moseyed back into the real world in search of food.

And that is when we got ripped off.

Exiting the immediate vicinity of St. Peter's puts one among a dizzying array of gift shops and restaurants.  People are everywhere coming and going.  Priests and nuns in habits mix with vacationers, cars, scooters, students, and ever-present restaurant proprietors "hooking" customers into their establishments.  If you've never experienced this quaint little cultural phenomenon, here's how it goes.

"*Buon giorno, signore!* Hungry? Come on in, air conditioning."

You stammer and peer inside. *Air conditioning certainly would be nice right about now*, you think, close to passing out from the heat.

"Come on, I have a table for you. *Prego, prego,*" says the proprietor.

By now he might even be pulling you inside by your arm, or your wife's, at which point it might be beneficial to realize that if someone pulls your arm, they're probably also pulling your leg.

There are only so many *pregos* one can resist when in dire need of air conditioning and refreshment.  So you think, *Why not?* and follow the nice gentleman inside, like prey into a Venus Fly Trap.

That's when you discover the prices. But by now, your kids are seated and begging for pizza, your dogs are barking in the shoes you've already loosened, and man, that air conditioning sure feels good!

*How bad can it be?* you ask yourself. *It's just a few bucks. I'm hungry. Let's just stay.*

And you leave with a bill for 150 euro, by far the most expensive pizza and water your family has ever consumed. When you inquire about it of the waiter, he is so unflappable it would make Al Capone blush.

*Rome*, you think.

But at least your pocket didn't get picked.

\* \* \*

Later that evening, after a much-needed recuperation in the cramped but cool quarters of our two hotel rooms (we found no place in Italy that would allow the six of us to share a room, so it was double the hotel cost at each stay), we strolled into the old quarter called Trastevere. This quaint area is full of charm and is supposedly inhabited by a group of people who consider themselves the only "true Romans." Perhaps it is these whom the Tuscans despise? We didn't ask. But we did ask about restaurants and found an excellent one.

A little front on a side street was all this particular ristorante boasted. Inside, however, it had excellent ambiance. Every table was, of course, draped with a beautiful combination of linens. A red brick vaulted ceiling and stone archways connected tiny little rooms to each other. None of these rooms was large enough for more than a few tables, so it felt like we were dining in the home of friends. Soft classical guitar played in the background, and the food was tremendous. I had *pici alla ragú* for my *primi piatti* (first plate) and Etruscan-style chicken for my *secondi piatti* (stuff-yourself-till-you're-too-full-to-breathe plate). Along with my meal, I treated myself to a glass of Nobile di Montepulciano, one of Italy's top three wines. Every morsel of my food and drop of my wine was delectable. If I didn't watch myself, I could almost slip into becoming a "foodie."

We strolled through cool evening air as the sun set and the traffic thinned to a whimper, offering us only a couple more Smart Cars for our count. We bought gelato from a young Romanian who spoke four languages and was working on a fifth (Mandarin). Then we drifted off to sleep in one of the most fascinating cities in the world.

## CHAPTER 25

# "OH, YOU SHOULD SEE THE COLOSSEUM, SPANIARD!"

*The Roman Colosseum was the fruit of Roman victory over the Jews. It was, in effect, the Temple of Jerusalem transformed by Roman culture, rebuilt for popular pleasure and the ostentatious display of imperial power.*
– Keith Hopkins and Mary Beard

Good things just kept rolling our way. We discovered a breakfast (of sorts) in the basement of our hotel.

"Breakfast in Italy?" we asked the desk clerk.

"*Si, signore.* It is rare. But many nicer hotels, such as our one, do this to accommodate tourists."

"We're glad your one does."

So we began Day Two in Rome on full stomachs, stuffed with something other than croissants and Nutella, for a change.

With due respect to the Vatican, I was even more excited to show my family the treasures of ancient Rome. I have long been interested in the history of the Roman Republic, its decline, and its transformation into an empire. The history is nearly bottomless and full of sweeping tragedies such as Sulla's genocides, Crassus's defeat of Spartacus, Pompey's triumphs in the east, Julius Caesar's incredible takeover, the saga of Cleopatra, the defeat of Marc Antony, the murder on the Ides of March, the rise of the unlikely first real dictator Caesar Augustus, Tiberius, Nero's descent into madness, the martyrdom of the Apostle Paul, the Flauvians and the age of gladiators, the philosophical Marcus Aurelius, the whole gallery of good and bad emperors mixed in, Constantine's removal of the heart of the empire to Byzantium, and the ultimate fall of it all. We had gotten a look at the daily life of Roman citizens when we walked the streets of Herculaneum. Now we would be at what was once the epicenter of Western civilization for hundreds and hundreds of years.

And we were going to do it in one day.

Nobody in his right mind thinks he can see ancient Rome in one day. So don't even try. Allow yourself many days, if you can. A lifetime, if possible. Seriously. As I indicated earlier, however, parenthood often clashes with fantasies,  and for the best of us, parenthood wins out. I must admit, though, the struggle would be a tough one on this particular day.

We grabbed taxis to scoot us over to the Roman Forum where we would begin. Trying to find one taxi for six people was impossible, so we called ahead for two. They were right on time, thirty-five minutes after the appointed time. No problem—we had expected that by now. Terri took two kids with her in one car, and I did likewise in the other. Then we went racing off. Literally.

I couldn't remember if I had used taxis in Rome before. Maybe I had blacked out, which would be understandable, because if we had been driven like we were now, the G-force alone could do it.

I tried to keep a close eye on the cab ahead of us containing half of my family, but it was nearly impossible. It would disappear behind a bus, then weave around motorcycles, pass on the right, and anything else one usually sees in a movie chase. Trying to be polite, no doubt, and keep me at ease, my cab driver was intent on staying with the leader. This was accomplished sometimes by drafting, sometimes by running red lights, and usually with shouting at someone along the way. Eventually, I relaxed and began enjoying the spectacle. My senses were on overload, and I'm pretty sure by the end of it, I was grinning. Nathaniel in the back seat said, "Dad! This is awesome!"

Our two cabs slid sideways in front of the Colosseum with tires squealing and burnt rubber smoke flying up behind us like drift cars in a commercial, then jerked to a stop in perfect unison. Well, almost. The drivers immediately jumped out, and I could have sworn they looked at their watches and gave each other high-fives. Were we part of some new record?

"I guess we'll start with the Colosseum," I said.

"Dad! Look at those soldiers!" squealed J.R. with delight, pointing toward a group of my old friends: the fake Roman soldiers. I was sorry to have to break it to him that they were bad guys freshly escaped from jail, and they fed on the bones of little children from America. Once in a while, Dad has to be the bearer of bad news. The soldiers didn't even approach us after that. I think they could sense the suspicion in my children's eyes.

Nathaniel wanted to go inside the Colosseum in the worst way. So, having learned a lesson from the Vatican, we hired the guided tour to bypass the lines and then gave the guide the slip once inside. I wouldn't really recommend this technique because the tours are generally very good, but I knew we were running on limited time with the two little ones and the rising heat of the day, so I was making calculated sacrifices. If I could let them see the Colosseum in say, half the time of a guided tour, we just might squeeze more in before Brady-kid-melt-down set in. We were also early enough to have beaten many of the crowds that would soon descend, so we had the freedom to roam largely unimpeded and just enjoy some serenity inside one of the world's top monuments—a rare treat indeed.

Rome is in ruins. While that's probably not a news flash, it was still a surprise to me when I first saw it. I'm not sure exactly what I expected, but there was just *less* of everything than I wanted. The Colosseum, too, is literally a ruin. But there is more of it than there is of almost anything else from the original Roma, and that alone makes it special. However, determining exactly what is original and what is a restoration is difficult. There are so many odd "tamperings" that comprise what we see today of the Colosseum that one is often left imagining more than admiring. The situation reminds me of those fractal prints (autostereograms) where a figure emerges if you stare long enough and in just the right way, crossing your eyes, of course.

The first thing that destroyed the Colosseum was neglect. The expensive free public spectacles held there were difficult to maintain as the empire slid into decline. Once the empire fell, the Colosseum went through a myriad of different uses, including housing for indigents, a factory, a market, and finally a quarry for church building projects across the river. Purposely pilfered as a show of Christianity's triumph over the pagan entertainments once held there, the Colosseum was literally picked apart. The iron straps that once fastened the huge marble blocks together were removed, leaving the "Swiss cheese" holes one sees throughout today. By the Victorian era, travelers were writing books about the vast number of wildflowers and weeds growing inside. One expert put the number of different variants growing within at three hundred fifty. Talk about a distressed property!

Pilferings and neglect were bad enough, but some of the many restorations attempted over the years were almost more damaging. In one section, there are marble seats intended to show what the originals were like. Historians say these are a terrible farce. Way up high on the west rim is a mix of different color, shape, and size marble blocks used to reproduce the original height and shape. These look okay from the outside but bizarre from within. Large sections of the stubbled surface of the sloping interior have been paved over, producing a strange asphalt appearance, like part of a skateboard park, where the real seats once were. Worst of all, however, are the tan brick buttresses built during Mussolini's time to strengthen the exposed edge of the upper rim. However, the intentional destruction and poor restorations inflicted on this building over the years don't rob it of its power. It is still a magnificent architectural marvel, designed and built by people of whom we know absolutely nothing—not even a single name.

Whoever they were, they certainly knew their business. The Colosseum is pure in its design and symmetry. It is comprised of eighty entrance arches all of the same width and height. Ringing the inside are corridors designed to funnel crowds from the various status levels of Roman society into their proper seats: senators and vestal virgins up front, patricians next, then plebeians, and finally slaves and women farthest back. Estimates usually say its capacity was 55,000, but historians can't agree. The arena floor was built over passageways and stalls, trap doors, and entrances for animals and combatants. Today, looking down into this area, the original floor is long gone (except for a partial reconstruction), and this labyrinthine network of passages is clearly discernible, if not decipherable.

The outside is as beautiful as the inside is functional. It consists of four tiers of arched openings ringing its circumference. Columns flank the arched openings, with each of the first three floors featuring a separate capital order.

"Oh, you should see the Colosseum, Spaniard! Fifty thousand Romans . . ." I muttered in the ears of Nathaniel as he stood in rapture, staring at the reconstructed arena floor. With the fast-forward button in hand and ready to zip past gory parts (fully half the show, I'd say), I had watched the movie *Gladiator* with Casey and Nathaniel as preparation for what they would see here today. Quoting lines from it throughout our tour was just Dad's way of building the drama. They liked it, too, until about the twentieth time.

I also struggled, as I guess most do, with the purpose behind this amphitheatre. This enormous, beautiful structure was erected as a showcase of cruelty. Only God knows how many murders occurred here, how many innocent victims, how many ferocious animal fights, the scope of the tragic destruction—all this, shockingly, in the name of entertainment. According to Hopkins and Beard, "A grand total of 8,000 deaths in the arena a year is . . . our best tentative guesstimate . . . mostly of trained muscular young adult males. Seen in these terms, the death of gladiators constituted a massive drain on human resources. Gladiatorial shows were a deadly death tax." As I stared down into what was once a celebrated killing field, I wondered what the Romans' unashamed bloodlust had to teach us about our own society and ourselves. Were they worse than we are or just more public and shameless with their atrocities? I tried relating a little of this to the children, but with a five and a six-year-old, the answers didn't exist for their predominant question: "Why?"

Why, indeed?

It was a sober moment in which it was impossible to forget that the power of Rome came from its violent conquests. Just as in the arena where its people delighted in blood sport, Roman ascendency came by conquering, slaughtering, subjugating, enslaving, and systematically thieving. Although Rome is famous for developing an effective system of jurisprudence, the "glory that was Rome" was anything but just, and it certainly wasn't glorious.

We asked a passerby to snap a photo of us together as a family, and then I had Terri take one of me with each of the children individually. These are some of my most cherished photos of us together. There, bathed in the strengthening Italian sun, we were relaxed and together, just enjoying our blessings and each other's company. I think you can see all that and more, perhaps even a little of the sobering lesson taught by the Colosseum, clearly on our faces.

Our tickets to the Colosseum allowed entrance to the adjoining Palatine Hill as well, the site of most of the palace ruins. Here the remains are sparse and leave many questions. Some signs indicate main attractions, and guidebooks are helpful. However, there are many questions that enter one's mind while strolling along roads once walked by emperors. The most predominant: What did it look like *then*? Who could possibly tour this place and not want to drop back in time for a quick peek? Mind you, I wouldn't relish the idea of being arrested for trespassing, sold as a slave, forced into gladiatorial combat, mugged, or horror of horrors, pickpocketed. But ancient dangers aside, how wonderful would it be for a historical mind to gain more of a sense of what it was really like than what these few brick walls and foundations can convey. I am certainly not the only one to want more of a picture of what once was. In fact, there is a pretty good rendition of precisely that available at some of the many souvenir wagons nearby. There is a foldout bird's eye reproduction of Rome at its zenith, as well as a DVD with computer graphic animation depicting the same. I found these quite helpful and interesting. Christine liked the huge movie star sunglasses we bought her there better.

From up on the Palatine Hill, one gets an excellent view of the Roman Forum below. This was the center of Roman public life, where senators met, speeches were given, trials were held, religious rituals were observed, and daily markets were set up. The Via Sacra was the road that connected the Colosseum to the Forum, through the Arch of Titus. From this high perch, all of this can be clearly seen. Standing there looking at so much history is staggering. This stuff is real. It really happened. They were *here*.

I was wishing for much more time.

J.R. was wishing for a bathroom.

Did they have public bathrooms in the Forum? We had no choice but to find out, so we descended near the Temple of Vesta and searched the ancient ruins for modern plumbing. I thought it strange how so much of our existence is reduced to physical necessities. It made me wonder if public restrooms were available during the days of the Caesars. Or did they just relieve themselves against a column or temple somewhere? I couldn't ever remember hearing *this* talked about on one of the tours.

By now, it was well over 100 degrees Fahrenheit, and the merciless sun was sapping us all. I tried to keep the troops moving but was fighting a losing battle. We stopped in the shade of the Arch of Titus, and the little ones sat down immediately, Christine picking wild flowers like a draft dodger from the sixties.

"Look up, kids, at the carvings inside this arch," I said. "See the soldiers carrying items from the Jewish temple in Jerusalem?" I explained the sack of Jerusalem in 70 A.D. by Titus, the emperor's son, who would soon be emperor himself. I related this event to things they had learned in Sunday school. I told how much of the marble of the Jerusalem temple—the very one at which Jesus had turned over the moneychanger's tables—was taken to build the Colosseum. I explained how this dispersed the Jews, put many of them into slavery, and ended the temple sacrifices. I tried to be entertaining, dramatic, funny, and informative, everything Jennifer at the Vatican had been the day before. I looked at four sets of brown eyes looking back at me. Then I quickly glanced into those big blue eyes of Terri.

I had lost them all.

They were toured out.

Rome had conquered yet again.

I thought for a moment about all that was left to see. There was the Mamertine Prison where legend says the Apostle Paul was kept (although some argue that it was Peter put there instead); there was Trajan's Market, the Capitoline Museums, the Piazza del Campidoglio, the Palazzo dei Conservatori, the Spanish steps, Castle Sant' Angelo, Tiberina Island, Trevi Fountain, the Pantheon (my favorite), the Baths, and the Circus Maximus. It had all been around for centuries, waiting—waiting for us to come see it.

It could wait a little longer.

"*What say we* get some ice cream and head back to the pool?"

"Yay!" they all yelled in unison. And Terri gave me one of those smiles that make being a daddy worth it all.

CHAPTER 26

# DAYS WITHOUT DESIGN

*We do not know the true value of our moments until they have*
*undergone the test of memory.* – Georges Duhamel

Montepulciano is another of Tuscany's delectable hilltop medieval towns located directly across the Valdichiana from where we were staying. With a little stroll down into the terraces of the olive trees at *La Contea*, getting far enough past the ridge to the west, one can look across the patchwork quilt of ambers, beiges, and sages of the valley and see Montepulciano like a sandstone wedding cake resting atop a hill of dark green felt. We just had to go check it out for ourselves.

Distances in these open spaces are still hard to judge for a person like myself who grew up in a state of forests. Perhaps someone from Kansas might have it easier, but I am still surprised that a town one can see so clearly can require forty-five minutes of driving to reach it. But what a drive! The winding roads leading across the valley and snaking up the hills approaching Montepulciano have to be some of the best we had taken.

It was just toward the end of siesta when we pulled to a stop near the arched entry through the city walls. We had timed things well and, incredibly, found a parking spot two places from the wall. It was right next to the sign boldly pointing to the "Secret Passageway." "Not so secret," Casey laughed. I had an urge to pump a thousand euro into the parking ticket machine to hoard the great real estate I had obtained. You find a parking spot this good in Italy, and you're prepared to sleep in your car. Then I popped the lens cover off my trusty Canon SLR camera and shamelessly took a photo of twelve old men sitting peacefully together along the ridge wall on the sidewalk. These old men began to feel like a talisman to me, appearing like an apparition at every stop, showing me a future I could have if I would just come back to Italy when I was old. *Maybe I could just keep this parking spot until then*, I thought.

I was in a photo-happy mood, too. Everything looked picturesque; every store, quaint. The smell of cheese from one shop was wonderful. The bell clanging the hour somewhere up ahead was symphonic. It occurred to me this must be what simple happiness feels like. I was now a prodigious noticer without having to work at it. I was seeing everything with eyes like a child. It had worked. My vacation had decompressed me into a real human being. I was alive, free, healthy, and thankful, but also hungry.

We ate on a wooden deck behind sound-deadening glass that reminded me of the stuff they put around drummers in rock bands to keep them quiet in relation to the rest of the instruments. All it accomplished was an amplification of the sounds of the other tourists around us. But I didn't care. We were sitting under an enormous umbrella, possibly the largest in the world, right in the Piazza Michelozzo at the foot of a building with a glockenspiel on its roof. The mechanical figure had a spear in his left hand and a mallet in his right and was wearing a kilt and, to top it all off, a witch's hat.

"What's that all about, Dad?" Casey asked pointing up at the strange figure.

"Not sure."

"He needs a paint job," Casey added.

I looked up. "Yup. And a fashion consultant."

Undeterred, the strange figure began ringing his bell again. *Sticks and stones*, he seemed to be saying.

We were speaking better and better "restaurant Italian" by now, confidently ordering our food and even asking a question or two. I ordered what I thought was a glass of the local wine, the Nobile for which this area was famous. What I received, however, was a tiny triangular glass filled with kerosene. I smelled it and would have immediately failed a Breathalyzer test.

"What's wrong, Dad?" asked Christine.

"Oh, nothing, it's just that they brought me some liquid from the very bowels of hell," I answered.

"What do you mean?" asked J.R.

"I think Daddy needs to work on his Italian," Terri said.

Pride goeth before a fall.

I wasn't the first tourist to get overly confident in his ability to order, apparently, because the nice waitress simply took the glass of poison and exchanged it for some red wine instead.

"*Vino*," she said as she plunked it down in front of me. "*Non grappa*."

*Grappa*, I thought, *so that's the Italian word for kerosene*. One word at a time, I was going to learn this language, by golly. I would later discover that *grappa* is the customary drink of choice at the very end of a meal. That is, after the *bruschetta*, after the *insalata* (salad), after the *primi piatte*, after the *secondi piatte*, after the *dolce* (sweet, or dessert), after the wine consumed throughout all this, *and* after the espresso, which was usually reserved for after dessert. *Grappa* was the final shot of apparently the only thing capable of reviving a person after so much eating.

*Non grappa*, indeed.

\* \* \*

Our days eased into a comfortable routine. We would go sight-seeing if we were in the mood, or we would just hang around the villa. Terri would serve deliciously simple lunches of salami, sausage slices, *prosciutto*, bread, green olives, grapes, melon, and Edema cheese. We would take naps in the sun by the pool while the kids frolicked. We read; I wrote a little; we played games as a family (*Scrabble* turned into an all-out war); and we finished watching the World Cup. Maybe in the afternoon, I would zoom away on the motorcycle and try to get lost.

One such time, I rode up into a town I thought was Arezzo, only to discover later it was the little village of Castiglion Fiorentino, a delightful town with a splendid piazza at the top. Along one side of this piazza is a wall with large arches. Through these arches, one sees a sloping hill with terracotta-roofed houses dotting its face. I stopped. I shifted my position along the arched wall to change my angle. I looked away and then looked back again. Reaching for my camera, looking through the lens, zooming in and zooming out, framing the scene without the arches, I became convinced this was the exact view painted on our wall in Florida. Had to be. I felt like a treasure hunter whose spade had sliced through soft sand and hit metal.

Once, while zipping around on the motorcycle, I spotted a castle high on a hill across the farmland I was traversing, so I snaked around little tiny gravel roads until I found its approach. It turned out to be Castello di Montecchio, closed for renovations. On another occasion, I came across market day outside one of the little towns nearby. Trucks and trailers and awnings and tents were set up everywhere, offering a dizzying array of everything from frilly underwear to green beans. I chose the beans and loaded up the bike's saddlebags with fruit and vegetables to impress Terri. I could always go back for the underwear, should she need further impressing.

I had talked so much about my beautiful motorcycle ride

around the fifty-four-kilometer perimeter of Lake Trasimeno that I conned the family into reproducing my experience with the mini-bus. We took a leisurely trip and stopped at a few of the lookout areas along the way, snapping pictures like mad. We found several roadside sites commemorating the battle of Lake Trasimeno. Large signboards featured colored illustrations of battle scenes and troop positions. Of course, this turned into an impromptu history class for the Brady kids. School was always in session.

"Imagine Hannibal, down to just one elephant, and thirty or forty thousand men. These were tough men, crazy men, mean and smelly men, who'd come from tens of different nations all around and had somehow crossed the Alps in winter to attack Rome in its own backyard. They had no provisions, no supply lines, and they probably didn't brush their teeth. And when an organized army of locals met them here, the Carthaginians massacred them. Can you imagine?" I asked, with the faint sound of the *Braveheart* soundtrack ringing in my ears.

"Yeah, Dad, cool."

"What's the Alps?"

"A mountain range to the north. Very dangerous. Very cold. Anyway, think about this," I continued. "You know that town we are staying right next to? That little one called Ossaia? Do you know what that means? It means *bones*. The Romans—fifteen thousand dead—had to be buried somewhere. They heaped them up in mass graves right there in that very town. People still dig up bones once in a while all around here when they're building houses and stuff."

"Wow. How do you know all this, Dad?" Nate asked.

"Just read these signboards," I answered with a gesture. And bless their little hearts, all four of them lined up and looked at the pictures with rapt attention and read at least some of it. I think it was the bones that got 'em.

"It was right here, along the shore of this lake, which was a lot bigger back then, where the Romans were trapped by the Carthaginians. Look around you and try to picture that happening."

Passignano sul Trasimeno was the next town, encamped right along the lakeshore like an American resort town. Ferries come and go here all day taking tourists to the three large islands in Lake Trasimeno. Shopping is supposedly very good, but we were in the mood for cruising, so we got a quick gelato and kept rolling.

We drove through the beautiful town of Magione and its Castle of the Knights of Malta and the Lombard Tower, yet another period of history begging notice among the many layers. Then, we went through the little towns of San Feliciano, San Savino, and Sant' Arcangelo, all crowded close to both sides of the road with views of Monte Bellaveduta and Monte Marzolana in the background. Next, we scaled the heights to Panicale, a sleepy town with a high and mighty view of the entire lake and Tuscany beyond to the north. Continuing clockwise, we drove inside the small city walls of Castiglione del Lago, the castle town so prominent in our view from *La Contea*. I had motorcycled through this town briefly but was very interested in taking some time here. Again, we found an incredibly good parking spot, and the entrepreneur in me wondered if I could start a business grabbing them during siesta and then selling them later when the rest of the world started rolling in for dinner.

"This is the best town yet, Dad, *fer* sure," said Nathaniel.

"Oh, yeah?" I said. "And why's that?"

"Because it's got five *gelaterias*!" he answered with that coy smile of his.

He was right. The per capita amount of ice cream shops is the highest we had seen. But there is also an interesting assortment of wine shops, cheese shops, pasta shops, and the usual touristy shops. In front of one of these, a very friendly man named Giovanni approached us with a tray of meats and cheeses.

"The best in Umbria," he said, pushing a piece of meat in my direction. "*Prego, prego.*"

I almost cringed at the *prego*s, but this wasn't Rome. So I took a piece and felt it dissolve in my mouth. Delicious.

"I can't believe this!" said Terri. "We have got to buy some."

"*Prego*. Come inside. My own family makes. I wrap some for you."

It was *cinghiale* (wild boar). We purchased some and walked on.

Throughout the trip, signs at various towns advertising different music festivals had caught Terri's attention, including, of course, the Pig Party. We had managed to attend exactly none of these so far, so we inquired at an information desk about details of a symphony concert supposedly scheduled for the following evening.

"*Si*," a curt woman reading a magazine told us, "*domani sera*," (tomorrow night).

I asked, "*Dove?*" (Where?)

"*Rocca Medievale*," she answered pointing.

"The medieval castle," I said to Terri. "It's right at the end of this town. Perfect. Hey, kids, how'd you like to hear a symphony tomorrow night?"

"Sure," said Casey, quite the musician in his own right. There were varying levels of interest expressed by the others. No problem. This wasn't a democracy.

"Let's do it," I said to Terri.

So we marked down the time and cleared our schedule for the next evening. We were going to see a symphony in a castle.

CHAPTER 27

# SYMPHONIC BLUES CONCERT

*Our happiest moments as tourists always seem to come when
we stumble upon one thing while in pursuit of something else.*
– Lawrence Block

That evening Terri and I revived ourselves with a walk up the
hill behind *La Contea*. The kids stayed back and kicked a soccer
ball around, which was fine with us. We probably needed a little
romantic sunset walk.

Up we climbed, all the way past the iron cross and right up to
an orange construction fence. We stood catching our breath for
a moment. Terri saw me looking up the hill at the church being
restored at its crest, at least another hundred feet or so higher.

"I wonder what's going on up there?" she asked.

"Let's go find out," I smiled.

"It says we can't enter," she said, pointing to a rusted old sign
nailed to a canopy pine.

"No, it doesn't. It's totally silent. Not saying anything. Besides," I said, holding up the thin plastic construction barrier for
her to duck under, "I can't read Italian. Remember?"

She hesitated, but made me proud when she finally limboed

beneath and started trucking up the dirt two-track toward the mysterious church on the hilltop. We had ogled it from below many times on previous trips up here. The curiosity was too much.

"What if there's a wild animal or something up here protecting this?" Terri asked, only half joking.

"Or a troll. Or some snipers. Or an entire SEAL team, perhaps."

"Stop. I'm being serious. This is a little unnerving."

"Exactly what makes it so exciting. Now come along like a good pirate."

We trudged upward in the dust, glancing sideways every now and then at the sinking globe in the distant sky. The breeze was refreshing, and the color of the sky was streaked rust with smeared gray. It was serene.

The road got steeper as we got closer to an old stone structure. It was obviously an old church, and out front was a bronze statue of a monk with his back turned to the valley. Something very important was written about him below, I think. There were some words there, at any rate.

The church was made from the same old stone all the other buildings around here seemed to have. I guessed it to be at least six hundred years old, maybe older. Its bell tower was partially intact, and a courtyard out back showed at least some evidence of being rebuilt by masons . . . or it once had been. In the whole time we had been here, we had seen absolutely no sign of life up here at all. Except for a few old trucks and tractors parked around, and the construction fence, you would never know anyone even knew about this place.

"What a view," I said, snapping some photos.

"I'll say."

We stood there with arms around each other for few moments appreciating yet another dramatic masterpiece in the making. The gray in the sky was winning out against the orange, and the light was fading, slowly pulling the color out of everything below.

Then we heard it.

"What was *that*?" Terri asked with a start.

"I don't know."

"But you heard it, didn't you?" she asked.

"Yep. Doesn't mean I know what it is, though. Probably the troll."

"I'm heading down," she said.

In the quiet solitude way up high where we were positioned, any noise would have been a violent disruption. The sound we had heard was also extremely strange, kind of a deep and guttural burble. Exactly like a troll, actually.

"Or a sheep," I said, spotting five or six freshly sheared sheep moving quickly toward us from behind the church.

"I told you there'd be wild animals up here," Terri said, already high-tailing it back down the path.

"Yeah, fierce ones. Are you actually running from *sheep*?" I asked incredulously, chasing after her.

Then I saw why the sheep were so disturbed. Down the hill, directly in the path of Terri's descent, were some lambs. Baby sheep—probably the babies of those mad mother sheep crashing down on us. In Terri's hurried departure, she'd positioned herself exactly between some moms and their offspring.

Those momma sheep were the most aggressive sheep I had ever seen. Not that I'm much of a shepherd, but I wouldn't have expected sheep to yell and scream at us and run straight toward us with blood in their eyes, flipping their chins at us and saying, "*Porca miseria!*" Their bleating was a mean and eerie sound, and it was sufficient to propel Terri down the hill in record time. I followed after her, rock in hand (just in case), laughing until I nearly cried.

At the bottom of the hill, past the construction barrier and canopy pine, Terri finally stopped and looked back. *Are they gone?* her eyes seemed to say.

"That was a close one!" I mocked, dropping the rock behind me where she couldn't see.

"You ran, too!" she said, always the keen observer.

"Just protecting you, babe, and getting the best angle for a good laugh." I had also gotten a priceless photo of the fierce beasts, just as a kind of proof.

We walked farther down, more slowly now, quiet for several minutes. The closing drama of the day's sky was almost complete—steel gray dominating all.

"I told you there would be wild animals guarding that place," Terri said under her breath.

We laughed all over again.

* * *

The next day, Terri took Christine shopping while the boys and I juggled the soccer ball in a park in the center of Camucia. A boy named Ben (at least we think that's what he said) joined in, so I was free to push J.R. on a swing and then play paddleball with him. Well, a little paddleball. It consisted mostly of J.R. whacking the ball a mile and me chasing it into the street. Nevertheless, he was quite good at this.

Shopping in Italy has to be an international sport. There are leather goods, silks, textiles, ceramics, wood products, iron works, wines, cheeses, breads, olive oils, designer clothes, and just about anything the heart desires. Unique items and authentic local products are easy to come by and often extremely high in quality. Purchasing them on location is also pretty reasonable. Today, however, Terri was after some dresses for Christine and a little mother-daughter time.

When we met at our rendezvous spot outside a little girls' clothing store in Camucia, Terri and Christine emerged with faces aglow and shopping bags swinging from their wrists. It reminded me of a scene from *Pretty Woman*.

"*Molto bella*," I said as Christine twirled proudly, displaying a white and silver sequin cotton summer dress. Christine just loves to dress up and beautify everything she touches. Every day of her life, she wakes up and chooses either a skirt or a dress to wear. When Terri wears pants, Christine asks her, "Why would you wear pants when you could wear a dress?" So a special day with mommy dedicated to dressing each other up Italian-style was one of the highlights of the trip for both my girls.

However, Terri was also looking forward to the symphony that evening. Music is one of the threads running throughout Italian history, as well as the current culture. An elderly lady told us one evening, "Music is very *importante* to *Italia*." About which Terri commented to me later, "She meant more by it than it sounds to us. *Importante* to her was more like central, or *crucial*."

This should all be quite obvious, actually. After all, the violin was invented in Italy. Opera, too. And most of the musical annotations on sheet music: *diminuendo, forte, crescendo*, and the like, are all Italian.

Thus far on our trip, music had taken a backseat to architecture, visual art, topography, food, and just about everything else. Terri and I were both itching for some authentic local cultural musical experience. We dressed accordingly, Christine with her new white dress, Terri in a new summer dress of her own, and I in some khaki pants and a lightweight white shirt. The boys dressed up, too, donning soccer shirts and gym shorts—their standard attire.

"Hey, at least they're clean!" they protested when I asked why they hadn't dressed up at least a little.

"We're going to a symphony, guys. Customarily you dress a little nicer for something like that."

"Okay, Dad. We will next time."

We arrived early, expecting the unexpected and wanting to

leave plenty of time to find the right place, get tickets, or whatever else was required. One never knew. Operating like we were in a foreign tongue was a little like having one eye closed or one ear plugged. You had a pretty good idea of what was going on but could never be totally sure you had picked up everything. Only the bigger stuff was discernible. As for the subtle stuff? No way.

So, one of the subtle things we had somehow missed was that there was no symphony concert taking place that night at the castle. Actually, there didn't seem to be a symphony performing anywhere in the nation at all. What had happened to all the posters we had seen? What about the oh-so-friendly information office lady?

"Sorry, *signore*," said the man at the ticket booth. "There is no symphony here tonight."

I looked at Terri incredulously. She addressed the man directly.

"Do you know where it is?" she asked.

"No, *signora*. Sorry. This is a blues festival. Every summer. Trasimeno Blues," and with that he proudly handed her a shiny black and blue pamphlet. She looked it over. He was right. It read, "Trasimeno Blues."

Terri played saxophone in a jazz band in college when I met her. She had previously won the state competition for saxophone in high school. She plays all the woodwinds, and she plays them well. A blues concert would have been right up her alley. Still, we had come expecting a symphony.

We both started laughing. It was a little like the old trick when someone put tap water in your soda can at school. There's nothing wrong with tap water; it's just that you were expecting soda when you put the can to your lips.

"I guess we're going to see a blues concert," I said.

"Who's performing?" Terri asked, almost to herself while opening the brochure.

Meanwhile, the man at the ticket booth was waiting with typical Italian patience. He smiled and allowed us to decide. People in line behind us didn't seem to mind our delaying the entire line.

"*Va benne*," I said and handed him a wad of euro.

"You will love," he reassured us. "Tonight is our biggest night. Featuring the main attraction. Dr. John."

I had never heard of Dr. John. Terri couldn't remember if she had or not. She had been a little out of the jazz scene since the whole wife and mommy thing had hit. Her musical expression was now limited to playing the piano at home and occasionally accompanying someone at church on the flute, or perhaps issuing threats in a sing-songy voice as she chased kids up the stairs to their rooms.

"I'm sure it will be good," she said.

"Says here this guy's from New Orleans," I added, reading the brochure.

We had come to Italy to hear some blues musicians out of New Orleans.

"Well, I've never been to New Orleans," I said. "So they're traveling thousands of miles to come to me. Just the way I like it."

"You still need to go there," Terri said.

"Oh, yeah. No problem. This is just a little appetizer."

The old castle had been turned into an outdoor concert arena. Stone steps were placed neatly into a terraced hill. Tents and concessions were set up at the higher level, and the stage was at the lower end directly against the castle wall that flanked the lake. The sun gradually set, and the moon took its place like stage lighting in preparation for the show. Stock music played through the sound system as the crowd slowly filed in, and Christine and J.R. danced wildly next to us while we waited. The temperature dropped down toward perfect, and a gentle evening breeze came in from across the lake, smelling of water and night.

We waited a long time, but none of us grew restless. Everything was perfect.

Finally, the night totally black, the moon entirely bright, we saw movement to the left of the stage. Out from behind some tem-

porary walls emerged a few gaunt figures. They climbed the stairs
to the stage and began tuning instruments: electric guitars, a base,
some drums, an electric keyboard, and at the center of it all, an upright piano draped in red tasseled velvet. The warm-up complete,
another figure emerged from behind stage. This one, not so gaunt.
He wore a custom suit of red suede, matching shoes, and matching
hat. Puffing out the last bits of a cigarette, he ambled toward the
stage steps feebly. The crowd started cheering madly.

Dr. John had been around the block a few times. He had the
look of a man of hard miles, a heart patient with a few rehabs in his
past, if I had to guess. Saying nothing, nodding only briefly to the
crowd, he made straight for the upright piano and began playing
the moment he reached it.

Amazing.

His fingers owned that keyboard. He lit the darn thing on
fire. No piano could be sufficient for his ability to run the length
of those keys, playing fast and with a precision only the best could
ever hope to achieve.

Dr. John could sing, too. He had the kind of voice that immediately made one think of New Orleans. It was rough and edgy,
full of soul and expression, but all the while seeming to not be trying at all, merely expressing the truth, because truth was all there
was.

Song after song. Style after style. Dr. John played the organ.
He played a mean blues guitar. He sang. And he was merciless
on that piano. There was upbeat stuff, and there were ballads,
tear jerker blues, and even a few funny songs. The kids danced,
the adults clapped, and a crowd that had to be filled with twenty
different nationalities all enjoyed witnessing the real thing. This
was music. It may not have been Italian, it may not have been a
symphony, but it was a treat, nonetheless. Soulful. Solid. Real.

My kids hadn't been exposed to much of this genre, so it was
a cultural broadening they quite enjoyed. For months afterwards,

we would be together in the car, imitating Dr. John's raspy voice and singing, "Up there they got seven-day weekends, thirty-hour days . . . the Greenwich Village Swing."

Dr. John used exactly one Italian word all evening long: *Grazie.*

*No, sir*, we thought, *grazie lei* (thank you).

It was the best symphony we had ever heard.

## CHAPTER 28

# HAIL IN CORTONA

*Our goal was to slow down our hearts and minds until they synched up with the circadian rhythm of the Italian countryside.*
– Michael Tucker

Italian food is famous the world over, of course. I have seen Italian restaurants almost every place I've ever traveled. But I have come to realize there is no Italian food like the Italians' food. It is usually simple yet delicious, local, organic, and unforgettable.

Terri loves to cook, and we love what she cooks. One of the things she really wanted to accomplish on this trip was to learn how to cook authentic Italian food. She hit the local markets, grocery stores, and fruit stands, but she knew she was missing the inside scoop. We all loved what she was making, but she wasn't satisfied. She wanted to dig deeper and find out how these people did it.

Enter Alessandra. She had been highly recommended by one of the villa owners, so we scheduled Terri for one of her all-day cooking classes. From the email communications it appeared Alessandra spoke English but we weren't sure, and we knew little else.

So when the morning arrived, I took Terri up into Cortona on the back of the motorcycle and pulled into the city through the Porta Colonia, down the Via Dardano, and as far as the barricades would allow since the main shopping district was closed to traffic.

All we knew was that Terri was supposed to meet up with Alessandra in her table linen shop under the Teatro Signorelli, wherever that was. I pointed Terri in a likely direction, and she began walking away. Then I decided to quickly ask the parking policewoman standing nearby, and she pointed up directly behind me. We had pulled right up in front of the place and didn't know it. Above the columns of the fascia over the portico in huge blue letters was: Teatro Signorelli. *Tourists*, the policewoman had to be thinking. But by now, I was getting quite used to making a fool of myself.

I drove down the hill and left Terri alone in her adventure. Returning to the children at the villa, we passed the morning playing games and reading, and then I loaded them up and took them to the beach at Lake Trasimeno, near the base of the castle walls where we'd had our symphony concert. They splashed and played and enjoyed the shallow sandy shoreline. A small breeze blew in off the lake, and I hunted for some shade, but the heat was intense.

"Man, Dad, it's hot out today," Nathaniel said.

"Sure is. Thermometer in the car here says it's thirty-nine degrees Celsius."

"What's Celsius?" asked Christine.

I explained the temperature scales while Casey did the conversion.

"That's 102 degrees Fahrenheit, Dad."

"This heat has got to break soon," I said.

And it did, like Grandma's priceless vase toppling off the mantel, right as I rode the motorcycle back into Cortona to retrieve Terri from her cooking class. Dark clouds rolled in low overhead, thunder cracked, the temperature dropped mightily, and the winds kicked up.

I parked the motorcycle along the wall of what I now knew to be the Teatro Signorelli and decided to stroll around while I waited for Terri and the storm. I was a few minutes ahead of our five o'clock rendezvous, and I had my cell phone so she could call me when she was ready.

I walked through two excellent art galleries on the Via Nazionale, stopped for a Coke Zero at one of the cafés, and looked at a bulletin board of local villas for sale. Then a display rack of souvenirs blew over. Next, some signs in front of the Museo della Accademia Etrusca toppled over, too. Shutters high above me began banging in the wind, umbrellas in front of cafés wafted violently, and people were scurrying for cover as if they had heard an air raid siren. They must have known something I didn't because seconds later the hailstorm began. I made it back to the portico of the Teatro Signorelli just in time to avoid being pelted like a little kid in a snowball fight, and I crowded into a doorway with an old man who couldn't understand a thing I said. Obviously his Italian wasn't very good. Stubbornly, however, I pressed on in my bid to communicate, asking if this type of storm was unusual in these parts. He somehow managed to indicate that he didn't understand me but was also, at the same time, offended by what I'd asked. That's the power of hand gestures for you. I chuckled in wonder at what I might have actually asked him. So in silence, we hunkered down together to wait out the storm, sharing our tiny space like two children in time out.

I appreciate a good storm. When I lived in Japan during their rainy season, I remember getting so frustrated at days on end of steady, gentle rain. It never would get mean and violent, but it wouldn't quit, either. It just rained. Steady. Unceasingly. *Come on!* I remember thinking. *Let loose! Show us what you've really got!*

But it never did—not a rumble of thunder or a flash of lightning the whole summer, just that miserable, unending drizzle. But here in Cortona on this afternoon in July, there was no such problem. It was truly letting loose and showing us what it could do. And it was doing it with style—so typically Italian.

Everything loose was being blown around or away. Petals were being sheared off flowers, leaves ripped off trees. Small pieces of twigs blew down the old stone streets. And the hail, about a half-inch in diameter, pelted down hard and steady for over twenty minutes, bouncing high off parked cars and making a tinny banging noise that echoed up the faces of the old buildings. It was loud. People on the leeward side of the wind kept their windows open and stood looking out. Every storefront and café housed refugees peering outward with the same curiosity. We were all united in a moment of trapped waiting—a moment that would last at least an hour.

Suddenly a man in the café near me began playing a violin. He was an excellent violinist, and the music was beautiful. The sound drifted out of the café and echoed throughout the portico, mesmerizing a little group of us who now sat at wet tables and simply listened. No one said a word. We were in a Bellini film.

As the storm abated and the sun came back out, the people did, too. Windows opened; storefronts spilled customers back out into the streets; cars and motorcycles began moving again. The noises of the storm receded, and the sounds of a bustling city re-emerged. The air was cool and damp, and the city looked shiny. But every crook and crevice was spattered with debris, mostly leaves and twigs. From where I emerged down the steps of the theatre, I couldn't see any trees, but the evidence that they had taken this storm particularly hard had blown all through Cortona.

Terri and I had swapped a couple text messages during this ordeal. She was happily at table in Alessandra's home down the hill and in no hurry to leave; some new friends she'd made during the day (no surprise there) had offered to bring her home whenever things finally wrapped up. A cab without a customer, I rode back out of Cortona to check on the kids. I was confident they had weathered the storm without incident, but with no way to communicate with them, I wanted to get back just to be sure.

As I navigated the winding roads snaking down the steep hill out of Cortona, I couldn't believe the amount of leaves and twigs scattered across the road. The wet pavement and the millions of tiny cypress tree leaves made the surface dangerously slippery. I proceeded with caution down to the lowlands and the straight road back to the villa. But that straight road was flooded in big long sections. Some cars were attempting to cross these stretches, while others were turning back.

*Cool*, I thought, *a water crossing*.

I proceeded through the first flooded section, which was probably over a hundred yards long, and the BMW handled it superbly. By resting my feet up on the tops of the cylinders, I managed to stay completely dry while crossing a mini-lake.

*What a blast*, I thought and began picturing myself on one of those motorcycle circumnavigations, where a few friends and I were off on a fifty-country trek. "The water crossings were particularly dangerous in Cameroon," I said into my helmet in my best film-documentary voice. "Often, the men would have to ride for miles at a stretch with their bikes sunk up to their axles, unsure of what they'd encounter next. Would it be alligators? Quicksand? Trench foot?"

Just then I encountered a driver of a car coming the other way who didn't realize there were *No Wake* rules on open waterways. Going way too fast, he was absent-mindedly splashing up huge waves of water from the sides of his car, one of which soaked me completely. Some people are just not polite boaters.

"Didn't see that one coming," said the announcer. "He sure looks miserable down there. For once, I'm glad to be safe and dry up here in this helicopter . . ."

CHAPTER 29

# COOKING WITH CLASS IN ALESSANDRA'S *CUCINA*

*Here in Italia, the customer is right when the customer is right;*
*and if the customer is wrong, then he's wrong and I am right.*
– Alessandra Federici

I made it back to the villa to find the kids safely inside with towels on certain parts of the floor.

"What are these?" I inquired.

"Rain was coming in all over. You wouldn't believe the hail! Smashing down like crazy!" They were all talking at once. After they'd finished delivering their excited version of the storm, we loaded up the minibus.

"Mommy's had a really good day at her cooking class, so we're on our own for dinner as she finishes up." And we were off to try a new restaurant called Bastian Contrario. The word *Contrario* was written backwards, which I liked, and the place was very close to our villa, which I also liked.

We were a bit early, as usual, so we killed time in the parking lot by watching cars splash through a flooded section of road directly in front of the restaurant.

"Cool!" yelled J.R. as a blue Fiat Panda was nearly brought to a stop by hitting the deep section too quickly. Huge plumes of muddy brown water shot off both sides and high into the air. Car after car did the same, much to the delight of my children. *These Italians even have style while crossing floods*, I thought. I didn't see anyone else doing it on a motorcycle, however.

By the time we returned to the villa, stuffed with yet another excellent restaurant meal, Terri had returned and was full of stories. We sat in a circle as she portrayed a fascinating day from start to finish . . . and the remainder of this chapter is as she told it:

Because in the original email, Alessandra had indicated she was available June 29, and I had to correct her to July 29, I was a bit afraid I had the wrong day, even if I had the right place. I was five minutes early. Her store, *Il Girasole* (The Sunflower), which was under the theatre, was still boarded up like a storage bin. I found a quiet place in the shade to wait, watching the street full of Italians and foreigners of all languages.

Soon, a Jeep pulled up, and a shorthaired woman in her late forties walked toward the garage featuring the *Il Girasole* sign. She hefted the large green barricade and hid it away into the ceiling, revealing an adorable shop of table linens.

"Alessandra?" I asked from behind.

"*Si!*" she said.

"I'm Terri Brady. Here for cooking class?"

I laugh at how although I speak English as my only language, somehow while speaking to foreigners, I tend to chop it up as if I am only allowed nouns and hand gestures. "Me: Terri" (pointing to me). "You: Alessandra" (pointing to her). "Cooking class?" And I stir an imaginary pot.

"Sure!" she says. "Wanna come into my store and wait for the others?"

It was the most American English I had heard from a native. *Wanna* was such casual slang.

"You drive a Jeep?" I asked, surprised by the American car but sharing a love for her particular choice.

"Yes," she said, "and a motorcycle."

I am not sure what I had expected: More prim? More fashionable? I don't know, but I was feeling silly that I had fretted over what to wear, if I should have smoothed my hair, and whether I would be offending someone if I turned down wine due to my own dislike of it. But Alessandra was real. I knew immediately I would like her but wasn't sure if she'd like me.

She got out her laptop and busily printed color photo-quality recipe books and information packets for the day's class. I was amused by the irony of my iPhone and her photo printer in the middle of Cortona, which, as one of the oldest hilltop towns of Tuscany, rivaled Siena and Arezzo during the Middle Ages.

The next class members walked in, and an attitude-full preteen was ambiance changing. The mother in her fifties, beside her two daughters (ages thirteen and twelve), hurriedly explained that the reason they were late was that the "trafficko" in the mountains was horrible—as if adding an "o" to a very American pronunciation of a word made it Italian—and as if someone had asked her why they were late. The newcomer went on to explain that she had been coming to Italy for twenty years and had bought a villa, or two or three, on the other side of "the mountain"—as if someone had asked. Pride is unattractive in all its forms. I'm afraid my annoyance may have been equally unattractive, so I attempted to hide it.

The twelve-year-old stood with one hip jutted and arms crossed, as if someone had better prove to her soon that today was worth her time. When Alessandra spoke to the girls, the younger's position and tone didn't change, showing a lack of respect that can make everyone within the room cringe. I suppose it wasn't an option to leave the younger girl at home; the older clearly had more of an interest in cooking.

Alessandra went back to her computer while I browsed the hundreds of tablecloths and cloth napkins.  So beautiful! Yet they were so impractical because my four children would stain them within one meal.  They were true linens—the kind you handwash in cold water and line dry for three minutes before ironing to dry the rest of the way.  I owned four placemats like these once but ruined them in their first and only meal and have lived with plastic ones and no tablecloth ever since.

"Alessandra!" a man said, in full recognition of his old friend as he and his wife entered the store with beaming smiles.  She left the computer and went to receive her guests with a kiss on each cheek.  Randy and Brenda completed our set of six students, and they blew into the room with a fresh ray of sunshine, breaking through the pollution that had hung there moments before.

Based on that excited greeting, I asked Randy when he had met her or taken the class before. He said he had never met Alessandra; he was just excited to be there.  *How refreshing and contagious is enthusiasm*, I thought.

We walked from *Il Girasole* to the coffee shop across the town square.  Alessandra told us to go inside and pick out a pastry and then come outside and order a *caffè* or whatever we preferred.  The American preteen controlled the conversation from there.  "I want a hot chocolate!"

"Baby, what do you want to eat? Do you want a cressy?" her mother asked. I later realized she was referring to a croissant.

The twelve-year-old followed us to the display case and said she wanted a chocolate-filled croissant.  Alessandra told her it didn't look like there were any chocolate ones left, but the baker could probably put some Nutella inside a plain one for her.

Baby resumed her strutted hip, folded arms position and said, "Nutella is disgusting!" offending everyone within earshot, even those who didn't understand English.  Alessandra asked the baker if he had anything chocolate, and he was both accommodating and able to find something that seemed to satisfy Baby.

I picked something that looked scrumptious and appeared even more so as the tongs compressed it nearly 50 percent when the baker picked it out of the display case. The sugar crystals made the whole surface area shimmer and my mouth water like Pavlov's dogs. We went to the table and ordered five *cappuccini*—with one hot chocolate—and one "coffee, as cold as you can get it," for Alessandra, who began to tell us all about Italian cuisine and herself. She started by saying she didn't care what anyone thought of her and the saying "the customer is always right" is only true in America.

"Here in *Italia*, the customer is right when the customer is right; and if the customer is wrong, then he's wrong and I am right."

I liked her more and more.

"Italian cuisine is really 'make do with what you have,'" she explained. "*Risotto* was really a poor man's dish, invented because northern Italians could solely grow rice."

The man brought our drinks. My cappuccino had a heart drawn with cocoa powder on top of the milk froth—consistent with the art that was behind all of their food, as I was beginning to notice.

Alessandra went on to explain that milk in Italy is a food, not a drink, so Italians don't order cappuccino *with* food, but *as* food. *Espresso* (Italian coffee) more likely accompanies food, as in dessert, but is usually "thrown back" as a shot of whisky is, not sipped like we Americans do. In her science and art of coffee, she helpfully explained that Italian coffee has less caffeine than American because of its fast brew time and low volume.

"American coffee takes more time and caffeine from the beans, and it shows by the quantity."

I was amused with the confidence in her statement, as if she had just completed her degree as a dietician, and her thesis was on "caffeine consumption comparisons." I grinned despite myself and socked away all this new coffee truth.

She continued to elaborate as we intently listened, notebooks emerging from purses. "Pelegrino Artusa was the original cook in Italy and responsible for the cuisine's fame." I was surprised and encouraged when I learned that Italian cooking was truly simple, made from few ingredients.

"I laugh when I find recipes online claiming to be Italian, yet they have so many ingredients! Obviously made up by a foreigner!" she said, as she told us that pasta had three ingredients, bread four, and as we would see later today, *tiramisu* had five.

"Do you like *panzanella*?" Alessandra asked Baby, trying to engage her, since she had clearly lost interest once her chocolate was gone. Baby scrunched her nose with more muscles than she seemed to have applied to any work in her life, made sure her body didn't leave its slouched position in the chair, raised her right eyebrow and allowed a disrespectful "Huh?" out of her cockeyed lips.

Less than thirty minutes into the day, and we were about to watch Alessandra's law that "the customer is not always right" in action.

"Look here!" Alessandra said forcefully, getting the girl's attention and almost changing her posture through the force of her words. "You give that look to your sister, your friend, and maybe your mother, but you don't give that look to me, ok?" She waved her pointed finger in front of the girl's face as if to say, *No, no.* "I'm going to treat you the way I treat my own daughter, and you will not look at me that way."

There. The customer was wrong, and she let her know it. I was embarrassed for the mom, and yet embarrassed by her, too. The mother said nothing to Alessandra or either of her daughters. Randy, Brenda, and I looked awkwardly at each other until Randy raised his eyebrows and pursed his lips as if to say, *Someone had to do something, so good for her!*

From then forward, the ice had been broken. We could bond as new friends from far locations. I watched as the woman who didn't care what people thought caressed her client with kind words: "I like your daughters—especially that one. She reminds me of me. That's why she's not getting away with it. But I am glad they came."

We rose to begin our day of Italian cooking—beginning with shopping. At home, my shopping for our family of six involves approximately a two-and-a-half-hour escapade once a week. I fill almost two carts and pay about $400. There are some fresh items that last maybe two or three days, and then we live from the apples, bananas, and the pantry or freezer for the other four days.

Italy grocery shopping was completely different. Chris even went to the grocery store here! I can count on my fingers the number of times he has done that during our marriage, but this was the first time he had ever gone without a list from me, since he had been out on his motorcycle alone. He came home so triumphant and proud. It was as if he had killed a bison with his bare hands— making cheese from the milk, slaying it for its leather, carving knives from its bones, filling its bladder with drinking water, and cutting meat from it for a year of family provision. Of course, he came home with about a day's worth of groceries, but that does feel like quite a victory when battling a crowd with a different language and customs.

Apart from the difficulty of reading the ingredients made necessary due to Nathaniel's food allergies, there's the fact that you weigh your own fruit and vegetables and label it with a sticker— preferably before you enter the checkout line with ten people behind you. Also, here you must estimate how many sacks you will need because you have to purchase them while you are buying your items. Families are small here, so quantities are, too. Milk comes in one-liter bottles and is almost always the shelf-stable variety to save refrigeration costs in the store. Chicken breasts come four filets to the quarter pound.  More common meats are wild boar, any part of a pig in sausage or *prosciutto*, and rabbit.  Of course, Alessandra was shedding light as to why we, the foreigners, were the only ones in the supermarket who actually rented a cart (you have to temporarily pay one euro to use one) and bought bags.  Everyone else must do their shopping almost daily as she was showing us.

"Italians like to buy everything fresh daily and 'make do' with what's available," she said as we walked down the cobble streets of Cortona in an ensemble of seven.  The old town seemed so alive with people.  I had been to Cortona before, but as a tourist seeing everything for sale as a trap for us.  This time was different.  I was walking with a native Italian who said hi to her friends and gave to the beggars whom she seemed to know by name.  They didn't ask her, just expected it.  We were buying fruit, vegetables, and meat from the *frutteria* and the butcher shop within the old city, not the supermarket down in the newer part of town where our family had been going.  These stores, by which I had walked so many times when we toured these old towns, now had personality and purpose, as I saw the way the locals convene there.

The outside front of the *frutteria* was laden with familiar fruits as well as some not so familiar.  Alessandra warned us that the storeowners prefer to do the fruit touching, so I supposed I would not be taste-testing the grapes that seemed to be calling my name.  We entered through a narrow door for a skinny person, down three stairs to the real store, as the storeowner put some fruit in a bag for the beggar.  The store was lined floor to ceiling with trays of fruits and vegetables, and the stench was such a combination I could not identify one ingredient.  Alessandra said aloud her list, and the worker busily went from basket to basket gathering the items.  No refrigerator doors were there to slow her down.

"*Carota, sedano, cipolla, zucchini fiori . . . che? No fiori?*"

What? No zucchini flowers? What would we do? I had never heard of a use for them, so I didn't know what she was planning anyway. Despite that, I didn't trust my Italian enough to know if we were really disappointed that she had no zucchini flowers.

"*Sette fico* . . ." Seven figs?! Oh! Just the sight of the figs made my heart skip! I had been introduced to them in Maori, when the fruit shop owner was shocked that I had asked what they were.

"*Fico*?! You don't know *fico*?!" He seemed appalled as he broke one open with his thumbs and insisted my daughter and I try a bite. There was no charge—as if his only payment was watching our enjoyment at such a wonderful new taste. I had had figs in the States before, but they were classified more as weapons than fruit. These figs were amazing, almost dissolving in our mouths with no chewing required. I wondered what we would be doing with figs today during our time in Alessandra's Italian *cucina*.

Next we went to the butcher shop. I have seen a couple of these in every old hilltop town we have visited across the Tuscan countryside. Large legs of cured meat are strung from the ceiling and walls. It had not dawned on me until this moment that clearly these shops were not the tourist traps I had labeled them. I had never seen a tourist carrying an animal's cured leg (or shoulder, as ours turned out to be) while walking down the street behind a tour guide. The shops were real, active suppliers of fresh foods for the locals.

After greeting her friend the butcher, Alessandra explained to us that all of the meat was labeled due to law, with the serial number of the animal, the farm from which it came, and the day and hour when it was killed. The label was proudly displayed inside the glass case, or hanging on the hook with its meat.

There was chicken—whole ones, not the thin filets of the grocery store—and also goose, ostrich, *prosciutto* (hind quarter or shoulder), sausages, rabbit, and various cuts of beef, all with the serial number and dates attached to ensure freshness. The sausages have come to be a local favorite of mine—a flavor I haven't had in the States, lacking the processing and preservatives for which sausage is infamous at home.

We bought an eye of round beef for the stove top roast and some chicken and beef to mince for our olive meatballs and *ragú*. We took our purchases, along with some others (flours, etc.) that Alessandra had bought elsewhere and headed to the taxi waiting for us at *Il Girasole*.

As our taxi headed out of the old town of Cortona on the narrow one-way exit road, a motorcyclist zoomed past us and waved with a smile. It was Alessandra, driving faster so she could hit a different vegetable stand and get some zucchini flowers so we could "make do."

We drove ten minutes to arrive at her home, a humble abode on a bumpy road amid a cluster of similar two-story typical country homes with large wood shutters. Walking in, I was struck by the fact that it was air-conditioned, which was a treat, given that the temperature outside was reaching into the high nineties (Fahrenheit).

The front door opened into a marble-top dining table with a well-organized kitchen and preparation island behind it. A couch and television to the right made the family room and the kitchen into a rectangle. The stairs left of the table led to the only bathroom and three bedrooms upstairs. The door beside the stove in the back right led out to the garden, with a garden shed and an outside dining area for cooler days than this. Although a small home (perhaps 1300 square feet) by American standards, the only hallway closet visible was filled with table linens.

The family room was lined with shelves of books and a shelf of DVDs—from which Baby selected *Harry Potter* when she was "tired of cooking" at 12:30. It amused me to see John Grisham and Anthony Robbins in their Italian form on her bookshelves, but it explained a bit of her evident American familiarity.

Alessandra's husband, her thirteen-year-old son, and nine-year-old daughter stayed outside for the majority of our eight-hour home takeover. I hope she left them some food!

We began our cooking as I presume most cooks do: chopping. Celery, carrots, and onions were chopped, or at least prepared for the food processor. I felt smug because the night before (without any Italian cooking class) I had stir-fried celery, carrots, onions, and zucchini and then tossed them with basil, tomatoes, and extra virgin olive oil in pasta for the family. Maybe I wasn't that far off from becoming an authentic Italian cook. Maybe I was a natural.

"Italians never stir-fry," Alessandra began, as if reading my mind and zapping my obnoxious pride. *Soffrito*, as she called the three-vegetable combination, is cooked slowly in olive oil so it gets flavorful but never brown. I smiled, inwardly remembering how my browned vegetables had colored the whole pasta the night before.

We would be using the *soffrito* for the *Polpettine di olive* (olive-flavored meatballs), as well as the *ragú*, which literally translates as "stew," although they serve it on top of pasta. She said it would cook slowly, unattended, for forty-five minutes before we would even add anything else.

In the meantime we put her week's worth of stale bread in a bowl full of water to soak in preparation for *panzanella*. This salad, which is layers of bread and vegetables with herbs and oils on the top, would traditionally be carried to the farm fields or picnics and tossed upon its arrival.

Next, we went to the marble table where a large wooden board and a flat plastic spatula-type tool awaited us. Alessandra took out a large container of semolina flour and dumped four medium scoops onto the board. We separated it to make a hole in the center like a large volcano. Being the only male, Randy would be the center of much attention today, and he was chosen to begin the pasta making. He cracked four eggs into the center of the mound, added some olive oil, and began mixing the ingredients, using the flat tool to keep the liquid from escaping.

"Have you ever kneaded?" Alessandra asked.

"Only love, here and there," Randy replied.

Alessandra rolled her eyes, said, "*Mama mia!*" and then continued in Italian with some words of pity toward Randy's wife Brenda.

He kneaded it into a soft ball, and Alessandra added more flour
pronouncing the dough "too soft—pasta dough must be stiff." The
newly stiff ball was then plopped into a lightly covered bowl to sit
for hours while we continued the rest of the meal preparations.

"Follow me to the neighbor's," she said as she walked out the
front door. We walked down the street, and she yelled (no doorbell
required) into a second-story open window, "Can we take some
eggs?"

With permission granted, we headed into the barnyard. The
yard, which had more gravel than grass, contained chickens, ducks,
geese, and various coops of babies lining the borders. Bunnies had
been born two days before, but Alessandra corrected us: "These are
not bunnies; these are rabbits," meaning they are food, not pets.

Alessandra grabbed five eggs from the nests—perfect for the
*tiramisu* that would use raw eggs, so fresh ones were required. She
helped herself to several twigs from the rosemary bush (for the roast
beef) and sage leaves for us to fry. The new smells and concepts
had my tongue curious.

Back at her home, we minced the chicken and added sausage
and ground beef to it, and then we put it into the *soffrito* for the
olive balls. As I chopped the chicken, I was grateful for the sharp
knife—one of the twenty attached to her wall on the magnetic
strip—since I had been forced to cut with a butter knife all week at
our rental villa.

The knives were not the only utensils on display. Pots hung
on hooks on a grid attached to the far wall. A canister displayed
various ladles and pasta forks. A drawer contained fifteen matching
spice containers with labeled lids. Another held matching contain-

ers of grain: Spelt, all-purpose-flour, salt, sugar, and semolina were the only ones I recognized.

We took turns with the pasta machine, pressing it thin and then cutting it into *tagliatelle* strips. Alessandra told us it could be done with a rolling pin, but she had never figured out how, much to the dismay of her neighbors, whose average age was eighty.

Our cooking day continued: batter to fry the sage leaves and zucchini flowers, a ceramic knife (which I had never heard of) to cut the apples into thin slices to lay with cheese and honey; rolling and frying of meatballs (never served on spaghetti, by the way), assembling of the wet-bread salad; adding wine (which would of course burn off) to the *ragú*, and "drowning" the roast beef with rosemary.

When deep-frying, the oil got too hot and almost caught fire. "I'm *estupido*," Randy joked in Americano-Italian.

"You are not stupid—just dangerous!" quipped Alessandra in return as she threw out the half-liter of burned olive oil and started anew.

No flour was added to thicken the *jus* for roast beef; the sauce was just left simmering while we started eating our *antipasti*. No sugar was added to take the acidity out of the sauce because the length of cooking had created the perfect flavor.

"Americans rush cooking too much and then have to add helps to try to fix the problems they've created," Alessandra educated, with the authority of her whole country behind her.

As a working mother, she had no more hours in a day than we did, but she explained how she cooked *ragú* during and after dinner and then took it off and put it in the fridge for the next night's meal.

To my surprise, the herbs (rosemary, garlic, etc.) were removed from the dishes before we ate. Their flavor remained where it was supposed to be—in the sauces.

Too hot to eat outside, we set the linen inside for dining at the marble table. We lined up seven plates on the island to "decorate" each one with the six *antipasti* we had created.

As we took our plates to the table, Alessandra put on a big pot of water to begin boiling. It was 5:00, the scheduled end of the class, but we would "make do" and happily continue. Chris had texted me to stay as long as I liked, so I sat to enjoy conversation and food with new friends.

The wine was opened, and after Alessandra turned it down, too, I knew my own refusal would not offend. After *antipasti* (of which I devoured every bite), we cooked and drained the home-made *tagliatelle*, never rinsing so the porous pasta would soak up the *ragú*, not the water. We tossed it with the sauce, then one more ladle on top before serving with cheese, never bread. *Delizioso!*

We went on to the beef, thinly sliced (*carpaccio*) topped with the cooked-down sauce beside a simple salad dressed with oil and apple vinegar. The entire meal came from local ground within a few miles of the table. *This is how food was meant to be*, I thought, savoring every mouthful.

The meal was completed with our five-ingredient *tiramisu* and *caffè*. Yum! *Grappa* was served, supposedly to "aid digestion," but that shot is so strong I think it only burns the calories before they digest and burns the stomach lining, too!

It was more than two hours past our ending time, as we enjoyed company and let a storm roll through. I think the day was truly *perfetto*, and when this customer is right, I'm right.

## CHAPTER 30

# FRANCIS OF ASSISI WAS NO SISSY

*I have been all things unholy. If God can work through me,*
*he can work through anyone.*
    – Francis of Assisi

"Preach Christ with all your might, and if you must, use words." That little quote, often attributed to St. Francis of Assisi, was the only thing I really knew about the man before this vacation.

Other interesting things are also attributed to this rascal believer, including legends that he conversed with the birds and talked a wild wolf out of terrorizing a little mountain town. The more believable aspects of his life are fascinating enough, however, and the deeper I researched into the life of this little man, the more respect I gained for what he accomplished.

Born the rich kid of a textile merchant father and a French mother, his "normal guy" name was Giovanni Francesco di Bernardone. Growing up today, we might call him Johnny Fran or something catchy like that. One can only imagine a life with such a moniker, so Francis did what all rich kids with funny names do: He lived it up. He went in for all kinds of exciting things, such as fighting in a battle to defend Assisi, getting captured and spending a year in prison, becoming seriously ill, recovering, and then taking a trip to Rome to tour St. Peter's, much as we just did (except he got to see the original basilica, not the "new" one, of course, it being the thirteenth century and all). Only instead of strolling around admiring architecture and the like, Francis decided to join in with the beggars he saw everywhere. Apparently this life either appealed to him or appalled him so much he was never the same again.

When Francis returned home after his pilgrimage to Rome, he refused to go back to his profligate way of life. As a result, his former friends teased him. It seems Francis wasn't interested in playing sports anymore. When asked if he was planning to settle down and marry, Francis supposedly answered, "Yes, to the most beautiful bride." What he meant by this was the bride of poverty. *Oh, that Johnny Fran is such a jokester*, his former friends no doubt thought. But they were wrong. Francis's vow of poverty was sincere, and his way of life consistent with his new views.

He began tending to the needs of the local lepers—the lowliest and most avoided people of his day. In the church of San Diamano near Assisi, he had a vision in which he claims he was told, "Francis, Francis, go and repair my house, which, you can see, is falling into ruins." Francis took this vision literally and launched himself into one of the original fixer-upper projects: the church in which he'd been praying. Surely pleasing the local priest, Francis began helping with restorations. He made a little miscalculation, however, when he sold some goods out of his father's store to pay the construction costs (always exorbitant in Italy . . . I guess even in his day). His father didn't take too kindly to this misappropriation, however, and attempted several popular tactics such as assault, battery, and lawsuits, to get restitution.

In a hearing before the local bishop, Francis renounced his father and his inheritance, in the process even removing every stitch of clothing from his person. Departing the scene entirely naked,

Francis went to live among the beggars once again, this time with a more authentic material situation.

Slowly he was able to expand his fixer-upper activities, restoring several more local churches. Then he heard a sermon that changed his life even further, compelling him to officially renounce a material life and to spread the word that the kingdom of heaven was at hand. He dressed in a simple rough garment, which lots of painters have since reproduced, and went around to all the towns in the area preaching repentance and faith in Christ. Francis was sincere, and by the end of one year had gained eleven followers. He refused any official ordination as a priest, and he and his followers began to be known as the "lesser brothers" because they refused to act with pride or take their place above anyone else.

Of course, such offensive behavior got them in trouble with the powers that be: the Church in Rome. It seems that preaching at that time was illegal unless one had obtained official sanction. So back Francis and his eleven went to the city that had started it all for him. Incredibly (and thanks to a dream he'd had), Pope Innocent III gave them an audience and an approval, of sorts. Francis was instructed that as his group grew, they could come back and gain official acceptance from the Church. In other words, "If you can convince more people of your ideas, then maybe we'll be convinced, too," or something like that. This quasi-approval from the Church was pretty important because it allowed Francis and his eleven to avoid the complications of being declared heretics. This was nice, since it meant they could remain alive, which was very helpful in gaining new followers.

Francis continued to demonstrate his life of poverty and preach his gospel everywhere he went, many times attempting to spread the message outside Italy, and even purportedly preaching to the Sultan of Egypt. His order of followers, ultimately called the Franciscans, spread around the globe, and the order he co-founded for women, the Poor Claires, was also successful. Francis was involved in many pioneering movements of the faith, both big and small, including the interesting Trivial-Pursuit-type fact that he was the first to set up a three-dimensional nativity scene, complete with live animals.  It was two years after he died that he was officially pronounced a saint and, therefore, got the name he is best known by today: St. Francis of Assisi.  He lived a life consistent with his doctrine and has been a hero of the faith down through the ages.

As soon as I realized how close we were staying to Assisi, the town made famous by this fascinating man nearly eight hundred years ago, I knew we had to go check it out.  Only a short drive into Umbria past Lake Trasimeno, we began to notice the change in stone color as indicated in all the guidebooks.  Where Tuscany is typically the orange of terracotta tiles and the brown of the stones found throughout the region, stones of pinker and whiter hues characterize Umbria.

We spotted the gorgeous little town from the expressway, off to our left a few miles away, cozily nestled into the side of a large ridge.  The sun was already running out of steam for the day, and the dimming colors reflecting off the Umbrian stone made a pleasing contrast to the dark green all around the town.  It was beautiful.

In keeping with our form, we managed to park in the wrong place, as some polite residents in lawn chairs told us.  So in standard fashion, I unloaded the family and drove down yet another hill in search of a berth for the minibus.

The first thing that struck us as we shopped our way into the city was just how marvelously clean it was.  This was true of most places we had been, but for some reason, Assisi was so prim we felt as if we were walking around in a dollhouse.  There were also plentiful photo opportunities, and I was kept busy at the shutter throughout the evening.  One in particular featured three large, identical trees on a ledge behind a fountain on which two young men wearing fedoras, facing the opposite direction, were posing side-by-side for a photo of their own.  From my angle exiting a small tunnel, it looked like a Beatles album cover. It is still one of the favorite shots I've ever taken.

It took a searching eye to see the reconstructions and repairs from the devastation an earthquake caused here over a decade ago. One or two buildings were undergoing massive restorations, but I wasn't sure if this was the last of the repairs or just more of the type of ongoing construction one sees throughout these towns of old in Italy.

Terri really got into the shopping in Assisi, finding a mono-gramming store to customize some aprons for friends and relatives. We picked up a few more gifts and found a little out-of-the-way place for dinner, taking our seats at long picnic tables in the front by the bar area. This was also where one had to pay at the end of a meal, and a funny photo opportunity presented itself. I looked up between my first and second plates to see a nun standing at the cash register waiting to pay her bill. From my vantage point, the cash register was not visible, and it looked like she had sidled up to the bar for a drink. I decided not to take the picture, she not having actually incriminated herself, and instead enjoyed a private chuckle at the arrangement of some of these restaurants.

After dinner, we strolled the main streets, and I especially liked the Tempio di Minerva, the remains of a Roman temple dating back to the time of Caesar Augustus. It has been incorporated as the front of a more "modern" building, an amalgamation done hundreds of years ago. This made me think of a similar arrange-ment in Castiglione del Lago and served as a constant reminder of the many layers of history enveloping us throughout our travels.

Unfortunately, the hour being late, we ran out of time and light. I would have loved to have seen the twenty-eight panels of frescoes depicting the *Life of St. Francis* by Giotto, some of his most renowned work, in their original position in the lower part of the Basilica di San Francesco. Also in this church rich in art treasures are frescoes by Martini, Lorenzetti, and even Cimabue. Knowing that we were only scratching the surface with our abbreviated evening visit, I made a mental note to return some day and "do" Assisi correctly. Besides, with the kids in tow, we had bypassed many a museum and church interior during this trip, missing out on huge amounts of painted masterpieces. Perhaps a future visit, Lord willing, could revolve around an itinerary of Italy's best frescoes. Talk about running the risk of sensory overload!

I made do with what we had to work with, however, and leaned against a ledge and watched the sunset. The reflected light from the changing sky almost made the buildings of Assisi glow. As I snapped a few last photos, trying desperately to capture with the lens what the senses themselves could barely take in, I thought about the ground upon which I stood. How many pilgrims had migrated to this city throughout the centuries, searching for inspiration from a man who actually practiced what he preached? I found it interesting that in a world with no shortage of self-promoting, greedy, selfish, power-hungry, materialistic, and glory-hungry people, that a humble, dedicated little man from a tiny hill town could have gained so much acclaim, much less have had such an impact. About him, author Robert Clark wrote, "He'd given Christ a face people hadn't seen before: the peasant's face. Until then Christ had been the Redeemer as the judge and king of the universe; he was painted enthroned, stern and impassive. Now he was the Redeemer as the Man of sorrows, the God who became human to the quick and the marrow in order to lay claim to human wretchedness." In fact, in my reading, I discovered that many historians believe the Franciscan Revolution begun by this humble man, which brought people back to a basic, simple faith, served to delay the Reformation by nearly three hundred years.

This land is adorned with centuries' worth of ostentatious displays of questionable piety. Faithfulness is not measured by the height of a spire or the flute of a column, but rather in the quiet, heroic walk of obedience.  Perhaps this is why Francis stands out so much here, especially in this place.

Is it that rare for someone to preach Christ with all his might, and if he must, use words?

Maybe, especially if what is meant by the quote is not a limitation on speaking the truth of the Gospel (for after all, faith comes by hearing, and hearing by the Word of God) but, rather, actions that back up the words.

Or perhaps this is not rare; it's just that obscure "lesser brother" types away from the camera lens of Hollywood or the national news are the ones who do it.

Or, maybe it's supremely difficult, requiring the kind of meekness described in the Bible: enormous strength held under control, the animal appetites tamed and subdued.

The more I thought about it, the more I realized what a tough, heroic figure St. Francis really was.  The thousands of pilgrims throughout the centuries had chosen a worthy figure to emulate on their own journeys homeward, and I was glad to be numbered among them.

# PART III: DIMINUENDO

CHAPTER 31

# FLORENCE, Y'ALL

*Italy contained half the significant art in the West and Florence contained half of that.*
— Robert Clark

If you drive through Ohio on I-75 and cross into Kentucky, you'll pass a tall water tower near the expressway with big letters proclaiming, "FLORENCE Y'ALL." The little town of Florence, Kentucky, probably never would have stuck in my brain were it not for that sign with the southern expression. For whatever reason, I just couldn't get that little saying out of my head as we finally set out one beautiful July morning for the original Florence—as in, the one in Italy.

Florence to me is mind-boggling. For starters, it's not even named Florence. It seems the Italians have their own ideas about what to call their cities, so to them it's *Firenze* (and always has been), which is actually a lot more cosmopolitan sounding, if you ask me. Saying you've just returned from Firenze has much more punch than plain old Florence, which, let's face it, sounds like it could be some small town in Kentucky. Just why there is this anglicized version of the city's name is a mystery to me. But wait, there's more.   Concentrated in this tiny spot in a compressed window of time were once gathered some of the greatest minds the world has ever known. The sound bite version is that Florence was the birthplace of the Renaissance, but the full story is infinitely more interesting than that.

The Medici family dynasty, made wealthy primarily through banking and predominantly through their biggest clients—a succession of popes—is a thread that runs consistently through the story of Florence.  It was largely their patronage that launched the Renaissance and years later, once they'd solidified control of Tuscany as a string of Grand Dukes, advanced science by supporting Galileo and others.  The Medici coat of arms, comprised of large spheres (balls, or *palle*) mounted to a shield (symbolism dating back to the original apothecary guild from which they rose), can be found on buildings, piazzas, and in churches throughout Tuscany, a reminder of their widespread influence.  In a word, their predominance is obnoxious.  One contemporary quipped, "He [Cosimo il Vecchio] has emblazoned even the monks' privies with his balls."

Dante Alighieri always comes first in my mind in the parade of Florentine greats.  He was trapped between the long feud of the Guelphs and the Ghibellines and exiled from his beloved city.  His masterpiece *The Divine Comedy*, written in the Tuscan vernacular, did much to establish the language we know today as Italian.  Next came Cimabue and his work recalling classical times, as well as his great apprentice Giotto, architect, designer, and artist extraordinaire.  Then there was the competition between Brunelleschi and Ghiberti to see who would win approval to fashion the bronze doors of the baptistery.  Ghiberti won and would spend the rest of his life constructing two sets of doors that are a marvel to this day.  Brunelleschi lost and instead demonstrated his genius with an infinitely clever methodology for constructing the beautiful dome of the Duomo, the largest of his time.  In the process, he would also invent many machines and devices still in use today.  Historians argue that some of these have been incorrectly attributed to the famous painter and dabbler, Leonardo da Vinci, another giant who spent much time in Florence. Vasari, the painter and architect, is best remembered as the chronicler of the great artists of his city. There's the writer Boccaccio, who depicted the life of an interesting cast of characters fleeing the plague. Niccolo Machiavelli, the last Republican chancellor of Florence, wrote the still controversial classic *The Prince*. There is the master sculptor Donatello, and Pisano, and Ammannati, and Giambologna, and both Giovanni and Andrea della Robbia, the painter Masaccio; also Lippi, and Ghirlandaio, and, of course, Botticelli, poet and philosopher Lorenzo the Magnificent, the fire-and-brimstone preacher Savonarola (later burned at the stake), the incomparable Michelangelo Buonerotti (my favorite), the two Medici popes—Leo X and Clement VII; Catherine de Medici, who married into the French dynasty and gave birth to two kings and introduced the fork to the French; Galileo, who confirmed the postulate of Copernicus that the earth revolves around the sun, among other significant advances, and on the list could go. All of these either called Florence their home, invested a significant amount of time in their work there, are featured in its galleries and museums today, or some combination of the three.

If such a litany of talent is staggering, one can begin to imagine the near impossibility of touring a city saturated in the works of so many great minds. A day spent in the Uffizi Gallery alone can nearly blind its viewer with beauty. So where does one start? On what does one focus? Is it possible to see so much and still come away with any sense of it all as a cohesive whole?

I have no idea.

I've happily been to Florence several times and still can't comprehend it all. I have concluded that there are only two proper approaches to experiencing Florence:

1. Live there.
2. Just drop into the middle of it at random and start admiring.

We decided on option two, having some commitments back home and all.

One advantage of our location near Terontola is its train station on the rail line heading north to Florence. My children love shuttle busses and airport trams of all sorts, so I knew just riding the train to Florence would be a thrill. The promise of a train ride also made it easier to awaken them early enough for us to get a good start on the day.

Purchasing tickets at the window was a snap. All I had to do was stand in a little line, wait my turn, and then strain like crazy to hear through two-inch thick bulletproof glass, which in sleepy little Terontola was about as out of place as a Hummer at an Earth Day rally. What the man on the other side was saying was, "Mmmm, nnnennnm, treeeeeeeen, onnnnnnnnnnly, mumm."

I didn't know the Italian for "What the heck are you saying?" so I made the universal face for "Huh?"

Understanding me immediately, the man stood up from his chair, placed his face near the glass, and spoke much louder—an exercise I imagine he had to do fifty thousand times a day.

"The only inner city train is seventy and fifty," he barked in frustrated, broken English.

Okay, great. Now I could hear him, but still had no idea what he meant. I must have exhibited the universal sign for idiot, because he got even closer to the glass and shouted it again, except this time slower and even louder.

"Theeee onlyyyyyy innnner ceeeeteee traaaaain is seeeveeenty and feeeeftyyyy!"

At which time Terri rushed to my rescue.

"He's saying the only express train leaves at seventeen and fifty, military time for 5:50 this evening," she explained.

So I said a bunch of *va benne*s, and the man began moving his mouse around on his computer a lot. I had indicated the size and ages of our family, something that was proving to be extremely difficult for him. He indicated seventy-five euro, so I handed him a hundred. Then he handed it back and started moving his mouse around again.

For a long time.

The line behind me was growing. People were spilling out onto the sidewalk. But the "inner city train" guy was feeling no pressure; he just kept sliding his mouse around like he was in a world championship Tetris match. Finally he emerged from his electronic trance to charge me one hundred fourteen euro this time. I didn't balk—just slid the money through the tiny slit in the bulletproof glass and made a quick escape.

We were in. *Whew.*

Then we boarded the train.

The car onto which we stepped was totally full. So we crossed to another, being shown the green button that opens the doors at the ends of the cars by two *carabinieri* (military police) who were helpfully standing nearby with their machine guns. The next car, featuring cozy little compartments with closable doors and drapes, was full as well.

At about this point we were stuck in a traffic jam of other travelers similarly attempting to find seats. One was another humongous American family like ours, also with the staggering number of four children. The mother was cool, calm, and helpful, pointing out to us that our tickets were actually for assigned seats on a particular car.

"Here," she pointed. "Carriage number two. These numbers here are your seats."

Extremely thankful for this bit of insight, we about-faced and squeezed past people back onto car two, the one with the compartments. And wouldn't you know it, two train conductor employee types were camping out in *our car*. They had their briefcases and jackets spread out shamelessly in our space.

I knocked on the glass and waited for it to open, then proudly showed them our tickets. One man stood, the other remained seated, and they both began jabbering. The standing one got out his cell phone and stabbed through a bunch of menu options. The seated man waved his hand in the air dismissively. Then, the standing man took out an instrument from his pocket and punched a hole right through our ticket. I was still trying to decide if this was good or bad when he put both tickets back into my hands and said, "This is wrong ticket, for return train. This one for now. Carriage three."

*Oops.*

"Um, sorry, *signore, mi scusi. Grazie.*"

So off we squeezed to car number three, our cover as secret tourists entirely blown. We were out in the open now, obvious to a whole train of people that we had absolutely no clue what we were doing.

Then at car number three, our specific compartment, we found the door closed and the drapes pulled. Through a crack in the drapes, I could see a man in a suit with his shoes off and feet up, sleeping. We all hesitated. What if we were wrong again? Should we risk waking this man?

We did.

He at first looked at us incredulously, but then remembered he was Italian and immediately became polite. He looked at our tickets, made a bit of a headshake, began getting dressed, counted the six members of our family and realized he wouldn't even be able to stay in the compartment, all six seats being filled. We had bagged ourselves a freeloader.

The kids were all smiles and wonder as we jerked out of Terontola and eased through the morning countryside, riding in our own compartment on a passenger train. And to think we'd already contributed to the cause of justice by booting out a freeloader. We streaked past the landscape we had been admiring for weeks, seeing it quite differently somehow from the train.

I have long thought trains give one a true sense of the local reality. One generally sees the backs of buildings, the underbellies of cities, laundry hanging out windows (where one really gets to see what people wear), and the best of the local graffiti. This ride confirmed my opinion. We rattled through Tuscany and got to see the industry, the farming, and the daily lives of its people, making us feel like peeping Toms as we rambled past. We arrived in Florence at the end of the line, Santa Maria Novella station, where J.R. took a look around and proclaimed, "Hey! This looks just like an airport!"

After touring so many tiny hilltop towns, Florence seemed large to us. This was the year before cars were outlawed from the center of the city, and the bustle and busyness was a constant clamor. The crowds were also bigger. One advantage of having been off the beaten path as we had been was the freedom from packs of other tourists. But we were back in the mainstream flow again and felt it immediately.

We strolled without hurry down the Via Degli Avelli past the church of Santa Maria Novella, ducking in shops lining the piazza as the mood dictated. From a Korean woman, we bought J.R. a little backpack to replace the bulky, unmanageable one he'd brought from home. It cost us all of ten euro.

The kids were hungry so we had an early lunch, something only possible in the larger towns. The service was fast, the kids proclaimed the pizza to be the "best in all of Italy," and I had the finest glass of Brunello I had yet tasted, even considering all my previous "excellent choices." There was a large party of people at a long table next to us who were impossible to ignore. They were a group of teenaged American girls: the sisters of soccer players here competing in a tournament. The two chaperones were middle-aged women who could do nothing the whole meal but complain about their tour guides. This negativity quickly spread to the girls who each clamored to add something derogatory of their own, thereby demonstrating their maturity and sophistication.

We were heading directly for the Piazza del Duomo, to me the heart of the city, where first we entered the Baptistry, the octagonal and oldest of the church complex. The original portion of this little building supposedly dates back into the tenth century. This is also where Dante was baptized. The ceiling sparkles in gold as the eight-hundred-year-old mosaics portray *The Last Judgment*. I took a few flashless photos and lingered a while in the quiet, beautiful place. Outside, a teenager was trying desperately to sell us a watercolor of the Ponte Vecchio. He mistook Terri's politeness for interest (or weakness) and wouldn't rest until I paid him five euro for his originally fifty euro painting.

Next, we waited in the long line to climb up Brunelleschi's Dome at the top of the Duomo. By now, I knew the Brady kids of all ages had the ability for these types of endeavors, after their performances in Siena and San Gimignano.

The climb up the dome is a captivating ascent that first takes one up normal stairs, then through narrow passages that allow walks around the lower and upper interior circumferences of the drum (the cylindrical base upon which the dome rests), then onward up cramped and leaning steps between the inner and outer shells of the dome. It is here where one gets a glimpse of the herringbone brick pattern, the inner and outer shells, and the ring of chains that comprised Brunelleschi's remarkable achievement. Any student of engineering or architecture will find even a quick study of this structure interesting. It is also here where much noteworthy graffiti can be viewed, some of it quite old. One such inscription, claiming a date in the nineteenth century, reads, "Someday I'll actually be here with someone." One can only wonder at the loneliness of this individual, or if the objective was ever achieved.

The views from inside the drum are wonderful. They provide a bird's eye view into the shadowy church far below (where a Mass was being conducted as we watched) with its inlaid marble flooring and a close-up look at *The Last Judgment* frescoes begun by Vasari and finished by Zuccari that comprise the entire underside of the dome. Especially graphic in these frescoes is the enormous representation of Satan eating his victims, complete with severed torsos and spilling blood.

"Eww," said J.R.

"Yuck," added Christine.

The best view, however, is reserved for the end of the climb. Here, at the base of the marvelous lantern, one steps out into fresh Florentine air and is rewarded with a stunning panoramic vista of terracotta roofs and narrow streets, the Arno River running through town, jagged green hills ringing the city, and the distant countryside for miles and miles. Each of the magnificent Florentine churches can also be discerned from this vantage point, their spires reaching proudly above the rooftops.

"Can you imagine how they built this dome way back in the 1400s?" I asked the children. "Think what it would have been like climbing all those steps every day, maybe a couple of times a day, carrying bricks and mortar and tools and your lunch."

They looked at me, looked down, thought about it, and then one of them replied, "Yeah." I couldn't blame them; I was a little speechless, too. Or maybe I was just out of breath from the climb. Either way, or both ways, it was breathtaking.

Again we lingered, wondering where the line was between lingering and loitering. A Polish couple asked me to snap their picture. An American from New Jersey asked if I'd been here before. And I sensed an unusual camaraderie among a group of strangers who seemed to feel the solidarity of being together in one of the coolest places in the world.

The descent from the top of the dome is not as much work as the climb, but perhaps more dangerous. The steps seem quite a bit narrower when heading down. Once we emerged into the sunshine in the Piazza del Duomo, Christine and J.R. wanted their pictures taken in front of their conquest. They were both so proud of having climbed all the way to the top. It looked big enough to me; I can only imagine how enormous it looked to them.

Next, we walked to the Piazza della Republica where I was asked to sign a petition. There was a little card table set up and two young people administering a very systematic process of obtaining signatures from foreigners for some undecipherable political cause. Or maybe it was a handwriting contest. I couldn't tell. But they seemed happy enough to have my signature. Perhaps I helped to topple a government somewhere.

From there, we took the short walk to the Orsanmichele, the church that had once been a public grain dispensary. We looked at its statues (many are now replicas of the originals that were once there) in niches between the columns, and I thought how it was the most unlikely looking church we had yet seen in all of Italy. I don't know—to me it looked like a grain dispensary that had been converted into a church. But that's just my own crazy interpretation.

Walking north, we went to the street markets around the church of San Lorenzo, which features the Medici tombs carved by Michelangelo, his marvelous and bizarre staircase, as well as the walls, ceiling, and desks in the Biblioteca. Although Michelangelo submitted several designs for its completion, the façade of the church is unfinished and remains a rustic-looking stone. Where else could a building go unfinished for five hundred years and nobody would seem to care?

The street markets themselves almost obscure the church. Umbrellas and tarps, little wagons and stands line both sides of the streets to the northeast of the church and fill much of the piazza out front. This unsightly commercialism didn't seem to deter my children, however, who scampered among the wares in search of just the right replica soccer jersey for some guy whose name I can't pronounce. Christine was into the purses and silks, and Terri found a lambskin jacket at one of the stores behind the market that made her look like she was in a magazine. We then split up to better focus upon our particular areas of interest, and I took the opportunity to select some of the nice silk neckties. These have become one of my favorite gifts to give my friends back home, partly because they sell at the unbelievable price of about three euro each. I loaded up with an embarrassing amount of these: the ties that bind.

We rendezvoused on the steps of San Lorenzo, shared a soda, and then moved on to the Piazza della Signoria. Here a replica of Michelangelo's *David* stands where the original once did (it's now down the street and inside the Galleria dell' Accademia), and in the nearby Loggia dei Lanzi stands the bronze statue of *Perseus* by Cellini, as well as the marble *Rape of the Sabine Women* by Giam-bologna, and several statues of people with no arms. Right out in the piazza is the Fountain of Neptune. This dedication of space to statuary, especially in the loggia, feels extremely foreign and eclectic. My birthplace of Flint, Michigan, certainly never had anything like this.

Looking around the piazza, one gets a sense of the Renaissance: a wide-open piazza framed by beautiful buildings and marked by statuary. Yep. One could almost imagine Leonardo da Vinci and Michelangelo striding into the Palazzo Vecchio for the fresco competition between them that never fully materialized.

*What history has walked here?* I thought, and looking around, I couldn't help but wonder at the variety of people walking here now. There was a group of Japanese standing in a clump, politely awaiting something. Italian teenagers—mostly boys—ambled through the center of the piazza in a big group, wearing designer jeans and tight tee shirts. Two teenage girls apparently thought "mall hair" from the eighties was back in style and, tragically, maybe it is, this being fashion-setting Italy. An enormous man with a gray hair comb-over was licking a yellow ice cream cone in short, choppy little strokes, as if his tongue would burn with longer ones. Two middle-aged women with long dark hair loudly greeted one another with kisses on both cheeks. A toddler was crying while walking alongside a stroller with a sleeping sibling inside, the mother mumbling something angrily while pushing the stroller as if it were the source of her ire. Tour guides walked while holding all manner of objects high over their heads so they could more easily be followed through the crowd. Cutting through the tourists, I saw a man smartly dressed in a dark suit talking on a cell phone. We were hit up by the same beggar woman with the long black braid we had seen the year before, still seven months "pregnant" (surely some kind of record) and, attempting to pull our heart strings, pointing to children in a photo, ostensibly her own (the children, that is, not the photo). There was a large group of elderly but incredibly fit bicyclists all wearing matching green helmets. A couple dressed in suits walked arm in arm. Many people just sort of wandered, cameras around their necks, heads tilted upward toward the buildings or down into guidebooks, deciding what to see next . . . or when to eat. Several men sported the fashionable European man purses, while women showcased the entire range of clothing options from "prime meat" to "past their prime." And two policemen wearing white Keystone Cop helmets strolled around as if they wished they had something to do.

I entertained myself wondering what all those great art masters so long ago would think about the clamoring crowds and waves of tourists like us, cramming together these many years later to view their work. Maybe, especially by the time of the High Renaissance, they had an idea of the admiration to come. I have always thought the portraits of the United States founders reveal them to be posing for more than just the artist, meaning also for the admiration of their posterity. Perhaps these founders, too, in their own way, were posing through their works.

Buying tickets for the museum inside the Palazzo Vecchio, the old town hall and center of Florence's government for centuries, we had to check J.R.'s new backpack into a locker, it apparently being dangerous to the artwork. At the top of the steps, we entered a huge room with a high ceiling and enormous frescoes all around by Vasari honoring—who else but the Medici. This was the central meeting spot for all those heated town meetings in Florentine history. Displayed around its perimeter are full-size sculptures of Greek gods doing what Greek gods do best: fighting and killing and such. The most interesting of these is located right next to the steps heading up into Pope Leo X's bedrooms and features a man ready to slam another to the turf in true WWF style. Not so fast, however; while one man appears to have the upper hand, the other has snuck in an underhand, taking a firm grasp of the other's naked manhood. This is graphic, painful-looking, and bizarre and must make any male viewer wince. I tried hard to recall this event from my apparently too limited studies of Greek antiquity, while also attempting to quickly steer away my daughter. Was this the famous battle between Hercules and Antaeus, whose strength only lasted while he remained fixed firmly to the ground? If so, and even though Hercules clearly had his opponent lifted clear of the earth, the grip of Antaeus appeared to still be plenty strong! J.R., all of five years old, noticed the situation and said with a smile of embarrassment and crinkled up nose, "That would *hurt!*"

After this educational art lesson, we purchased our now almost daily helping of gelato and retreated to the shade of the Palazzo Vecchio adjacent to the Uffizi art gallery, where we relaxed and soaked up the atmosphere. Should we go into the Uffizi? Should we cross the Arno River and tour the Pitti Palace and Boboli Gardens? We kicked around several attractive options, our minds dull from beauty, our bellies full of calories, and our skin mugged by the sun.

That was when we heard the music.

"Ooh, where's *that* coming from?" Terri asked, standing up.

"I don't know but let's follow it," I said.

We rounded a corner and walked all of fifteen feet before finding the source of that wonderful sound: a lone man on a stool playing a classical guitar. He was fortysomething with thinning hair and had a friendly round face that seemed to feel the music as he played it. He closed his eyes and rocked ever so slightly while his hands effortlessly plucked and picked individual notes so clear and precise they almost sounded digital. The song he was playing was "*Con Te Partiro*," and it was absolutely mesmerizing. Without saying a word, Terri and I found a little spot on the side of the building on which to rest, and we both sat down.

It has been said that music is the language of the soul. I have always appreciated it as such, but in the frustrating years of my youth, in which I was subjected to harsh music teachers with chains on their glasses to hold them onto their noses as they looked down them at me in disgust, or the retired nun who tried her best to teach me piano while her little yappy dog barked from atop his "time out" stool, somehow the soul got taken out. What remained, like a fish cleaned of its meat, were the bones of mathematics and a bunch of heartless technique. I swapped music for motocross and left it behind forever. Until I met Terri, that is. Here was a girl who could not only play music, as in technically being able to hit the right notes, but she could express it, too. She wasn't just someone who could play an instrument. She was a musician, an artist. Music had come back into my life, figuratively and vicariously, even romantically.

This man humbly seated before us now was a musician, a master. There was so much sincerity and feeling to what he played that we were transported, transfixed, and a whole bunch of other *trans* words, probably, too. At any rate, we liked it. Others did, too, as a little group of thirty or forty had gathered to stand in rapturous silence with us. Even our children sat in quiet enjoyment.

We let the songs proceed one after another without stirring from our front row seats. The crowd changed faces but never shrank, while our six faces remained. The kids took turns putting money into the man's guitar case, each gift received with a polite nod and a smile. And the music played on.

I whispered to Terri, "Remember the last time I was in Florence, when I told you about our stroll through the Piazza della Repubblica one evening?"

Terri shrugged.

"You remember: There was this young woman—couldn't have been twenty-five years old. She had a little head strap microphone and a tiny amp, and she was singing some of the most beautiful operatic music I've ever heard."

Terri nodded, perhaps remembering, perhaps just being nice.

"Anyway, we stood there and listened to her and totally enjoyed it. Then, for some reason, we just walked away without buying any of her CDs or even getting her name."

"Okay?" Terri whispered.

"Well, I've always regretted that. There's no way of ever finding out who she was. But *this* guy!" I said thumbing in his direction. "We've got to find out who he is. We've just got to buy some of his music."

"I agree," she answered, not taking her eyes off him. "You can probably do it right there. He's got some CDs set up for purchase, it looks like."

I swiveled my head and chuckled. A little poster and stand offering CDs for sale stood humbly behind his guitar case. I had been too busy listening to notice.

We stayed until he stopped playing and then clapped and clapped, expressing our appreciation as best we could as we departed, carrying away our new Piotr Tomaszewski CDs. This humble, decorated master from Poland could have had no way of knowing it, but he had provided us with our sound track for the vacation. Everywhere we drove after that, we played his music, and it became the emotional, beautiful, "just right" accompaniment to match our growing feelings of attachment to this land and its culture.

The city of art had worked its charms once again.

FIRENZE, Y'ALL.

CHAPTER 32

# DIFFERENT DIFFERENCES

*The Italian way of life cannot be considered a success except by temporary visitors.* – Louigi Barzini

We began to grow accustomed to a great many things as the days slipped into weeks. Hills, for one, became our constant friends. Everywhere, all the time, there were always more hills and winding roads awaiting us. It's not that we didn't have hills back home, just not hills like *these*. Other things that at first were totally foreign but began to seem normal were small parking spaces, tiny gas stations, and paying for public toilets. Even the word toilet (which sounds crude to us compared to the more refined and totally dishonest "bathroom") as a moniker for the facilities took some getting used to. Always paying in cash was at first strange, considering that at home I use a credit card for nearly everything, but after a while, I found I actually preferred it. Paying with actual cash (and the euro are so pleasingly colorful) never allows one to get far from realizing just how much is being spent.

One tendency in Italy is that if something can be beautified, it will be. This applies to all sorts of things including public walls, balconies, steps, doorways, arches, windows, and especially tables.

Linens for tables are a must; nearly every restaurant uses them, and entire shops are dedicated to tablecloths and napkins. One wonders how long a store like that would survive back in the land of fast food. By far, though, the most interesting beautification we witnessed was a cell tower. I had spotted it from the Auto-strada one day heading north but couldn't get a long enough look to verify what I thought I was seeing. On a return trip, I noticed it again and, sure enough, someone had gone through the trouble of camouflaging the unsightly tower with large synthetic pine boughs. We had to agree a nice symmetrical pine tree was more pleasing than a big metal post.

Living out of doors, nothing new for American southerners, is still more of a way of life in Tuscany. Pergolas and pavilions are common, and almost always beautiful, decorated as with all things Italian to enhance both attractiveness and function. Every villa seems to have covered porches, grapevine or lemon-tree-draped pergolas, and/or shaded pavilions, often out by the pool. Restau-rants almost always feature outdoor seating, the indoor sections entirely unused on better days. There must be more tables with umbrellas in Italy than anywhere else on the planet. Weekly out-door markets, common throughout the little towns, quickly be-come preferred to hundred-acre fluorescent light "super centers" with mile-long aisles and shelves to the ceiling. Come to think of it, the American tendency toward bigger stores, bigger cars, and bigger homes seems mocked by Italy's successful attractiveness of the opposite. Smaller somehow seems more appealing than bigger, especially when smaller is done right.

Every now and then, these beautifications backfire, though. At a quaint little restaurant in Licignano, a fourteenth-century town with streets concentrically constructed around the contour of its hill, we sat happily on a small wooden deck that jutted into the narrow street. Large umbrellas provided shade from the midday sun, and a polite waiter trying his best to speak English was helping us enjoy exquisite meal number 278. Then someone flushed a toilet in an apartment above the restaurant. We know this because the waste pipe was routed directly down the outside face of the building. It made a bend back into submersion within the rock wall ten feet above our heads. This bend worked to enhance the, um, ambience of the sound.

This collision between the quaint and the absurd is everywhere in Italy, in spite of, or perhaps because of, the tendency toward beautification. As author Tim Parks put it, "You can hardly help wondering . . . at the way this . . . people so infallibly reproduces . . . two starkly contrasting environments: anarchy without, ceremony within." We ate in a restaurant with a dark red stucco wall that was also the final resting place for a bright pink antique hutch. Another with an enormous outdoor eating area also featured a mechanical bull attraction (four euro per ride) right out by the street. In Rome, our hotel had a magnificent view of the ancient skyline and also about eighty rusty TV antennas. The biggest displays of kids' toys are always in front of tobacco shops. The police are the friendliest I've met anywhere in the world, and they carry machine guns. I already mentioned the bulletproof glass at the train station, but there was no security check for passengers whatsoever. There *was* a security check, however, at the entrance of the Pitti Palace in Florence, and even though I forgot to remove my cell phone and a wad of change which set off the metal detector's loud screech, the policeman remained in his chair and just smiled me through. There are expensive, luxurious villas located at the end of tiny two-track dirt roads so rough one needs to wear a kidney belt, and so narrow and close to other houses it feels like trespassing just driving through. Many towns have elaborate escalator systems and tunnels leading into the ancient city center, perfect for tourists. But these are generally closed by the time dinner is through and it's time to get back *out* of town. In Piazza Signorelli in Cortona, there is a wonderful fruit market where, chained to an exterior wall adjacent to picturesque produce, there is a crude white bucket labeled "Used Battery Return."

Language slip-ups were a constant source of entertainment, as well. One evening, while talking with Giulio and Daniele, we thought they asked us if we had eaten. We replied in the affirmative, giving a complete description of our meal. After all, we were the most accomplished in our Italian food vocabulary, and it felt good for once to actually say something intelligent. Reflecting upon this conversation later, we realized they had actually said they needed to leave because *they* had still not eaten. That was funny enough. But then they proceeded to inform us about a nearby store featuring a takeout window (we think). They kept repeating the word "penny" in their usual style, confident that repetition was the key to comprehension. I pulled out my language conversion smart phone app and typed in the word I thought they were saying, laughed, and showed it to Terri, who also stifled a laugh. Were they really saying the word *penis* over and over again? Eventually, we got it. Penny was the name of the market. Someday, when we are fluent in Italian, we will tell them this story and laugh deep into the evening.

Italian styling is known the world over, and they do have a certain flare for fashion. There are a few things Italian, however, I will likely not adopt. First among these is the man purse. While it's no doubt very practical, I just don't have the shoes to go with it. Another item that has no power of attraction over me is what passes for a man's swimsuit. No matter how buff I could ever become, it would be impossible to look at home in one. Trust me, I know this to be true, having been shown many examples against my will on the beaches of Italy. And while we're on the topic of men's clothing, I'll probably be staying away from tight designer jeans and armpit hugging tee shirts with accent color sleeve and neck hems. Also, I'm striking off my list the tight white long pants that seem to go so well with Neil Diamond hair and big sunglasses.

Driving in Italy is different, too, as I've already partially covered in these pages. But there is one other major distinction I've noticed. Back home in the States, approximately 15.6 percent of the population is afflicted with what I call Left Lane Driving Syndrome. No respecter of persons, this condition seems to affect all ages and types of people. It manifests itself in the dangerously annoying result of the victim driving slowly in the left lane of a highway, thereby blocking up traffic behind for miles, like an old sewer pipe. Usually sufferers of this affliction are entirely unaware of its effects. Happily, they putt along in their lane of choice while hundreds of drivers harbor the not-so-secret wish of an intervention followed by immediate placement in a twelve-step driver's education program. I am pleased to report that I find this condition entirely absent in *Italia*. However, there does seem to be another affliction nearly as annoying that has made its way onto the peninsula: Line Straddling. This peculiar condition results in the driver being unable to drive his or her car within a single lane, clearly painted lines to the contrary be damned. Instead, the victim clips along mindlessly with one side of his car completely in the next lane with no intention of actually *changing* lanes. Generally, as in the case with Left Lane Drivers, Line Straddlers gaze at their fellow drivers as if they haven't the foggiest idea why anyone would be displeased with their driving. I am not sure which of these two afflictions is worse, but I am sincerely hoping the two countries do not export their ailments. One can only imagine a highway system with *both* of these symptoms in combination.

Another driving peculiarity of which I've become aware has to do with all those curvy mountain roads. It seems that when the roads curve, Italian drivers feel duty-bound to pull up to the bumper of the car ahead of them and just generally push it down the hill. With every possible opening in the road, they try to pass and scoot around as if rushing a pregnant woman to the hospital. Out on the open road, however, where things are straight and smooth, nobody seems to be in much of a hurry, sometimes giving farm tractors a run for their money in the slowness department.

There is another feature of this landscape I've already mentioned often enough: the abandoned farmhouses. All over the place, one finds perched in perfect settings rather large brick or stone homes in dilapidated condition. Some still have roofs, others' walls barely standing. This population of ghost homes dotting the landscape is the result of economics and government many decades ago, when families abandoned their farms and headed to the cities for factory jobs. When the "fix up a villa" craze hit, foreigners started buying them up, and the prices went through the roof. Now, there are many, many such places fully restored with new gates out front and Germans or Americans sunning by the swimming pool. I suspect this to be the source of all those Audis on the road. However, even though twenty or more years of restorations have taken place, there are still hundreds of the things all over. And it is downright impossible not to be drawn in to the allure of owning one, too. This is especially true when riding a motorcycle—the most efficient vehicle ever for hunting ruins. On many occasions, nearly lost, I would spot an abandoned farmhouse in a perfect setting atop a hill and roar up its gravel driveway like an explorer in the new world. Never sure what I'd find at the end of the trail, I had no trouble whatsoever imagining owning one myself. *Just look at these beautiful, fully mature umbrella pines lining both sides of this mile-long road leading directly to the buildings*, I'd think. *Wouldn't this be a gorgeous approach? And look at those outbuildings, what perfect guesthouses those would make. Oh, and the pool could go over there. And a courtyard? Perfect! All we've got to do is rebuild those walls.*

Every so often, a construction crane perched silently a hundred feet above one of these old beauties interrupts the landscape, the sure indication that someone else has taken the plunge and is in restoration mode. I wonder what would happen if we bought one of these, too, hired a restoration crew, and got our own crane?

Could Tuscany or Umbria handle one more family? Do the natives ever resent those of us who drop in out of the sky and get starry-eyed about their hometown, treating their country as our own open-air theme park?

Overall, those who live here have welcomed us warmly. We are often confused, lost, in the way, and, one would think, annoying from time to time. Nonetheless, we are treated almost universally with kindness and respect.

A woman with pretty white hair and a quick smile sat next to us one evening at a patriotic musical performance in Castiglione del Lago. We were listening to a brass band, a local choir, and readings recounting the struggle for Italy's independence. She and Terri struck up a conversation in which she conversed in very broken English, and Terri did the same in reverse. In so many words, she officially thanked us for coming, adding that Cortona is filled with Americans (something we noticed, too), and their economy would be in real trouble if it weren't for those of us who come and spend money.

"*Grazie*," she said with a warm smile.

"No, *signora, grazie lei* (thank you)," we replied.

CHAPTER 33

# "I FORGOT MY SHOES!"

*You need to be good at contingency plans to live in Italy.*
  – Chris Harrison

On days without the *il sfumato*, that smoky cloudiness that often graces these landscapes, we could see clear across the Valdichiana to Montepulciano.  At the top of our hill and looking north,
we could see Cortona.  From our vantage point, these two towns
of old look like twin sentinels guarding the lush farmland between.
In the mornings, when the sun made its ascent behind us, the sun-
flowers in the fields of the valley dutifully turned to face us, like
soldiers saluting a flag.  This made spectacular rectangular fields of
yellow in the patchwork valley spread before us.

"When we were in Montepulciano, did you see that next town
westward?" I asked.

"I don't know," Terri answered.

"It sat atop the next big atoll, and we wondered what it was.
Well, the guidebook says it's called Pienza.  It used to be called
Corsignano, but Pope Pius II had the architect Bernardo Rossellino
totally redesign its town center.  It seems this pope was born there
and had the name changed in his own honor."

"How pious."

"Well, I think we should go see it. It's famous for its cheeses, too, I guess."

"I'm in."

So we took the beautiful drive across the valley once again and wound our way up those fabulous hills approaching Montepulciano.

"It's so beautiful here," Terri said. "I can't figure out how to describe it."

"Me either. And don't you just want to share all this?"

"Exactly."

It was a constant urge. Experiencing so much, seeing so much, we wanted to transport it home and share it with others. That explained all the photos and gifts, I suppose.

We were now in a groove. We'd begin a boondoggle by choosing a target town, such as Pienza. Then we would calculate driving time in order to leave appropriate hours for exploring first by car, finding the ever-elusive parking spot, walking into town, doing a little shopping, and then locating a suitable place for dinner. Pienza turned out to be a snap. We parked down the road in the middle of a normal residential neighborhood. But we had blown our plan a little by arriving late, and most of the shops were closing as we arrived. Still, we were able to walk the clean little town with narrow streets and quaint little buildings and get an idea why old Pius II liked it so much. If someone like Rossellino could similarly transform my birthplace of Flint, Michigan, who's to say I wouldn't be in favor of someone naming it after me as well? However, neither is any more likely than peace in the Middle East.

The cheese shops were delectable. You could smell them long before seeing them. There were all kinds, shapes, colors, and sizes of cheese offered, more than I ever knew existed. There were enormous wheels and big triangles, long rectangles, and stout squares. Some cheese was for grating, and some for cutting into slices.

Some cheese was available already cut. For the most part, though, the customer was expected to cut his own cheese.

We purchased some representative samples and moved onward to the small piazza. It was neat enough, but I found it nowhere near as pleasing as Cortona's, or San Gimignano's, or even the tiny one in Monteriggioni. *Funny*, I thought, *how we are starting to learn this area well enough to make comparisons.* We settled on a little restaurant near the town's arched entryway, and people watched as the sunlight faded to gray—a perfect way to end a day.

At about noon the next day, we set out for Gubbio, located about an hour and a half to the northeast. Having enjoyed Assisi so much, we decided to take in another Umbrian town. It was a gorgeous day, not too hot, just warm and sunny, with big, bright white cumulus clouds decorating the sky. We played the Tomaszewski CDs while we drove, which rounded out the ideal environment. Everything was perfect, and we were about halfway there when a little voice from the backseat interrupted with, "I forgot my shoes!"

It was Christine.

Then, before I could respond, J.R. said, "Me, too."

Any parent knows getting kids out of a house and into a car wearing shoes is an effort difficult enough to drive one to drink. Why is it so hard? I was reminded of the schtick by comedian Tim Hawkins who said; "I don't care if you've got a rain boot on one foot and a flip-flop on the other. *Get in the car!*" We didn't even have the rain boot or the flip-flop.

I reviewed our options as we sped along the highway. Getting out of sync with the Italian schedule was not a good idea, so turning around and losing ninety minutes wasn't very advisable. On the other hand, finding a shoe store would be no easy feat either, as it was already nearly lunchtime, and stores of utility are not that plentiful in these tourist-trap towns. We would have to find a section of "real" stores catering to "real" people in order to find two pairs of shoes in little kid sizes. Doing this could throw us off even worse than turning around and going back.

*Hmmm.*

"Should we just bail on the whole trip and head back to the villa?" I finally asked, perplexed.

Before Terri could answer, Casey said, "Here's something!" and he held up the pair of terry cloth slippers one of the kids had taken from the hotel in Sorrento our first night in the country. They were huge one-size-fits-all adults type things, and for some reason, they had been jostling around in back of the minibus the entire trip.

Terri, always the trouper, said, "Well, one kid could wear those while we carry the other. Then they can switch off. We *might* just find a shoe store somewhere during our day."

It was as good a plan as any, so we motored onward.

We parked in Gubbio on its mountainside, near the beautiful green rise of the Apennines, so at first, the town itself didn't look like much. What we kept noticing was the sky. That day, it was the purest blue. And those cumulus clouds were building a tall tower out of themselves and reflecting snowy white in the sun. Again, the camera couldn't capture it, but that didn't stop me from trying.

We wandered through some narrow streets past furniture re-furbishing shops, a wine shop, and another carpenter shop of some kind. All closed. Christine was shuffling along in the hotel slippers without lifting her feet, the backs sticking out six inches behind her heels. Terri was carrying J.R. piggyback. The camera had no problem capturing all of this.

Then, before we reached the piazza, an old man approached us. He had piercing blue eyes and a grandpa grin.

"Welcome to Gubbio," he said in English.

"Thank you."

"Where are you from?" he asked, shaking my hand and tussling J.R.'s hair with a smile.

"Florida," we said, never sure exactly which state we should say.

"Oh, Florida. I have a son in Florida," and he took out a picture to show us the dark-haired young man attending university there.

"You been to Gubbio before?" he asked.

"Nope. First time."

"Oh, oh, my. You will *love* Gubbio. It will be your best visit. Your favorite."

And we chatted amicably like this for a few minutes, falling in love with the town we hadn't yet seen because of this voluntary greeter in one of its back streets.

The man was right. Gubbio was great. Originally founded way back in the third century B.C., it later became a Roman colony and then an independent commune. And wouldn't you know it, old St. Francis of Assisi had been here, too. This was the mountain town we'd learned of earlier in which he had spoken to the wild wolf to get it to stop terrorizing the town. The result today is a proliferation of St. Francis statuettes for sale in all the souvenir shops. Various renditions of the wolf are available, too, but he is not quite as popular.

The old city streets are gorgeous, quaint, and very medieval. They wind around nicely, first through small piazzas, then out to a large one and a nice central park near the old loggia, once used in the textile industry. There are ceramic shops, art galleries, leather goods stores, furniture shops, and the, by now, familiar magazine stores with toys out front too junky for a dollar store. The one thing Gubbio didn't seem to have, however, was a kids' shoe store. So Christine and J.R. took turns shuffling and riding piggyback while we went up and down hills and around corners. One lady in a souvenir shop was so intent on doting on our children I bought a St. Francis figurine just to please her. At a roadside magazine stand, Terri found a perfect ceramic gift for one of her friends. Then we wandered back into the older section of town and found a perfect restaurant on the piazza, complete with umbrella overhead and friendly waitress.

Also outside was parked the most beautiful touring motorcycle I'd ever seen.

"Order for me, Terri," I said as I went out front to get a better look.

"Ooh, Dad, can I come?" asked Nathaniel.

"Yeah, can I come?" asked Casey.

"Me, too?" added J.R.

So all three of my sons and I did what men have been doing for generations: We admired another man's ride. Its owner was nowhere to be found, but he was obviously on a real journey. The bike was outfitted with luggage boxes on both sides and propped high above the back of the seat. This particular bike had the "Adventure" package, with spotlights on the front and protective tubing around the engine's horizontal cylinders, as well as the large capacity gas tank that made the bike look intimidatingly huge. Still, I couldn't help imagining myself taking off through this countryside similarly outfitted on a serious cross-country bike with a bunch of my closest friends in tow—perhaps even with my boys someday. What a great way to see Italy. I began envisioning return trips in my mind, putting together an invite list and planning routes. What is it about Italy that seems to always demand a return trip, like a love interest with whom you can't part until you've booked the next date?

As we relaxed comfortably in the shade after lunch, without watches or the slightest respect for the passage of time, we discussed what to do next. We could go back to the villa and siesta and swim. We could stay around Gubbio and peruse its churches and museums. Or we could drive up to Perugia and see one of Umbria's most celebrated cities.

"I vote for Perugia," Terri said, and I completely agreed. This moment-to-moment freedom to wander was wonderful.

"Let's at least drive by the old Roman amphitheatre on the outskirts of town as we leave," I added.

So we did. Then we turned the minibus in the direction of Perugia and drove through the afternoon sun, Terri and the kids taking the opportunity to nap. They all looked so peaceful bobbing on their headrests, but I just had to wake them. Somehow, incredibly, I was driving past a shoe store. And it was open during the middle of the afternoon. Surely its owners had forgotten they were in Italy.

"Wake up, kids, time to get some shoes."

"Really?" Terri asked, having resigned herself to the program of carrying one kid while the other slipper-shuffled.

"Am I good, or what?" I asked, pulling in to park.

I must admit I was quite surprised to have seen it. I had been asleep myself.

CHAPTER 34

# FINALLY A MUSIC FESTIVAL

*Italy gave us not only the violin, the vibrant heart of orchestral music, whose timbre and expressiveness most evoke the human voice, but also the piano, the instrument fittest for accompanying the voice in song.*
— D'Epiro and Pinkowish

Just as with the city of Florence, Italians insist on naming their own provinces, too. Tuscany is actually *Toscana*. The province next door to the east, at least from a tourist standpoint, seems to have taken a backseat to its famous neighbor, but *Umbria* is deserving of adulation as well. However, it does not yet have an anglicized name. We had fun trying to come up with one, but the word *Umbria* is so much more foreign sounding than *Toscana*, and it was, therefore, surprisingly difficult to come up with anything at all. We soon dropped the project, as apparently everyone else had done before us.

One of the flagship attractions in *Umbria* is the city of *Perugia*. We arrived ahead of the dinner rush with plenty of time to walk the streets and get a feel for the city before the crowds hit. At least that's what we thought. From the moment we ascended the steps from our parking area, however, Perugia was a jumping place. A group of twentysomething young men were descending a steep street as we climbed it. They were whooping loudly, laughing, and just generally having a great time. But as they neared us and saw the young children, they calmed down, nodded at me, and apologized. I have no idea what they had to be sorry about but was duly impressed by the sentiment, nonetheless.

Reaching the top of the city and entering the broad, pedestrian-only street called the *Corso Vannucci* offered a pleasant surprise. The "livable space" was broader and more open than anything we had yet seen. Just how the city designers from the Middle Ages knew to put the buildings this far apart to make room for future tourists is a mystery to me. Still, I'm glad they had the foresight. The result is space freshened from the breeze blowing in from the Piazza IV Novembre and sweeping down between the buildings. The hottest evenings must still be a joy here.

We knew very little about Perugia, so everything about it was a new discovery. More than most of the other towns we'd visited, it had a blend of utilitarian stores mixed in with the touristy stuff. J.R. was quick to find an Apple Computer store, for instance, at which he pointed proudly, like a hunting dog at a pheasant. Also, much like Assisi and Gubbio, the colors of the stones in the buildings and walls were generally pinker and whiter than their Tuscan counterparts. Several buildings, all tied together as is usually the case in these old towns, actually formed a smooth curve. Why this was necessary I don't know. But it played tricks on the eyes when viewed at just the right angle.

There were placards and posters everywhere advertising musical festivals. The blues concert in Castiglione del Lago and the Piotr Tomaszewski experience in Florence had only whetted our appetite for more. So Terri began deciphering details and asking passersby for information. Eventually, we learned there was a piano concert this evening in the lower rooms of the Brufani Hotel. Finding the hotel at the end of the *Corso Vannucci*, we inquired inside about the piano concert. A polite lady in hotel uniform led us down a labyrinth of steps and narrow hallways to a room set up for the purpose. There were about one hundred chairs facing a black grand piano.

We were the only ones there for the longest time. Then a woman dressed like she was interviewing for a position in the oldest profession entered on the arm of a short, scruffy looking Dutchman in jeans. They spoke very little English, but seemed friendly enough and joined us as we waited for the beginning of the show.

It never happened.

What was our challenge with music festivals, anyway?

Tired of waiting, Terri and I dared Casey to go up to the piano and play a song. He hesitated, until the reward got to five euro. Looking at the unlikely couple sitting patiently with us, I guess he figured he had nothing to lose and euro to gain, so he did it— marched right up there and played *Solfeggetto* like a pro. The seven of us gave him a thundering ovation. I was even more proud of him for his gumption than his playing ability.

So after a musical festival of our own production, we exited the Brufani and fell into our normal pattern of gelato before dinner. Here Nathaniel went on and on about his banana-flavored triple scoop. It was something he would still be talking about a year hence. You just never know what's going to be memorable for someone.

Undeterred by our string of music festival no-shows, we made further inquiries. There were simply too many posters about town not to have something happening somewhere! Sure enough, a police officer wearing a white helmet informed us there was something happening at a place called the *Sala Dei Notari*, which was in the direction of his outstretched arm. It wasn't scheduled to begin for a few hours, however, because this was Italy, and there are apparently national laws against anything starting before 9:30.

So we did what we had learned to do so well on this trip: eat. This time we chose a restaurant with outside seating, of course, under big umbrellas in the direct center of the *Corso Vannucci.* Shoppers, tourists, and teens on patrol for each other walked down both sides of our table. A woman wearing a bleached blonde-colored wig and makeup so thick she made Tammy Faye look like milquetoast walked a ridiculously manicured black poodle on a leash. A street musician not quite in the same class as Piotr Tomaszewski had a tiny ukulele, a beard like ZZ Top, and bright orange overalls. He approached us, strummed the same cord repeatedly and sang the words, "*Piccolo amore, piccolo amore, piccolo amore,*" until we gave him several euro coins to take his *little love* somewhere else. I had a feeling a restaurant with this much ambience was going to charge a pretty stiff cover charge, but I wouldn't give up our seats for anything. This kind of entertainment was priceless.

While we waited for our Umbrian-style pizzas, featuring white cheeses and a thick layer of fresh and leafy arugula, Terri spotted a clarinet duet down the street. She popped up out of her chair like an American tourist running shy on music festivals. Christine and J.R. danced and whirled right in front of the two stunned musicians whose shyness seemed to indicate they had never had groupies before. They were saved only by the arrival of our food and our subsequent departure to the *Sala Dei Notari* for what I hoped would turn out to be something—*anything*—we could call a music festival.

We marched up the steps of what appeared to have been the town's hall, similar to what we had seen in Florence and Siena. An American college kid took our money at the door and said we were in for a treat. I certainly hoped so, but I didn't say it. He would never understand.

Inside the *Sala Dei Notari* is a beautiful large room ringed in frescoes, pretty much what we expected by now. But these frescoes are unexpectedly different; they feature massive colorful coats of arms of various former city rulers. Some are pleasingly out of proportion and, well, not that good. The lack of symmetry and consistent size of those across the front wall were amusing to me. I'm sure I'm offending some art expert by saying this, but I really enjoyed their dearth of perfection. This town was pleasingly unique in many ways.

Christine and J.R. sat on large benches that ran the length of both side walls, while the rest of us took our places in some folding chairs. A woman scurried over to shoo Christine and J.R. away. Apparently, she was guardian of the frescoes and their bottoms were about to do irreparable damage where the artists hadn't already managed to do so. I should have noticed that the benches themselves were painted in fresco, too. *Oops.*

We waited for it to be sufficiently late for a music festival in Italy to start. It was hot. I was getting sleepy. The noise from the street below sounded like there was a party going on, and we were missing it. Chatter and laughter grew louder and louder. But if music was going to be played in that building that night, I was prepared to wait it out. I passed the time by reading the brochure. The performers were a group of college music majors from around the world, each extremely accomplished and studying that summer in Umbria on special invitation. It was a bona fide music festival, by golly.

One young lady sang beautiful opera. There was a violinist—my favorite—from America, who was angry with himself afterwards for messing up, though none of us had detected it. And there were gobs of piano players, though I realize piano players probably aren't used to being classified in "gobs." They were all quite good—actually, exceptionally good. The only problem was most of the piano pieces seemed to have been chosen for level of difficulty instead of musicality and "listen-ability." Some of the pieces were so complicated and bizarre as to almost hurt my ears. One Korean kid, however, lit the keys on fire with a fun and fast rendition of something by Lizst. None of us had ever heard anything like it. When he was through, he literally jumped up from the bench as he expertly pounded the final chords. *Wow.*

We emerged from the *Sala Dei Notari* into a scene from the movie *Grease.* People were everywhere sitting on steps, sitting around the fountain, standing in little groups, strolling arm-in-arm, and sitting on park benches. Children, who all across Italy apparently have no bedtime, ran and played chase and laughed and yelled as if they owned the place. Which, in fact, I think they do. Never did we see a single correction administered to an Italian child the entirety of our trip. This may have something to do with Italy having Europe's lowest birthrate: most families having only one child apiece. We lingered for a while to take in the nightlife. This was so very different from anything we had ever experienced. This wasn't the American club scene, with its *Wild Kingdom* animal mating rituals, which, besides druggies and dealers and other shadowy figures, usually accounts for most of the movement in cities after dark. Rather, it was the whole town, from young to old, out mingling and messing around and laughing and simply enjoying their city and each other on a regular summer night. There was no festival, holiday, or occasion whatsoever. This was just how it was done. Sitting there, taking it all in, we kind of liked how it was done. There were still places in the world with a sense of community.

The evening could have ended right there. Instead, we had a hilariously hard time getting out of Perugia as our GPS seemed unable to comprehend the tiny winding roads leading down and out of town and seemed committed to keeping us in the middle of the town and its late-night festivities. One downhill turn was so sharp I had to pull backward and forward three times to negotiate it without scraping the sides on the high concrete walls. Throughout this whole "Escape from Perugia" experience, I narrated to make the kids laugh. We were in a silly mood indeed when the GPS directed us to pull into someone's driveway—a pathway so narrow the minibus scraped bushes on both sides as we drew near to this poor fellow's house.  Did he realize his front yard was featured in a GPS program for tourists leaving the city?  As I shifted into reverse, Terri spotted a mouse standing on a branch in the bush next to her window, not a foot from her face.  Unflappable, it held tightly to its branch and looked at us as if *we* were the ones out of place, which, come to think of it, I really couldn't argue.

CHAPTER 35

# THE SPACES IN BETWEEN

*It has been my lot in life to be dragged kicking and screaming into most of the really good things that have happened to me. But I finally came to see that hopelessly clinging to a way of life that was consuming me was the crazy part.* – Phil Doran

I had one day remaining with the motorcycle and took an extended ride to savor the last moments with my new friend. It's surprising the connection a man can develop with a vehicle, but I guess it's because shared experiences build bonds, and this bike and I had traversed many a twisty road, bounced down bumpy trails, zoomed along farm paths, and putt-putted through the stone streets of many ancient towns. It wasn't the best bike in the world, to be sure, but it had been my magic carpet of sorts as I'd used it to drop into stimulatingly unknown spots in this captivating country. To me, getting far off the beaten path is the best way to get an authentic feel for a place. This little motorcycle had provided a super enjoyable way to do just that. We had dead-ended in farmers' fields, families' driveways, and tiny piazzas in front of churches at the top of little hill towns.

I had adopted the attitude that acting like I belonged somewhere was half the battle of being allowed there in the first place.
I guess you could say I was adhering to the philosophy that asking forgiveness is easier than obtaining permission.  So I would
just pull up to an ancient town, watch what the local scooters and
motorcycles were doing, and then do likewise. This worked well
enough.  However, there were times when I could swear I was receiving looks of suspicion from people, as if somehow they knew I
didn't really belong. Thinking that to be impossible, I would simply nod and continue on my path, exploring like a conquistador.
Only after several weeks did I notice the huge sticker on my front
headlight bezel proudly proclaiming: "RENT ME."

The weather had turned a sharp corner; hot and muggy days
were suddenly only a memory as I donned my only two long
sleeve shirts and strapped on the helmet.  There was mist in the
air, and the sky was low.  Deep gray swirls ebbed under lighter gray
puffs, the whole canopied beneath yet another shade of gray.  As I
bounced down the rough dirt road from *La Contea*, I was actually
chilly.  It could have been snowing, however, and I would have still
taken that ride.

I motored up the pleasing switchback roads that led up into
Cortona, enjoying every turn, accelerating into the apex, braking,
downshifting, then powering out of the curve while straightening
the bike and accelerating again.  Then into the next turn the process would start all over.  There were no kids in the back seat to get
queasy, and there was no way any Italian driver was going to come
up behind me and "push" like they were so fond of doing when
I was in the minibus.  It was so much fun I got all the way up to
Piazza Garibaldi, turned around in front of the old men who were
already there at their posts, and went back down to do it all over
again.

On the second climb I shot up a road to the right I hadn't
explored before.  It led into a long, flat, wide expanse that looked

like a park but also a road. The surface was gravel; there was a car way up ahead going through it, but there were also pleasing park benches and lantern posts along both sides. It was bordered on its east side by a steep hill holding up the rest of Cortona above and on the west by a stunning panoramic view of the Valdichiana. I didn't see any signs prohibiting (not that they had *always* stopped me before), so I entered, keeping my speed slow and the engine quiet to preserve the serene setting. Then I popped out the other side on a narrow paved road flanked by cypress trees. Up ahead, high on the hill, with beautiful terraces and flowers that looked like they were dripping off of the balcony, stood *Bramasole*, the house that author Frances Mayes had purchased and restored and made famous in her book *Under the Tuscan Sun*. I had read enough of her descriptions to know it immediately. And besides, there was a biker decked out in obnoxious racing colors and logos, resting on his bike on the side of the road, shamelessly gawking up at the house. Across the little street from him, a car was stopped and a woman jumped out and started snapping photos. I slowed but didn't stop, thinking Frances and *Bramasole* had probably had more than their share of gawkers.

I proceeded up the hill following signs to the Medici Fortress, marveling at just how prolific those Medicis had been. This took me up more switchback roads, steeper this time, which gave an even more remarkable view of the valley below. Whoever thought to put Cortona up on this particular ridge of Monte Sant' Egidio sure knew how to appeal to future tourists. There were a thousand photo opportunities before I even reached the top—and this was on a gray and misty day. If I had only thought to come up here earlier on one of those endlessly hot and clear days!

At the top, the first thing I came to was the Basilica di Santa Margherita. Unlike many other churches we had seen throughout this region, this was an active place of worship. Nuns were filing in as I entered, but a priest assured me I was still welcome, even though they were assembling for a reading. I thanked him and left my helmet and gloves near the tall front doors. It took a while for my eyes to adjust to the dim lights, and while I stood there, a nun approached the priest to whom I had spoken and asked permission to go to the bathroom.

"*Prego*," he said.

I was glad for her because even masked in very appropriate demeanor, it was obvious she had waited too long. She quickly scurried out.

I strolled quietly through the beautiful church, listening to the monotone voices of the priests reading in Latin, while I tried to stay out of sight. Studying a highly decorated section, I noticed the top featured Christ with His arms extended, and below there were flowers and candlesticks and carved marble. Eventually it dawned on me that I was looking at a final resting place of someone; by now, I had grown accustomed to these tombs inside of churches. What I hadn't expected to see, however, was the body of the revered one herself. I stepped closer, blinked, and tried to let my eyes adjust further to the dim light. I had not been mistaken. There, through a coffin with a glass side reinforced with diagonal steel mesh, was old Saint Margherita, her head tipped forward slightly on a pillow and partially blocked by a white hood. My first thought was that she really didn't look that bad, considering. The Latin continued to echo around me as I thought of the cultural differences between my own life and what I was witnessing: adults asking permission to relieve themselves and others preserved in glass coffins.

Curious, I read up on Saint Margherita later. She had been a common farmer's daughter before joining the Third Order of St. Francis (there he was again), and had founded a convent, a hospital, and had been yet another individual who had apparently "preached Christ" through her life as much as her words. *Our present-day society often reveres sports stars for their very decadence*, I thought, and even though Italy's was a culture very foreign to me, I respected that individuals were held up for their godliness.

I exited the church in deep thought, not fully noticing that the sky had cleared and the sun was winning the battle for the day. Not really wanting to shatter the silence with the engine of my motorcycle, I strolled instead along the valley side of the church. As I was doing so, a shiny black Mercedes sedan pulled up. A driver remained seated as a passenger from the front jumped out and opened both rear doors. An older couple emerged. The man was dressed in clothing that looked like it came directly out of a safari outfitter catalog, while the woman had the overly coiffed look of the aged wealthy. They listened politely as the young man from the car explained the next few steps of their tour. It seems Miguel was going to take the car down into Piazza Signorelli in Cortona while the three of them first toured Santa Margherita and then walked down the "easy" steps into town.

"But first," said the tour guide, "I want to show you the best view in Cortona. Almost no one knows of this spot, and nobody is ever here when I bring people up. It's a chance at seclusion in one of the better views in all of Italy."

He said all of this while eyeing me. I had been walking from my motorcycle in the middle of the large, nearly empty gravel parking lot in front of the church and heading back in the exact direction he was now promising his high-euro guests would be secluded. This is just the kind of trouble into which a motorcycle can get a person. Feeling awkward now because I was already heading for "one of the better views in all of Italy," I sped up and tried to get there before them, hoping to take a quick gander and get out to leave them their space.

"Unbelievable!" I heard the guide exclaim quietly to the couple.

I turned. "*Mi dispiaci*, I'm sorry, I can wait for you folks. I was just . . ." I began to explain.

"Oh, nonsense, young man," said Safari Man. "There's room enough for all of us. Please, join in."

*Don't mind if I do*, I thought. So I thanked them and walked along a little sheepishly behind as the tour guide led us to the ledge overlooking Cortona below and the Valdichiana farther beyond. The guide, whose name I never did catch, explained some history of the region, how the valley was for a long time a malarial swamp, how the old cities around here were not only built high on these hills for defense purposes against attackers, but also against disease. It was felt that the air in the lowlands was bad for health. It wasn't until the fifteen hundreds that the swamp was drained by—who else?—the Medicis. It subsequently became a fertile farming heartland. Then the guide fell silent to let us enjoy the view from a spot "almost no one knows about."

Too embarrassed to make a formal introduction, I said goodbye and good luck to the wealthy couple, thanked the tour guide, and rode up the hill to the Medici fortress. Up there, I didn't run into any pesky tourists getting in the way of my solitude. This was aided, of course, by the fact that the castle was closed for renovation. I walked to the edge of a weedy ridge and looked down on the same view from now an even higher perch. A hundred yards below me, hobbling along slowly but happily enough, went the wealthy tourists and their guide. I hoped their steps truly would be easy.

As I stood looking out over the valley, the sky darkened once again and the sun looked to be losing after all. Wind kicked up the hill and wafted my double layer of shirts against my body. I looked down on the tile roof shingles of the church held in place against high winds by large stones spread all around. Suddenly, my mind shifted to architectural calculations of roof loads (which would have been snow loads back in Michigan), and I wondered if the original structure of the building had been made strong enough to support rocks on its roof.

*It's days like today*, I thought, *that are the most representative of what this sabbatical has been about.* In one moment, I'd been experiencing the simple fun of a motorcycle on a good road. But that road had led to an intrusion in my mind of a figure and a period in history that had radically changed my mood into one of deep reflection and pondering. Almost immediately, however, came a chance encounter with strangers that was as pleasing and informative as it was entertaining. Then rocks on a roof had prompted my technical side to life. All of this had happened within an hour or so.

I wanted it to continue. Whatever had happened to me by becoming free from my own self-imposed prison of busyness didn't have to die just because my vacation ended, did it? Couldn't I foster in myself a better awareness of God's world and all He was doing in my life on a daily basis? Couldn't I continue to see the little things, the chance encounters, the serene moments in between the "big" things?

If there was anything I learned from a tourist's standpoint on this trip, it was that the best touring is done in *the spaces in between*. Sure Florence and Rome had been great, but much more enjoyable to me were the deserted country roads, the old men playing cards under an umbrella in a little nameless town, and the forgotten spaces between the bustle. It was a metaphor for life, I was realizing. We tend to focus on the main goals, the biggest objectives: the crowded spaces. But life is perhaps lived best in the spaces in between.

As a tourist, the motorcycle had been the vehicle to provide that for me. Returning to my "normal" life would similarly require a vehicle, if I were to have any hope of retaining my new sense of awareness. I realized this vehicle would have to come from the way I oriented myself to my life. Instead of an endless pursuit of big objectives, I would instead try to model more of the behavior of the revered saints of this land. Instead of letting my accomplishments speak, I would instead try to speak more loudly with my conduct between the accomplishments. All this history had taught me that the accomplishments don't add up to anything anyway. What really matters is what those saints who were revered for their daily examples had shown me:  It's not so much what you accomplish but who you are as you live out the days you've been given.  I wasn't going to suddenly stop striving or working hard to fulfill my God-given potential.  No.  That's not what I was feeling.  But I also would never again rush forward into some promised great life of the future by bypassing the one I already had, either.  I had sacrificed too many *todays* on the altar of *tomorrow*, and I would never do so again.  I would be more like St. Francis. He had worked hard.  He had started monastic orders, built and refurbished churches, established a large community of followers, and taught his principles consistently throughout his life.  But it was his daily living, his daily conduct, his in-the-moment character and credibility for which he was respected the most.  He had certainly accomplished things, the biggest of which was who he was *as* he was accomplishing those other things.  Saint Margherita had evidently done the same.  They had lived right—Christ-like—in the spaces in between.

I strapped on my motorcycle helmet for that last ride back to the villa before Riccardo would show up in his van to take it away. I descended those wonderful winding roads, braking, downshifting, leaning, accelerating, up-shifting, and straightening, over and over again.  *A lot like life*, I thought.

CHAPTER 36

# LEAVING *LA CONTEA*

*"You flew by like a summer vacation…"*
  − 'I Think I'll Disappear Now "by the Crash
    Test Dummies

T he next day Riccardo came and got the motorcycle. He honked as he drove away, and I kicked at the stones on the ground like a little boy who had lost his ball over the fence. That night, we climbed into the minibus, and I took the family to the town I had once thought was Arezzo, only to find out later it was, of course, the little town of Castiglion Fiorentino. By now, you might not believe that it was an accident, but I drove straight into the arched entryway and directly up into the center of the old city. We next lumbered down the other side before parking outside the old city wall and walking back up that same hill to get dinner at the only restaurant we had seen. It was located off the central piazza complete with outdoor seating under the loggia with the view of our Florida house's mural. I couldn't wait to show Terri.

"See!" I said with a sweep of my arm. "What do you think?"

She stared for a minute before saying, "I think you might be right. That mural could be taken from almost anywhere, but still, the resemblance is inescapable."

"Told ya!" I thundered proudly. "Can you believe it?"

We stood resting against the stone wall, peering through those wonderful arches, watching the lights twinkle in the homes on the slopes as the sunlight faded. The brilliant orange of the sky faded while darkening the green of the hillside. We were in no hurry, partly because we were on this wonderful vacation and our frenzied sense of time was long gone, and partly because the restaurant wasn't open yet. After all, it was only 7:30.

The owner was not working too hard on opening his business for business, it seemed, but was more intent on arranging a small theatre of sorts. He cranked a video projector down from its position against the ceiling, connected wires and fussed with a remote. He must have noticed me watching him because he paused, smiled, and said, "*Futbal* game."

That was all that my boys needed to hear. Everywhere we traveled, *futbal* or *calcio* (soccer in the U.S.) was a universal language. While standing in line to climb the dome of the Duomo in Florence, for instance, people kept coming up to us and asking questions in Spanish. After three or four of these, Terri finally said, "It's your soccer jerseys!" The boys and I looked down at what we were wearing, and sure enough—each of us just happened to be representing a different Spanish professional team. Now, *futbal* was our ambassador with the owner of this pizzeria. He winked at me and guided us to the table with the best view of the screen.

"Can we stay for the game, Dad?" asked Casey.

"Please?" chimed Nathaniel.

At the rate things were going, our dinner wouldn't be ready anytime soon anyway, so I decided to work on my Father-of-the-Year campaign and said, "Of course."

The game featured top-level Italian professional team Juventus against the Shamrock Rovers, whoever they were. We watched as though we had money riding on it and stretched our dinner to over three hours. People at the other tables did the same, and once again, we felt camaraderie with total strangers as we cheered against those despicable Shamrock Rovers. Course after course, followed by gelato for the kids and espresso for Terri, we had finally become Italian diners. Our butts hurt from sitting when we finally got up from our chairs to walk down the hill to the waiting minibus. As we did, I noticed a sign with a red circle declaring the area off limits to non-resident drivers. *That's a lot like the one from Siena*, I thought fleetingly. It was months before the tickets started arriving in the mail, one after another, for violations of these little signs, including this one tonight, captured by automatic cameras. I also found out that rental car companies charge exorbitant fees for becoming the middleman in these transactions. Travel teaches so many unexpected things.

The next morning, we woke bright and early to pack and say our good-byes to Giulio and Daniele. They greeted us with hearty *buon giornos* and radiating smiles. What followed was the best conversation we had managed to have with them yet, in which we learned that Giulio had built *La Contea* in 1980 on the site of an old ruin. Had it been a castle? An old farmhouse? Another little church like the ones I had discovered all over these slopes? We couldn't get that part clear. The part that was perfectly clear was that this place had been a labor of love for this kind man for thirty years. His wife had died of a debilitating muscular disease five years ago, which explained the elevator at the end of the hallway. It also probably explained why he had decided to move out and turn it into an *agritourismo*.

The term *agritourismo* doesn't have a direct equivalent back in North America. With the tourist industry kicking into high gear in Tuscany a couple of decades ago, suddenly all those waning farms had a new source of revenue. The appeal for travelers like us is the chance to stay on a working farm and get a taste of Italy from the inside. We had expected to like that. What we hadn't expected was to fall in love with the people there.

At one point, Casey pointed to the many trophies on display on the high shelves of the library. Giulio explained they were his son's, a motocross racer of some renown, who was "always on his motorcycle all the time." That is, until he succumbed to the same disease that had taken his mother. When we asked how long ago that had occurred, Giulio looked down at the ground forlornly and held up one finger: a single year ago.

Unable to delay the inevitable any longer, we took a few quick photographs together. As we said our good-byes and *arrivedercis*, Giulio gave us the customary double kiss and waved a hearty *buon viaggi*. Daniele hugged us all, complimenting the behavior of our children. Giulio was keen to tell us to drive safely, pantomiming his words by walking slumped over and slowly. There are millions of crazy drivers in Rome, he seemed to be saying in warning, and I wondered if he had ever been to Naples. The clunky white minibus ambled down the bumpy gravel drive one last time as *La Contea* and all we had experienced there was transitioning into memories.

"I love people," Terri said after a kilometer or two.

We rode along in silence. There was nothing to add. With three words, Terri had summed up why it was bearable to leave this place we had grown to love so much. We were heading home to the people we love and miss. We would miss our new friends, to be sure, and we would never forget them. But our lives were with those back home. It was time to return to them.

The sun was already blasting the countryside, and the cold reprieve we had experienced for a few days had succumbed to the resurgent stifling heat. Swallows darted around in the sky above the olive trees, and birds everywhere seemed to be singing us away as in the closing scene of a princess cartoon. We rambled down past the tall cypresses, past the farmhouse ruin with the tall tower, and past the working farm with the tractor parked in the weeds.    In that bright landscape of greens and tans, of undulating hills and mountain peaks, of terracotta roofs and farmhouse ruins, of sunflower fields and canopy pines, of layers and layers of human history, one white minibus moved slowly through it all . . . driving in a mural.

There was, however, time for one last adventure.

"Montalcino," I said.

"What, Dad?"

"Montalcino.  It's where I'd like to go today before we get to our hotel near the airport in Rome."

"What is it?" asked Casey.

"Probably one of the most famous wine towns in Italy, and it has a long history of conflict and alliance with the other old towns around here."

"Smart Car!" J.R. yelled, pointing out the window.

"That's eight hundred seventy-one," said Nate.

"No, it's eight seventy-seven," said Christine, and the debate was on.

"Another Smart Car!" said Nate, and I decided everyone was all right with going to Montalcino.

So we finished this trip almost exactly as we had begun it: with a kid throwing up. This time, however, being a much more seasoned traveler, I managed to stop the van first, which was fortunate. What was unfortunate was that it was right at a busy intersection entering Montalcino.  Cars whizzed by, people gawked, and J.R. emptied his queasiness right there on the curb.

What struck me most about Montalcino was its views of the surrounding countryside, rivaled, in my mind, only by those in Cortona.  The geometric shapes of color and the long swaths of farmland far below are truly captivating.  As we climbed the hill leading to the central part of town, the now familiar restored stone buildings occasionally provided an opening from which to peer out far into that great expanse.  As I had done throughout this trip, I strained hard at the camera lens to steal away snippets of what my eyes were seeing. I aimed down narrow alleys trying to frame the distant valley with stone houses on either side. In one shot, I focused on a potted geranium, allowing the background to smear softly. The image didn't work. Then I'd step high on a stairway and take in only the distant vistas, but the shot looked flat and soulless. I was slowly succumbing to the reality that cameras can only do so much. Many native Americans once felt that a camera could steal away one's soul. *They needn't have worried*, I thought. *Photography is pitiful against the real thing.* So I surrendered, securing the lens cover for the final time. Another photographer utterly defeated by the relentless beauty of *Italia*.

Actually, that's not true. I did use the camera one more time to photograph a couple holding the leash of their pooping dog directly in front of a "No Dogs Allowed" sign. Some things are easier to photograph than others, I guess.

Wine shops line the little streets of Montalcino, which struck me as a quiet town barely worthy of its notoriety. But then I began tasting its wine, and immediately I realized what all the fuss was about. Without a doubt, Brunello di Montalcino is the best I sampled on the entire trip, and by now, I was confident in my ability since it was obvious I could blindly select the most expensive wine in any tasting. At one such event, while Terri and the kids ransacked a jewelry store next door, I was led down narrow steps into a cool cellar with a brick vault ceiling. Rough stone walls were pleasingly damp. The ceiling above the vaults was made of glass, allowing a view into the *enoteca* above. In the center of a little space was an old oak table on which were neatly arranged wine bottles, glasses, and the latest reviews of wine critics: people like me, who, obviously, had "the knack," too. I selected several "excellent choices" and filled out another shipping form, a lady with long fingernails and fancy clothes happily swiping my credit card. Whether or not I would ever see any of these shipments felt like a fifty-fifty proposition.

We progressed farther into the town, climbing higher and higher, to the *fortezza* at the peak. Originally constructed in the thirteen hundreds, it seems those busy Medicis had built its ramparts a couple of centuries later. I was not surprised, by now having formed an opinion of the Medici family as something perhaps similar to the Mafia in Sicily.

Lunch was delicious, as always, and we eventually emerged from the tiny *osteria* to procure one final gelato in a tiny crevice of a store farther down the hill. We had settled into a comfortable existence of hyper-caloric intake. *Who wouldn't fall victim to the seduction of this life?* I thought, licking like a dog with peanut butter stuck to the roof of its mouth.

The fact of our departure was beginning to settle in upon me now, a heavy realization laced with sadness. I had never lived through a month like this one. I had never had such an expanse of time and experience. I had rarely even dreamed of such a thing. Now, it was shrinking into powerless photos and pleasing memories. I looked at the buildings and people of Montalcino with eloper's eyes, knowing what they didn't: I was about to take flight and leave them behind. A couple of days of hassle and I would be dropped back into my previous life like an apparition. The razor blades providing death to the artist by a thousand cuts of emails, texts, faxes, voice mails, ringing phones, commitments, meetings, and deadlines were about to be given their chance at revenge. I knew they would be merciless. They wouldn't care what we had seen, what we had felt, how it had changed us. They wouldn't feel the metamorphosis that had taken place deep inside. It would be impossible to explain that there was a different way of life lived somewhere, in a place where time didn't as much "go by" as it folded up onto itself over and over, all the layers always present and simply getting thicker.

I knew I was entering a transformation as necessary as the digitizing of a document to enable faxing. First I had to withdraw, the sadness of parting setting in heavily like the heart tugs I felt as Giulio and Daniele waved us *buon viaggio*. Next came the dread of returning to the violence of the normal. Finally would come the yearning for the familiar and the needed awakening from the dream, in which I would mutter the only thought of consolation possible: "I'll be back. I'll be back. I'll be back. . . ."

CHAPTER 37

# RESTORED, BETTER THAN NEW

*Travel is more than the seeing of sights; it is a change that goes on, deep and permanent, in the ideas of living.*
– Miriam Beard

There is a momentum to the end of a trip. It begins with the counting down of last days. "Only five more days." "Now only four." This accompanies a growing sense of dread as reality beckons nearer and nearer. "This time next week, you know where I'll be?" Those gangly responsibilities, appointments, and commitments lurch closer in the calendar and gnash their relentless teeth. My entire life, I have fought what I can only call the End of Vacation Blues.

Then, right toward the end, when the constructive part of the vacation is truly over and nothing remains but the return travel and all of its afflictions, I just want to be home. Immediately. It is during such moments I long the most for teleporting to become a reality. In its absence, I buck myself up for sweaty check-in lines, sticky shuttle buses, no chairs at the terminal gate, cruddy airport food, the long flight home, a mob at Customs, messed up sleep, unpacking, and re-acclimating.

It would all begin with losing Kooshie.

At a gas station convenience store in Michigan, J.R., at the age of four, had spotted the furry little stuffed dog and bought it with his own allowance money. Of all his toys and possessions, Kooshie has reigned supreme. His little brown and white fur has been worn nearly through. J.R.'s grandmother has had to sew many repairs to Kooshie's seams. And in a cute little habit, J.R. rubs Kooshie's ear between his fingers and has several times worn right through the cloth. Needless to say, Kooshie generally goes with us everywhere. You might say he's the Brady family version of Flat Stanley, the traveling paper doll featured in photographs from all over the world. And Kooshie is most adept at getting lost. It's his chief life skill. Sometimes I think he stays awake at night, peering through his glassy little eyes, thinking of ways to elude J.R.'s care, scanning every nook and cranny for hideouts. He has been left under hotel beds, at Grammy's house, at church, in the cars of friends, and this morning, he was left behind in J.R.'s new backpack. It probably didn't hurt that I had already tipped the shuttle driver well as he unloaded our bags at the airport terminal because he very kindly offered to see if he could grab J.R.'s backpack on his next round to the hotel and bring it to us. Incredibly, all this worked out just fine, and Kooshie was once again reunited with his protector—the villain's diabolic plan foiled again.

When we finally made it to our gate, of course, there were no chairs. Fiumicino airport is famous for having about eight seats per gate for waiting passengers. So we casually sat on the floor with hundreds of others. The sun outside shown brightly and felt warm on the glass windows against which we leaned. I relaxed for the first time that morning. Shepherding a family of little kids through the intricacies of foreign travel can be a bit harrowing. There is constant checking for bags, passports, and making sure all the kids are in tow with shoes on their feet. Now, all we had to do was climb on this plane and settle in for the long ride home. I let out a sigh of relief.

I had almost closed my eyes when I saw the commotion. Two women had made a dash for one seat that had suddenly become available. Their sizeable hips crashed into each other, and a verbal catfight ensued, complete with expletives and dirty looks. They were at least fifty years old. One lady eventually lost out and huffed a short distance away where she maintained the most horrid angry stare at the victorious one, who in turn kibitzed with her friend seated next to her about the other lady being a female dog in heat. The hard feelings and tension filled the air around them as they boarded, still exchanging murderous looks. When we finally found our seats on the plane, the "victorious" lady and her friend sat right across the aisle adjacent to me. By now, embarrassment was setting in, and they chatted me up nicely to cover what had just occurred, as if a flurry of words could bury the deed.

That's when the man in front of them began swearing.

"I've got two hundred thousand frequent flyer miles with this airline! This is ridiculous," he said loudly enough for everyone to hear. Apparently, his seat was broken and wouldn't recline.

"I'm not about to ride eleven hours on a plane with a seat like this!" And he swore some more to emphasize how serious he was about being a big spoiled ninny.

First, a tiny female flight attendant tried to appease him, followed by a larger one with hairy forearms. Then, a male attendant made an attempt. Finally, the captain of the stewards himself had a try at the man.

"We're very sorry, sir, but the plane is completely full. We can try to compensate with some free snacks and beverages during the flight, and we can also offer you some additional free miles."

"I don't want any of that stuff. I want a fully functioning seat like I paid for."

And on it went.

"Our only option, sir, is to get mechanics in here to try and fix your seat, and that could delay our departure by who knows how long."

"I don't care what it takes; I want a functioning seat. I've got two hundred thousand miles with this airline and . . ."

Terri was trying to get my attention. I was entranced by the free *Jerry Springer Show*, thinking what a contrast the behavior we had witnessed in just the last half hour was to the Italian gentility to which we had grown accustomed.

"Tell that steward that our kids can switch with him," Terri said to me in a whisper.

*That's a great idea*, I thought, wondering why it hadn't occurred to me. No matter because I got all the credit for it as I spoke up and said to the steward, "Uh, sir? I think we can help."

He turned to look at me as if I was Ed McMahon from Publishers Clearing House Sweepstakes bearing the winning ticket. "Yes?"

"Those are my two little kids over there," I pointed. "They could easily switch with this man and his wife. They're too little to need seats that recline anyway."

And just like that, I was a hero.

They brought me wine. They brought me pretzels. They handed my kids little wings and extra apple juice. They gave me a bottle of champagne to take home. They gave me frequent flyer miles. I thought they might even get around to naming a terminal after me. Even the seat-stealing woman gave me a compliment about how nice it was to see someone being selfless. I grinned and nodded and eventually muttered to one of the flight attendants that it was my wife's idea. But by then, it was too late. I was the flight's official rock star mascot from then on.

The flight was actually great. We shuffled our seats around a bit, and I sat next to Christine for most of it. She made little dolls by taping soda cans and plastic cups together. We used my cell phone camera as a photo booth and made all kinds of crazy faces together. She wrote and read me a story about a cat that tours Rome. We played a castle battle game on my phone. And we wrote some poetry. It was these little moments of intimacy with my children I hoped would not disappear just because we were about to get busy with real life again. I counted my blessings and then tried to count her freckles. Both were impossible.

My rock star status with the flight attendants came in handy after we landed, too. It seemed the boys had gotten off the plane without the soccer ball that had entertained them so much in Italy. It was too good a souvenir to lose lightly. So as we stood in the cattle lines waiting to clear Customs, one of the flight attendants was nice enough to go back and search for it, but we had used up our retrieval Mulligan when finding Kooshie. The famous red soccer ball was gone, probably on its way to a new home with the children of an airplane cleaning guy.

As we snaked back and forth through the incredibly long wait at Customs, Casey and Nathaniel were snickering every time we passed a certain redheaded lady and her husband.

"What's up guys?" I inquired.

"That's the lady, right there," Nathaniel pointed subtly.

"She's the one who said it," Casey said and then they laughed again.

"Said what?" I asked, apparently having missed the explanation.

"At one point during the flight, she stood right up in her seat, turned around to look at us, and said, 'Did you take your shoes off or something? Because your feet *stink*! I can't *stand* it!' and then she sat back down!" Casey said, laughing again.

Then Nathaniel added, "Yeah, and I said something intelligent like, 'Uh, okay.'" And they laughed some more.

*What a reverse culture shock we're experiencing*, I thought.

"You know what you could have said, Nathaniel?" I asked.

"No, what?"

"You could have said, 'Yes, lady, my feet might stink. But after I shower, I'll smell good again, but you'll still be mean!'" And in total shock, my boys burst out laughing at their dad's inappropriateness. I then told them about Winston Churchill's famous joke with Lady Astor when she deridingly called him drunk. "I may be drunk, Lady Astor," he famously replied, "but in the morning I'll be sober, and you'll still be *ugly!*" And they roared some more. You see, it's on trips like this that history lessons really hit home.

Speaking of home, I was ready to get there. As the trip had wound to a close, the "foreign-ness" of Italy wasn't as quaint or alluring anymore. I longed for the familiar, for conversations I completely understood, for food I could order at any time of day or night, for the bigness of anything big, for my sport utility I could drive without my knees pressing up into my chest, for my own bed, and my pillow that isn't hard as a rock. I was going to eat a cheeseburger, dare to visit a store in the middle of the afternoon, and expect to receive the bill at a restaurant without first having to chase the owner of the place into the kitchen. I was going to walk through woods without thinking about vipers or scorpions, and pull into a parking lot and expect to find a space—wide enough to allow me to open my doors. There would be a shower big enough to turn around in, and soda that was actually cold. I was going to get on the Internet and expect the pages to load before it was time for the next meal. Soon, there would be air conditioning that truly was conditioned.

Then I thought about all I would miss. What would I do without those landscapes? Where would I find such architecture? I knew I would miss the roads, and ironically, the curvy hills. The layers and layers of history dating back thousands of years would be hard to leave. That I would miss the food went without saying. The friendly people, the Mediterranean sun, olive trees, vineyards, the museums, the evening festivity in the central piazzas of nearly every town, a place so utterly lost in time—I would miss it all . . .

and much more. Of all the places in the world I've visited, Italy demands the most sincere promise of "I'll be back." And what about that cozy little family cocoon to which I'd grown accustomed? As we returned home to our incessantly busy schedules, often going in several different directions at once, I knew it just wouldn't feel the same—we would be missing that little extra something, a togetherness that comes from . . . what? Time? Yes. That is what I would miss the most—not just quality time, *quantity* time.

Never in my adult life had I taken such a large swath of the calendar and declared it off limits to everyone and everything else that dared make claim to it. Never had I sequestered myself so completely. Never had I seen such a stretch of days out before me with nothing but freedom in how to spend them. Never had I slowed down to this extreme.

I had never dared.

Now, decompressed, fully recharged—heck, truly *changed*—I was hurling back into the real world with clear eyes and a clearer mind. I was ready to take on the world, should the world be willing. And if it weren't? Well, I was feeling so good I just might be willing to force it.

Interestingly, the world had gone on just fine without us. Nothing came crashing to the ground; all the pre-work I'd done before departure had carried through; new issues awaited my return, and a whole book of adventures for me was but a blip of a mere month to the rats in the race. Sure, there were some who had to cover for me. Many picked up my slack, for which I thanked them profusely (I hope). But it was nothing major, nothing that couldn't really have waited.

It was this interesting paradox of time that perplexed me the most as I eased back into my Mach V life. I had been gone the same amount of time others had stayed at the helm, yet my memories from this period were enormous, while theirs were mostly miniscule and ordinary. I had grown and changed and advanced in my understanding and appreciation of so many things, most of them small, while people wedged into the tight schedules of the daily grind were quite possibly no farther ahead. Sometimes haste *is* just waste, and I'm not talking about fast food, where haste literally makes *waist*. Nope. The "sharpening of the saw" thing was true.

For a period of my life, I was interested in restoring cars. I was into the old body styles but didn't really like the interiors or lack of technology. I remember going to car shows and seeing the finished output of the masters: cars restored so well, with clever modifications and enhancements, one could actually say they were an improvement on the original. The interiors were reconstructed and some of the latest technology was employed to boost horsepower and performance. These mechanical artists had not only breathed life back into worn out old cars, they had actually advanced them to a condition that was *better than new*. That's the best way to describe a vacation done correctly: It's not just restoration; it's coming back better than new.

People began asking me about the trip.

"How was it?"

"What did you see?"

"Where did you go?"

So in reply I'd sputter and kick around some answers, none of them sufficient. Maybe I would show a few pictures. I was blessed, fortunate, and thankful, and I desperately wanted to share all that we had experienced. I couldn't, however, figure out how to do it without sounding like I was boasting. At other times, I could tell I just wasn't explaining myself properly. *What do you mean?* their faces would seem to say. *I take vacations. I know how to relax. I take my trip up to the lake each year.*

It would require a whole book to convey what I saw, smelled, tasted, felt, experienced, learned, and gained. I would have to take some serious time to reflect on just what it was that made this the best month of my life. I'd have to find the means to tell the story in a way to help the other person benefit from my experience. I wanted to let people know there is a way to sharpen the saw and come back with a more effective edge than ever. I wanted people to rediscover the art of vacation.

Sure . . . it doesn't have to be Italy. That is just my particular infatuation. It can be anything or anywhere that will inspire and rebuild, replenish, and renew. But there is more to it than getting a campground or hotel reservation, taking a little time off work, and getting out of town for a few days. There is an art to it. There is an intentionality required if one is to obtain the biggest impact possible.

So I wrote it down—every word true, with big huge chunks left out to spare the reader's sanity. I had originally thought of giving some specific steps, action plans, and lists of advice. There are so many little tidbits I could have thrown in that may have helped the next traveler on this path. But that isn't really what it's all about. One can never make a masterpiece by following a dot-to-dot. Nope. That's what's so difficult about art: It doesn't hold up under analysis, and it can't be produced through copying. It only has power if one experiences it correctly, and that means with originality, wonder, and authenticity. If you have made it this far, you have a pretty good idea of what I'm trying to convey. Hopefully, nearly forty chapters have accomplished at least that much. I haven't lectured about how to rediscover the art of vacation—I've attempted to *show* you instead. It's just something you've got to *feel*. That's how art is. You have to blaze your own trail.

"Why was it the best month of your life?" people ask.

"Because of how it made me *better.*"

"And what is that supposed to mean?"

"You would have to win the lottery, recover from some sickness, or repair a broken relationship to have an inkling of an understanding of what I'm talking about. I am restored, refocused, and reinvigorated. I have reawakened to the realization that, by God's grace, I am still in charge of the time I've been given. I am going to be held accountable for how I live this life, and, therefore, I have got to be the one in charge of living it. Nobody else can live it for me, tell me how to live it, or impose upon me their expectations and requirements. That's between God and me. I know. We spoke a lot while I was gone."

"Uh, you'd better write that book," one of my friends said, looking at me as if he couldn't figure out if I was onto something or merely *on* something.

So I went back to Italy to write it all down . . . and it was even better the second time.

# JOURNAL ENTRY
## SATURDAY, JULY 31, 2010

Of all the places I've visited, Italy demands
the most sincere promise of:
"I'll be back."

**OFFICIAL SMART CAR COUNT:
987***

*disputed

# ACKNOWLEDGMENTS

It is with the memory of warm Italian sun on my skin and a steaming plate of pasta in front of me that I consider the many wonderful people who are part of this project. First and foremost in that consideration is my family. I would like to thank my wife Terri for her partnership, sense of adventure, and editing abilities—all of which were necessary for this book to become a reality. I would also like to thank each of my incredible children Casey, Nathaniel, Christine, and J.R. for their willingness to not only play a part in Dad's adventures, but also to submit themselves to being written about like characters in a novel. It is also with warm remembrance that I thank the many new friends we met along our journey. I hope I have done you all justice in these pages.

Thanks are due to my executive assistant Doug Huber, who not only keeps my life running smoothly, but was responsible for making all the travel arrangements for this Italian sabbatical in the first place. I also want to thank my friend and often co-author Orrin Woodward and his wife Laurie, who gave me such a great response to an early version of this manuscript that I was encouraged to continue. Rob Hallstrand, lifetime friend and COO at Obstaclés Press, does such an amazing job with a huge number of projects, as well as a whole host of things on my behalf, that I could never thank him enough. Bill Rousseau also deserves recognition for excellent project management and the impossible task of helping me hit deadlines. Special thanks are also due to my friends Tim

Marks, Bill Lewis, Claude Hamilton, George Guzzardo, and Dan Hawkins for picking up the slack while I was gone.  A heartfelt thank you is also due Oliver DeMille, who went above and beyond what was expected and provided excellent advice for improvements in the manuscript.  I would like to thank the very talented Norm Williams for the cover design and his ability to discern what I want with very little input. Lalanne Barber deserves special thanks for saving me from several embarrassing blunders, and thanks also go to Wendy Branson and Deborah Brady, who provided final editing. Tracey Avereyn, who manages and directs my social media presence, deserves my gratitude as well.  Thanks also to Dirk Rozich for designing the website and the programmers at RMR who made it work.  A special thank you also goes out to Emily O'Boyle, Ryan Renz, and Andy Garcia for creation of the video trailer.  Thank you to my friend Kyle Reeder for providing the music for the trailer and to Russ Mack for his promotional expertise and assistance. Also, I wish to thank Stephen Palmer, Sharon Lechter, Richard Bliss Brooke, Chris Gross, Dr. Gaetano Sottile, Lucio Malan, Jason Ashley, Venkat Varada, Vago Damitio, Karen McCann, Elizabeth Condelli, Diana Simon, Turhan Berne, and Art Jonak for reviewing galley copies of the book.  I would like to thank my parents, Jim and Gayle Brady for setting the model example of parenthood and now, grandparenthood.  Finally, I wish to give all honor and glory to my Lord and Savior Jesus Christ.

## ABOUT THE AUTHOR

Chris Brady is an avid motorized adventurer, world traveler, humorist, community builder, business owner, soccer fan, and dad. He also has one of the world's most unique resumes, including experience with a live bug in his ear, walking through a paned-glass window, chickening out from the high dive in elementary school, destroying the class ant farm in third grade, losing a spelling bee on the word *use*, jackhammering his foot, and, more recently, sinking his snowmobile in a lake. Chris and his wife Terri have four children and live in North Carolina.